The Industrial Revolution

PROBLEMS IN EUROPEAN CIVILIZATION SERIES

General Editor
Merry E. Wiesner

The Industrial Revolution

Edited with an introduction by
Steven M. Beaudoin
Centre College

Houghton Mifflin Company Boston New York

Publisher: Charles Hartford
Editor-in-Chief: Jean Woy
Senior Sponsoring Editor: Nancy Blaine
Development Editor: Julie Dunn
Senior Project Editor: Rosemary R. Jaffe
Associate Production/Design Coordinator: Bethany Schlegel
Manufacturing Manager: Florence Cadran
Senior Marketing Manager: Sandra McGuire

Cover Image: Interior of a factory for dying textiles, Vienna, Austria (nineteenth-century print). Courtesy of The Art Archive, London.

Credits appear on page 233, which constitutes an extension of the copyright page.

Printed in the U.S.A.

Library of Congress Control Number: 2001098674

ISBN: 0-618-22025-9

123456789-CRW-07 06 05 04 03

Contents

Preface

Any attempt to understand Europe and the world since the beginning of the nineteenth century would be incomplete without consideration of the Industrial Revolution. It was a fundamental transformation in history, with such wide-reaching impacts that it commands center stage in disciplines as diverse as international relations, sociology, and economics. Among historians, there has been no end to the study of its causes and impacts since the famed British historian Arnold Toynbee first popularized the phrase "Industrial Revolution" in a series of published lectures in 1884. Even before then, scholars had begun to ask pointed questions of the dramatic changes that seemed to be rocking the world around them: how was one to define the economic and social revolution occurring throughout much of Europe; what was the origin and nature of these developments; why did it begin in England and what might prompt similar changes elsewhere; what other alterations might follow in its wake. These are the same questions that structure this book.

After a brief introduction, outlining the history of industrialization in Western Europe alongside a chronology that lists some of the key technological developments in the eighteenth and nineteenth centuries, the selections fall into five analytical themes and key questions that have shaped the literature. Parts I, II, and III focus on giving meaning to the term Industrial Revolution and understanding why and where it arose as it did. In these sections, comparison offers its greatest rewards, shedding light on the factors that gave England its advantages while providing a definition that incorporates the myriad experiences and developments from across the Channel. In Part I, for example, David Landes's classic definition stressing dramatic technological innovation in England meets opposition from William Sewell's argument that the industrial organization of the workplace need not depend upon the advent of new machinery, as the French case demonstrates. At the same time, E. A. Wrigley argues that much of England's industrialization was slow and gradual. In Parts II and III, concerns with causation take historians as far back in time as the fifteenth century and as far from Europe as China. Joel Mokyr, for instance, traces England's head start to numerous factors that included a social, economic, and political environment that fostered invention and innovation, the roots of which Nathan Rosenberg and L. E. Birdzell Jr. trace back to the advent of laws guaranteeing private property. Keith Pomerantz, on the other hand, emphasizes the role of the Americas in his explanation of Europe's ability to overcome the same "land constraints" that stifled industrial development in China. Following this attention to definitions and causes, Parts IV and V focus on some of the most significant impacts that followed—primarily in the nineteenth century. Working-class formation and the recent concern with gender and family history take pride of place among these passages. In Part V, Louise Tilly and Joan Scott argue that the separation of work and home life significantly altered women's experiences, offering both new freedoms and greater risks. Elinor Accampo builds on this by exploring its impact on fertility and family relations, claiming that industrialization brought enormous stress upon working-class families. While this book's structure thus mirrors much of the current historical research, readers are encouraged to follow their own leads and make connections across existing boundaries. Finally, a list of suggested readings, like the excerpts themselves, gives the readers a means of continuing their own inquiries into a vibrant field that shows no signs of relaxing in the future.

Like a manufactured item, this book is the product of time and effort from many different individuals. It arose from the interest of Merry Wiesner, who first suggested it to me in 1999. Early reviews from Kenneth Mouré, University of California at Santa Barbara; Royce E. Walters, Indiana University of Pennsylvania and others then offered many useful suggestions that have made this a much stronger work than I first proposed. At Houghton Mifflin, Nancy Blaine, Julie Dunn, and Rosemary Jaffe oversaw the whole process with professional skill and great concern, answering many questions and gently coaxing me through the editing process. Along the way, I've benefited enormously from discussions with colleagues at Centre College and elsewhere, especially Lori Hartmann-Mahmud, Gina Hames, Mike Hamm, Rick Bradshaw, and Dan Stroup. My own understanding of the Industrial Revolution has been shaped most significantly by two sources, however: Peter N. Stearns, who first guided me through the vast literature, and my students, whose questions and interests have challenged me to think more clearly and coherently about this complex process. Finally, academic pursuits rely heavily on so much that is nonacademic. For all his attention to those other essential aspects of life, I thank John Rusnak, to whom this work is dedicated.

Steven M. Beaudoin

Editor's Preface to Instructors

There are many ways to date ourselves as teachers and scholars of history: the questions that we regard as essential to ask about any historical development, the theorists whose words we quote and whose names appear in our footnotes, the price of the books that we purchased for courses and that are on our shelves. Looking over my own shelves, it struck me that another way we could be dated was by the color of the oldest books we owned in this series, which used to be published by D. C. Heath. I first used a "Heath series" book—green and white, as I recall—when I was a freshman in college and taking a modern European history course. That book, by Dwight E. Lee on the Munich crisis, has long since disappeared, but several Heath books that I acquired later as an undergraduate are still on my shelves. Those that I used in graduate school, including ones on the Renaissance and Reformation, are also there, as are several I assigned my students when I first started teaching or have used in the years since. As with any system of historical periodization, of course, this method of dating a historian is flawed and open to misinterpretation. When a colleague retired, he gave me some of his even older Heath series books, in red and black, which had actually appeared when I was still in elementary and junior high school, so that a glance at my shelves might make me seem ready for retirement.

The longevity of this series, despite its changing cover design and its transition from D. C. Heath to Houghton Mifflin, could serve as an indication of several things. One might be that historians are conservative, unwilling to change the way they approach the past or teach about it. The rest of the books on my shelves suggest that this conservatism is not the case, however, for many of the books discuss topics that were unheard of as subjects of historical investigation when I took that course as a freshman thirty years ago: memory, masculinity, visual culture, sexuality.

Another way to account for the longevity of this series is that several generations of teachers have found it a useful way for their students to approach historical subjects. As teachers, one of the first issues we confront in any course is what materials we will assign our students to read. (This decision is often, in fact, paramount for we have to order books months before the class begins.) We may include a textbook to provide an overview of the subject matter covered in the course and often have several from which to choose. We may use a reader of original sources, or several sources in their entirety, because we feel that it is important for our students to hear the voices of people of the past directly. We may add a novel from the period, for fictional works often give one details and insights that do not emerge from other types of sources. We may direct our students to visual materials, either in books or on the Web, for artifacts, objects, and art can give one access to aspects of life never mentioned in written sources.

Along with these types of assignments, we may also choose to assign books such as those in this series, which present the ideas and opinions of scholars on a particular topic. Textbooks are, of course, written by scholars with definite opinions, but they are designed to present material in a relatively bland manner. They may suggest areas about which there is historical debate (often couched in phrases such as "scholars disagree about . . .") but do not participate in those debates themselves. By contrast, the books in this series highlight points of dispute, and cover topics and developments about which historians often disagree vehemently. Students who are used to the textbook approach to history may be surprised at the range of opinion on certain matters, but we hope that the selections in each of these volumes will allow readers to understand why there is such a diversity. Each volume covers several issues of interpretive debate and highlights newer research directions.

Variety of interpretation in history is sometimes portrayed as a recent development, but the age of this series in its many cover styles indicates that this account is not accurate. Historians have long recognized that historical sources are produced by particular individuals with particular interests and biases that consciously and unconsciously shape their content. They have also long—one is tempted to say "always"—recognized that different people approach the past differently, making choices about which topics to study, which sources to use, which developments and individuals to highlight. This diversity in both sources and methodologies is part of what makes history exciting for those of us who study it, for new materials and new approaches allow us to see things that have never been seen before, in the same way that astronomers find new stars with better tools and new ways of looking.

The variety and innovation that is an essential part of good historical scholarship allow this series both to continue and to change. Some of the volumes now being prepared have the same titles as those I read as an undergraduate, but the scholarship on that topic has changed so much in the last several decades that they had to be completely redone, not simply revised. Some of the volumes now in print examine topics that were rarely covered in undergraduate courses when the series began publication, and a few former volumes are no longer in print because the topics they investigated now show up more rarely. We endeavor to keep the series up-to-date and welcome suggestions about volumes that would prove helpful for teaching undergraduate and graduate courses. You can contact us at http://college.hmco.com.

Merry E. Wiesner

Editor's Preface to Students

History is often presented as facts marching along a timeline, and historical research is often viewed as the unearthing of information so that more facts can be placed on the timeline. Like geologists in caves or physicists using elaborate microscopes, historians discover new bits of data, which allow them to recover more of the past.

To some degree, this model is accurate. Like laboratory scientists, historians do conduct primary research, using materials in archives, libraries, and many other places to discover new things about the past. Over the last thirty years, for example, the timeline of history has changed from a story that was largely political and military to one that includes the experiences of women, peasants, slaves, children, and workers. Even the political and military story has changed and now includes the experiences of ordinary soldiers and minority groups rather than simply those of generals, rulers, and political elites. This expansion of the timeline has come in part through intensive research in original sources, which has vastly increased what we know about people of the past.

Original research is only part of what historians do, however, in the same way that laboratory or field research is only part of science. Historical and scientific information is useless until someone tries to make sense of what is happening, tries to explain why and how things developed the way they did. In making these analyses and conclusions, however, both historians and scientists often come to disagree vehemently about the underlying reasons for what they have observed or discovered, and sometimes about the observations themselves. Certain elements of those observations are irrefutable—a substance either caught fire or it did not, a person lived and died or he or she did not—but many more of them are open to debate: Was the event (whether historical or scientific) significant? Why and how did it happen? Under what circumstances might it not have happened? What factors influenced the way that it happened? What larger consequences did it have?

The books in this series focus on just those types of questions. They take one particular event or development in European history and present you with the analyses of several historians and other authors regarding this issue. In some cases the authors may disagree about what actually happened—in the same way that eyewitnesses of a traffic accident or crime may all see different things—but more often they disagree about the interpretation. Was the Renaissance a continuation of earlier ideas, or did it represent a new way of looking at the world? Was nineteenth-century European imperialism primarily political and economic in its origins and impact, or were cultural and intellectual factors more significant? Was ancient Athens a democracy worthy of emulation, an expansionary state seeking to swallow its neighbors, or both? Within each volume are often more specific points of debate, which add complexity to the main question and introduce you to further points of disagreement.

Each of the volumes begins with an introduction by the editor, which you should read carefully before you turn to the selections themselves. This introduction sets out the *historical* context of the issue, adding depth to what you may have learned in a textbook account or other reading, and also explains the *historiographical* context, that is, how historians (including those excerpted in the volume) have viewed the issue over time. Many volumes also include a timeline of events and several reference maps that situate the issue chronologically and geographically. These may be more detailed than the timelines and maps in your textbook, and consulting them as you read will help deepen your understanding of the selections.

Some of the volumes in the series include historical analyses that are more than a century old, and all include writings stretching over several decades. The editors include this chronological range not only to allow you to see that interpretations change, but also to see how lines of argument and analysis develop. Every historian approaching an issue depends not only on his or her own original research, but also on the secondary analyses of those who have gone before, which he or she then accepts, rejects, modifies, or adapts. Thus, within the book as a whole or within each section, the selections are generally arranged in chronological order; reading them in the order they are presented will allow you to get a better sense of the historiographical development and to make comparisons among the selections more easily and appropriately.

The description of the scholarly process noted above is somewhat misleading, for in both science and history, research and analysis are not sequential but simultaneous. Historians do not wander around archives looking for interesting bits of information but turn to their sources with specific questions in mind, questions that have often been developed by reading earlier historians. These questions shape where they will look, what they will pay attention to, and therefore what conclusions they will make. Thus, the fact that we now know so much more about women, peasants, or workers than we did several decades ago did not result primarily from sources on these people suddenly appearing where there had been none, but from historians, with new questions in mind, going back to the same archives and libraries that had yielded information on kings and generals. The same is true in science, of course; scientists examining an issue begin with a hypothesis and then test it through the accumulation of information, reaching a conclusion that leads to further hypotheses.

In both history and science, one's hypotheses can sometimes be so powerful that one simply cannot see what the sources or experiments show, which is one reason there is always opportunity for more research or a re-analysis of data. A scholar's analysis may also be shaped by many other factors, and in this volume the editor may have provided you with information about individual authors, such as their national origin, intellectual background, or philosophical perspective, if these factors are judged important to your understanding of their writings or points of view. You might be tempted to view certain of these factors as creating "bias" on the part of an author and thus to reduce the value of his or her analysis. It is important to recognize, however, that every historian or commentator has a particular point of view and writes at a particular historical moment; very often what scholars view as complete objectivity on their own part is seen as subjective bias by those who disagree. The central aim of this series over its forty-plus years of publication has been to help you and other students understand how and why the analyses and judgments of historians have differed and changed over time, to see that scholarly controversy is at the heart of the historical enterprise.

The instructor in your course may have provided you with detailed directions for using this book, but here are some basic questions that you can ask yourself as you read the selections:

- What is the author's central argument?
- What evidence does the author put forward to support this argument?
- What is the significance of the author's argument?
- What other interpretation might there be of the evidence that the author presents?
- How does each author's argument intersect with the others in the part? In the rest of the book?
- How convincing do you find the author's interpretation?

These questions are exactly the same as those that professional historians ask themselves, and in analyzing and comparing the selections in this book, you, too, are engaged in the business of historical interpretation.

Merry E. Wiesner

Chronology

1712	Thomas Newcommen invents a steam engine to pump water from mines.
1733	John Kay invents the flying shuttle, increasing the output of woven cloth.
1764	James Hargreaves invents the spinning jenny, which Richard Arkwright improves on with his water frame, allowing water power to work several spindles at once.
1769	Josiah Wedgewood establishes the Etruria bone china works, an early experiment with the factory system.
1776	James Watt makes great improvements to the Newcommen steam engine.
1779	Samuel Crompton invents a spinning mule allowing many spindles to be worked at once.
1784	Henry Cort patents a puddling process designed to convert pig iron into wrought iron.
1787	Edmund Cartwright builds the first wool-combing machine and an early version of the power loom.
1800	Alessandro Volta invents the galvanic cell, the first electric battery that converts chemical energy into electricity.
	Eli Whitney is credited with the introduction of interchangeable parts for manufacturing muskets, but his work builds heavily on earlier techniques devised by Simeon North.
1801	Joseph M. Jacquard invents a loom for figured silk fabrics, later introduced into the making of worsteds.

1802 Richard Trevithick builds the first high-pressure steam engine and patents the steam carriage for transportation.

1807 Robert Fulton sails the steamboat *Clermont* from New York to Albany, the first commercially successful operation of a steamboat (earlier versions included the Marquis Claude de Jouffroy d'Abbans's paddle-wheel steamer in 1783 and John Stevens's screw-propeller steamboat in 1802).

1813 William Horrocks invents a new power loom, which Richard Roberts improves in 1822.

1814 George Stephenson builds his first locomotive, predecessor to his 1829 *Rocket*, which wins a competition with locomotives of other design and sets the pattern for future locomotive developments.

1818 The Institute of Civil Engineers, the first professional engineering society, is founded in London.

1825 The Stockton-Darlington Railway opens—the first successful railroad system, using a steam engine built by Stephenson.

1827 Benoit Fourneyron develops the water turbine.

1830 Joseph Whitworth invents the standard screw gauge and a machine to measure one millionth of an inch, permitting greater precision in machine tools for planing, gear cutting, and milling.

1837 Charles Wheatstone and William F. Cooke patent the telegraph, which is also independently invented by the American Samuel F. B. Morse.

1845 William McNaught creates the compound engine by adding a high-pressure cylinder to the Watt engine.

1846 Elias Howe invents the lockstitch sewing machine.

1849–51 Samuel Colt and Elisha Root develop a practical system for manufacturing interchangeable parts.

1851 London hosts the Great Exhibition at the Crystal Palace meant to trumpet Britain's industrial prominence.

1851	Isaac M. Singer invents the first practical domestic sewing machine.
1856	Henry Bessemer perfects a technique (the Bessemer process) for converting pig iron into steel.
1860	Construction begins on the London underground railway system, which is electrified in 1905.
1866	Cyrus W. Field successfully completes laying the first transatlantic telegraph cable.
1869	Ferdinand de Lesseps completes the Suez Canal.
1873	Electricity is first used to drive machinery (in Vienna).
	The Remington Company begins the manufacture of the typewriter, patented by Christopher L. Sholes.
1876	Nicholas August Otto invents the first practical gas engine, which Gottlieb Daimler improves on in a gasoline engine he patents in 1885.
	Alexander Graham Bell patents the telephone.
1878	Joseph W. Swan of England makes the first successful carbon filament electric lamp; working independently, Thomas A. Edison patents his incandescent bulb a year later.
1882	Thomas Edison's electric generating station at Holborn Viaduct Station in England begins operation.
1885	Karl Benz produces the prototype for the automobile using an internal combustion engine.
1888	John B. Dunlop invents the pneumatic tire, supporting the development of automobiles.
1892	Rudolf Diesel patents a heavy oil engine and successfully manufactures it in 1897.

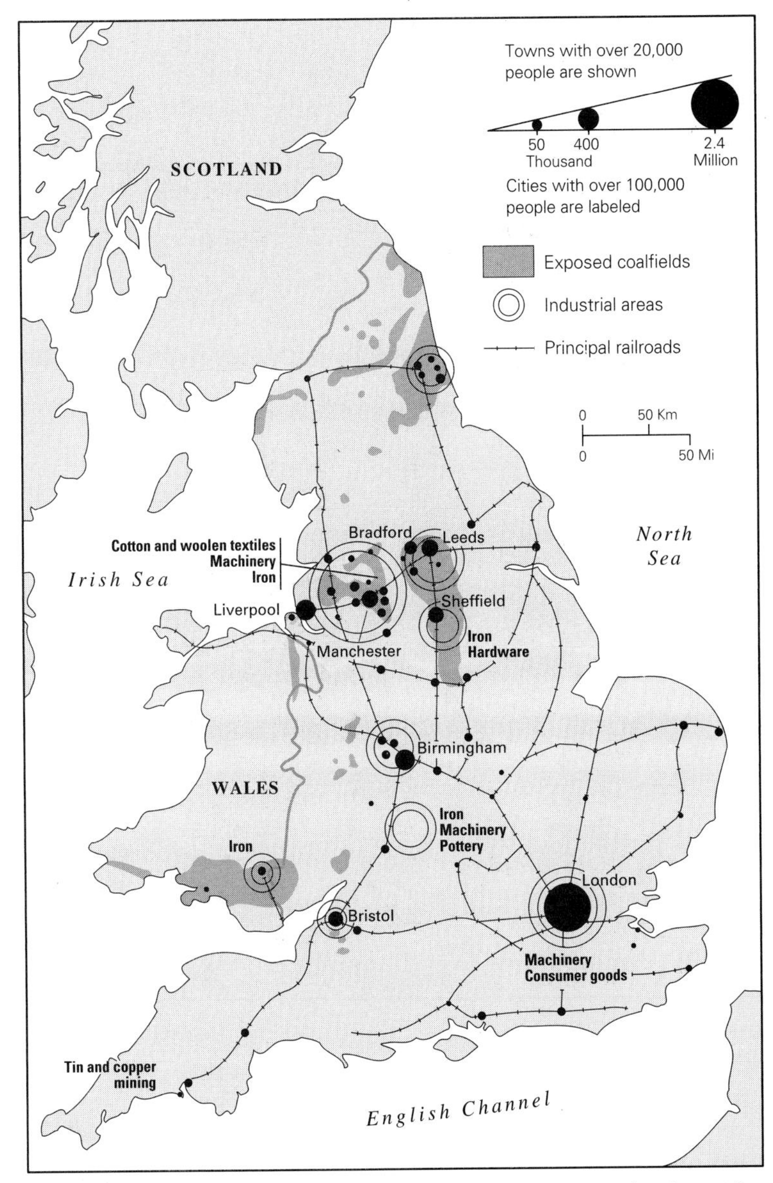

The Industrial Revolution in England, ca 1850 Industry concentrated in the rapidly growing cities of the north and the Midlands, where rich coal and iron deposits were in close proximity.

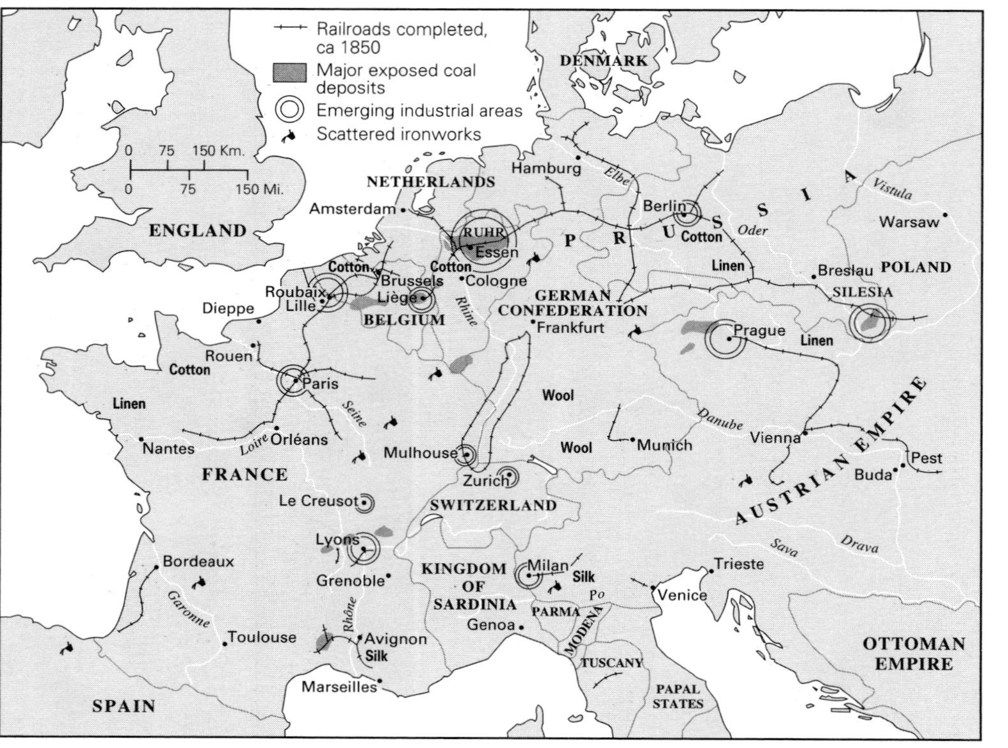

Continental Industrialization, ca 1850 Although continental countries were beginning to make progress by 1850, they still lagged far behind Britain. For example, continental railroad building was still in an early stage, whereas the British rail system was essentially complete.

The Industrial Revolution

Introduction

The Industrial Revolution was one of the most significant transformations in the history of humankind. In magnitude and scope, it is comparable only to the Neolithic Revolution, the seedbed of civilization and sedentary agriculture. The Industrial Revolution not only altered production methods and the overall nature of national and regional economies; it also initiated modifications in home life, demographics, social structure, and politics, to name but a few. Not surprisingly, then, historians and other scholars have scrambled to explain the various causes and impacts of this revolution since its first obvious manifestations in the early nineteenth century. Yet at some basic level, it is deceptively simple to understand. Whether in Asia or Europe, Latin America or the United States, industrialization concerns technology and organization. It is the adaptation of new technology to the manufacturing process, such as the replacement of human and animal labor with steam and electricity, and the invention of new machinery to harness that power more effectively for both production and transportation. This substitution results in the complete restructuring of both the manufacture and the marketing of goods. At the same time, the place of manufacturing in the overall shape of the economy shifts to accentuate the secondary sector.[1] In the European case, workshops gave way to factories, small shops yielded to department stores, and agriculture ceded its prominence to manufacturing—which itself witnessed further concentration in the rise of big business.[2] All of this spearheaded Europe's continued development as an industrialized society, capable of dominating world trade to an unprecedented extent.

According to most historians, this process began in England around 1750 and then spread to the Continent after the Revolutionary and Napoleonic Wars. Traditionally, the study of industrialization incorporates two major periods, designated simply as the First and Second Industrial Revolutions. The first entailed the dramatic transformation

[1]Scholars frequently divide economic activity into three sectors. The first entails direct extraction of natural resources, like mining and agriculture. The second includes the production of manufactured goods. The third involves economic activity that results in no tangible product, such as banking and wholesale or retail trade.

[2]Steven M. Beaudoin, "Current Debates in the Study of the Industrial Revolution," *Organization of American Historians' Magazine of History*, 15, no. 1 (Fall 2000): 7–13.

of three primary industries: textiles, metallurgy, and transportation. First in Britain and then in Belgium, France, and Germany by the mid-nineteenth century, the use of steam power and new inventions and techniques permitted manufacturers to increase production and reach wider markets. In iron forging and mining, for example, Henry Cort's puddling process made a stronger and purer wrought iron more accessible by the 1780s and prompted the widespread use of the steam engine to pump water out of coal mines and later to power locomotives along iron rails. But the true age of the machine emerged during the Second Industrial Revolution, after 1870, when the use of electricity and the internal combustion engine mechanized virtually all aspects of manufacturing. Inventions also created whole new industries, such as the chemical and automobile businesses.

At the same time, industrialization involved the complete restructuring of the production process. The most obvious innovation was the factory system, which separated work from home by grouping workers together and subjecting them to tighter work-discipline in order to increase production and cut costs. Frequently, factory organization followed the introduction of large machinery like spinning and weaving machines, but this was not always the case. Regardless of mechanization, the specialization of labor in factories increased the importance of wage labor to working families and introduced a certain amount of deskilling. Workers no longer learned an entire craft, only that small portion in which their employers asked them to specialize. Workers became semiskilled.

In addition to factories, industrialization promoted business consolidation. Maintaining competitiveness required a great deal of capital, especially during the Second Industrial Revolution. Small family firms that had been the mainstay of industrialization before 1870 found it difficult to remain innovative. So states provided the institutional frameworks necessary to big business, including laws creating corporations and limiting investor liability. Again, England pioneered such legislation in the 1840s, with much of the Continent following suit in the 1860s. Like the timing of this legislation, the process of industrialization in Europe witnessed wide variations, but remained true to this general outline for the most part. And as most historians agree, this transformation had significant ramifications for class formation and politics in nineteenth-century Europe.

Yet for all of this apparent simplicity and consensus, the Industrial Revolution remains at the center of great debate. This is due in part to its overwhelming scale. It has no clear beginning or end, there are few key dates to act as turning points, and it bleeds ceaselessly over the conventional boundaries separating fields like economic history and cultural history. In short, industrialization is a difficult process to integrate into the traditional framework of historical analysis; it defies easy periodization and categorization. As some of the following selections demonstrate, for example, some scholars argue that the true causes of the Industrial Revolution rest on a spate of technological inventions and innovation during the eighteenth and nineteenth centuries, while others insist that its roots go as far back as the fifteenth century. Similarly, historians dispute whether those same causes can be traced solely to social and economic factors or to changing patterns of business behavior related more to cultural phenomena such as religion. The numerous impacts of the Industrial Revolution spawn even more disagreement, given its apparent connection to all facets of life. As for a culmination, it is difficult to ascribe an end to the Industrial Revolution because continued change, especially in manufacturing technology, is a fundamental part of its essence.

These inherent difficulties create and enhance debate over the Industrial Revolution, but they are not the sole cause of disagreement among scholars. Another explanation arises from industrialization's policy implications. Long seen as the key to the modern West's power and success, industrialization has been the focus of intense study not just by historians, but also by policy analysts bent on understanding its causes and copying its achievements. In the early nineteenth century, continental powers sent spies to great textile cities like Manchester and Birmingham and wooed engineers and factory managers with hopes of transplanting British technology in their own soil. Later, delegations from as far away as Japan and China toured European factories and universities, aiming to borrow Western technical and commercial know-how so as to keep the "barbarians" from overrunning their countries. And currently, organizations such as the International Monetary Fund force Third World nations in need of loans to reform their economies in order to promote "development"—often a synonym for industrialization. It isn't surprising, then, that studying the Industrial Revolution generates intense disagreement. For many, the stakes are high and are more material than intellectual.

These different opinions form the backbone of this book. The selections it brings together are meant to acquaint the reader with both the basic outlines of industrialization and the different interpretations of those who research it. For the most part, the passages herein pertain to those developments associated with the First Industrial Revolution, from approximately 1750 to 1850, but certain selections on causation and impacts go beyond those dates. Like the Industrial Revolution itself, these excerpts also span the range of historical inquiry, from economic studies of its causes to social and cultural interpretations of its consequences. In fact, most parts combine selections from different analytical standpoints. In addition, although the selections include a few classic interpretations, particular attention has gone into choosing passages from the most recent literature. In particular, Part V is devoted to the growing interest in gender as a category of historical analysis and the new perspectives this affords on this already intensely studied subject. Together, the excerpts assembled here convey the continued challenge of understanding the Industrial Revolution and the powerful attraction it retains for all students of modern society.

Workers in the Baines Cotton Mills, 1835 Family members often worked side by side in early British factories, and the child on the left is quite possibly the daughter of the woman nearby. They are combing raw cotton and drawing it into loose strands called rovings, which will be spun into fine thread. (*Mary Evans Picture Library* #10015743/04)

PART

I Defining the Industrial Revolution

Acknowledging change is often far easier than defining it. No one disputes how significant the Industrial Revolution was to humanity. The very nature of the transformation, however, remains a matter of great debate. Some even question if the term *Industrial Revolution* is truly appropriate. The phrase, coined by a Frenchman in the 1820s, first gained currency in English with Arnold Toynbee's 1884 *Lectures on the Industrial Revolution.* By the twentieth century, even those who opposed the wording acknowledged the futility of fighting it. In fact, it acquired even greater force with W. W. Rostow's classic image of the industrial "takeoff." According to Rostow, industrialization is marked by a series of stages: an initial takeoff of technological innovation in certain sectors, a more extended period of adaptation during which technology spreads to different areas of manufacturing and produces higher growth rates, and a final, mature stage in which new technology can be used in all branches of production. But since the inception in 1960 of this interpretation, it has lost much of its allure. A new school of historians, relying heavily upon the tools of economic analysis, emphasizes the gradual nature of change associated with industrialization, which was itself more of a long, multifaceted process than a "revolution." This approach, too, has its critics, and in recent years the battle to define the Industrial Revolution has raged anew.

David S. Landes's influential book *The Unbound Prometheus* mirrors most succinctly the early paradigm of technological change and rapid transformation as the heart and soul of the Industrial Revolution. Focusing primarily upon the cotton, iron, and mining industries, Landes argues that a series of new inventions revolutionized production between 1750 and 1800. In its wake, this technology not only reshaped the organization of manufacturing by introducing the factory system, but also paved the way for significant alterations in society and politics. In this sense, revolution is a doubly appropriate concept. This interpretation is particularly noteworthy for its inclusion of the complex relationship between industrialization and modernization, a term many historians now reject for its vagueness and veiled ethnocentrism. Nevertheless, it captures the myriad transformations frequently enmeshed with the study of industrialization and thus makes the difficulty of defining and interpreting this significant development so understandable.

In his analysis, Landes also manages to tie together two different approaches to understanding the Industrial Revolution. The first emphasizes the social organization of both production and consumption. Industrialization entailed the mass production and consumption of goods and the final destruction of extra-economic relationships that had defined manorial agriculture and guild manufacturing. The second gives technology pride of place in bringing about such transformations, basing change on the invention and diffusion of new machinery.

In recent decades, Landes's emphasis on abrupt change has undergone significant challenges on a number of fronts. Emphasizing the slow and measured pace of industrial transformation, for example, practitioners of New Economic History have brought new tools to bear on this topic.[1] Using quantitative data on the per capita growth of output, they challenge any analysis of the Industrial Revolution that emphasizes its suddenness, its dependence on technological change, and its linear progression from earlier developments.

[1]The New Economic History refers to the school of history whose practitioners—self-styled cliometricians—began in the 1960s to apply economic theory and quantitative methods, like statistical analysis, to historical data.

This has been particularly true of French historians. Because manufacturing in France experienced relatively little technological change, earlier histories even posed the question, Did France have an Industrial Revolution? William Sewell represents a new group, however, that argues that low population growth translated into rates of output per capita that rivaled England's. French industry accomplished this largely by altering the organization of manufacturing and by carving out a niche for itself in the European market for handcrafted luxury items. Without necessarily creating factories, manufacturers in France began to operate growing workshops in a manner that increased production and that deskilled labor (see Part IV). Though smaller in scale, French workshops came to mirror the large factories of England in significant ways. Moreover, French citizens came to enjoy similar rises in per capita incomes and consumption. In the final analysis, then, France developed an industrial economy and society without a technological "revolution."

In the aptly titled *Continuity, Chance and Change,* E. A. Wrigley maintains a macroeconomic scope that hinges on aggregate data and places the mechanized sectors of cotton textiles and mining into the broader context of England's national economy, from agriculture to handicraft. The result is a continued emphasis on gradual change and a reevaluation of the nature of economic development. Wrigley's starting point is the curious observation that most of England's most prominent and astute eighteenth-century political economists, including Adam Smith and Thomas Malthus, failed to recognize the promise of the economic transformation occurring in their midst. In fact, many of the country's brightest minds wrote more as harbingers of economic gloom and dearth.

Wrigley explains this pessimism by distinguishing between two interconnected economies at work during the eighteenth century: an agricultural, or "organic," economy that was much more familiar to contemporary scholars, and an industrial, or "mineral-based energy" economy arising in certain sectors of manufacturing. England's political economists wrote more about the former not just because the latter was new and unrecognizable, but also because the two coexisted in inverse proportion to each other throughout the transition to an industrial economy. The process by which the latter managed to outperform and dominate the former was long and protracted. Besides acknowledging the continuity in English economic development, this approach also clearly and succinctly delineates the differences between agricultural and industrial economies. Finally, in an illuminating comparison of England and Holland, Wrigley argues that English industrial development was predicated upon the luck of having a readily available source of mineral-based energy—coal. In short, there was nothing rapid or natural about the progression from an advanced organic to an industrial economy. The Industrial Revolution was the product of continuity, chance, and change.

While gradualists like Wrigley currently seem to hold the upper hand in the debate over the definition of the Industrial Revolution, Maxine Berg and Pat Hudson have recently argued for a "rehabilitation" of the concept of and the emphasis on rapid, fundamental change. Berg and Hudson assert that the gradualists have overemphasized national and aggregate data while maintaining an artificial divide between the traditional and modern sectors of the economy. If historians focused on regions and examined the ways all manufacturing changed, they would find more drastic alterations, from innovation in "traditional" trades to life-altering variations in child and female labor. Finally, in an argument reminiscent of Sewell's, Berg and Hudson hold that a lack of groundbreaking technology in various trades did not necessarily indicate a similar lack of originality in organizational structure, which itself spurred significant transformations in social relations and consciousness. So while the sea change of the Industrial Revolution may have escaped detection by such luminaries as Smith and Malthus, millions of Britons living in the early decades of the nineteenth century could not and did not overlook the "revolutionary" new turns their lives were taking as England's economy shifted and grew.

David S. Landes

The Unbound Prometheus

When dealing with ambiguous terms, the first duty of a writer is definition. The words "industrial revolution"—in small letters—usually refer to that complex of technological innovations which, by substituting machines for human skill and inanimate power for human and animal force, brings about a shift from handicraft to manufacture and, so doing, gives birth to a modern economy. In this sense, the industrial revolution has already transformed a number of countries, though in unequal degree; other societies are in the throes of change; the turn of still others is yet to come.

The words sometimes have another meaning. They are used to denote any rapid significant technological change, and historians have spoken of an "industrial revolution of the thirteenth century," an "early industrial revolution," the "second industrial revolution," an "industrial revolution in the cotton south." In this sense, we shall eventually have as many "revolutions" as there are historically demarcated sequences of industrial innovation, plus all such sequences as will occur in the future; there are those who say, for example, that we are already in the midst of the third industrial revolution, that of automation, air transport, and atomic power.

Finally, the words, when capitalized, have still another meaning. They denote the first historical instance of the breakthrough from an agrarian, handicraft economy to one dominated by industry and machine manufacture. The Industrial Revolution began in England in the eighteenth century, spread therefrom in unequal fashion to the countries of Continental Europe and a few areas overseas, and transformed in the span of scarce two lifetimes the life of Western man, the nature of his society, and his relationship to the other peoples of the world. The Industrial Revolution, as it took place in western Europe, is the subject of this book.

From David S. Landes, *The Unbound Prometheus: Technological Change and Industrial Development in Western Europe from 1750 to the Present* (Cambridge: Cambridge University Press, 1969).

The heart of the Industrial Revolution was an interrelated succession of technological changes. The material advances took place in three areas: (1) there was a substitution of mechanical devices for human skills; (2) inanimate power—in particular, steam—took the place of human and animal strength; (3) there was a marked improvement in the getting and working of raw materials, especially in what are now known as the metallurgical and chemical industries.

Concomitant with these changes in equipment and process went new forms of industrial organization. The size of the productive unit grew: machines and power both required and made possible the concentration of manufacture, and shop and home workroom gave way to mill and factory. At the same time, the factory was more than just a larger work unit. It was a system of production, resting on a characteristic definition of the functions and responsibilities of the different participants in the productive process. On the one side was the employer, who not only hired the labour and marketed the finished product, but supplied the capital equipment and oversaw its use. On the other side there stood the worker; no longer capable of owning and furnishing the means of production and reduced to the status of a hand (the word is significant and symbolizes well this transformation from producer to pure labourer). Binding them were the economic relationship—the "wage nexus"—and the functional one of supervision and discipline.

Discipline, of course, was not entirely new. Certain kinds of work—large construction projects, for example—had always required the direction and co-ordination of the efforts of many people; and well before the Industrial Revolution there were a number of large workshops of "manufactories" in which traditional unmechanized labour operated under supervision. Yet discipline under such circumstances was comparatively loose (there is no overseer so demanding as the steady click-clack of the machine); and such as it was, it affected only a small portion of the industrial population.

Factory discipline was another matter. It required and eventually created a new breed of worker, broken to the inexorable demands of the clock. It also held within itself the seeds of further technological advance, for control of labour implies the possibility of the rationalization of labour. From the start, the specialization of productive functions was pushed farther in the factory than it had been in shops and cottages; at the same time, the difficulties of manipulating men and materials within a limited area gave rise to improvements in layout and organization.

There is a direct chain of innovation from the efforts to arrange the manufacturing process so that the raw material would move downwards in the plant as it was treated, to the assembly line and transmission belts of today.

In all of this diversity of technological improvement, the unity of the movement is apparent: change begat change. For one thing, many technical improvements were feasible only after advances in associated fields. The steam engine is a classic example of this technological interrelatedness: it was impossible to produce an effective condensing engine until better methods of metal working could turn out accurate cylinders. For another, the gains in productivity and output of a given innovation inevitably exerted pressure on related industrial operations. The demand for coal pushed mines deeper until water seepage became a serious hazard; the answer was the creation of a more efficient pump, the atmospheric steam engine. A cheap supply of coal proved a godsend to the iron industry, which was stifling for lack of fuel. In the meantime, the invention and diffusion of machinery in the textile manufacture and other industries created a new demand for energy, hence for coal and steam engines; and these engines, and the machines themselves, had a voracious appetite for iron, which called for further coal and power. Steam also made possible the factory city, which used unheard-of quantities of iron (hence coal) in its many storied mills and its water and sewage systems. At the same time, the processing of the flow of manufactured commodities required great amounts of chemical substances: alkalis, acids, and dyes, many of them consuming mountains of fuel in the making. And all of these products—iron, textiles, chemicals—depended on large-scale movements of goods on land and on sea, from the sources of the raw materials into the factories and out again to near and distant markets. The opportunity thus created and the possibilities of the new technology combined to produce the railroad and steamship, which of course added to the demand for iron and fuel while expanding the market for factory products. And so on, in ever-widening circles.

In this sense, the Industrial Revolution marked a major turning point in man's history. To that point, the advances of commerce and industry, however gratifying and impressive, were essentially superficial: more wealth, more goods, prosperous cities, merchant nabobs. The world had seen other periods of industrial prosperity—in medieval Italy and Flanders, for example—and had seen the line of economic advance recede in each case; in the absence of qualitative changes, of improvements in productivity, there could be no guarantee that mere quantitative gains would be consolidated. It was the Industrial Revolution that initiated a cumulative self-sustaining advance in technology whose repercussions would be felt in all aspects of economic life.

To be sure, opportunity is not necessarily achievement. Economic progress has been uneven, marked by spurts and recessions, and there is no reason to be complacent about the prospect of an indefinite climb. For one thing, technological advance is not a smooth, balanced process. Each innovation seems to have a life span of its own, comprising periods of tentative youth, vigorous maturity, and declining old age. As its technological possibilities are realized, its marginal yield diminishes and it gives way to newer, more advantageous techniques. By the same token, the divers branches of production that embody these techniques follow their own logistic curve of growth toward a kind of asymptote. Thus the climb of those industries that were at the heart of the Industrial Revolution—textiles, iron and steel, heavy chemicals, steam engineering, railway transport—began to slow toward the end of the nineteenth century in the most advanced west European countries, so much so that some observers feared that the whole system was running down. (At this point, the Industrial Revolution in these countries was substantially complete.) Similar dire prognoses accompanied the world depression of the 1930's, particularly by those Marxist critics who saw the capitalist economy as incapable of sustained creativity. In fact, however, the advanced industrial economies have given proof of considerable technological vitality. The declining momentum of the early-modernizing branches in the late nineteenth century was more than compensated by the rise of new industries based on spectacular advances in chemical and electrical science and on a new, mobile source of power—the internal combustion engine. This is the cluster of innovations that is often designated as the second industrial revolution. Similarly, the contraction of the 1930's has been followed by decades of unusual creativity, consisting once again primarily in innovations in the application of chemical and electrical science, plus advances in the generation and delivery of power—the abovementioned third industrial revolution.

A more serious cause of concern lies outside the productive system proper—in the area of political economy and politics *tout court.* Even assuming that the ingenuity of scientists and engineers will always generate new ideas to relay the old and that they will find ways to overcome such shortages as may develop (whether of food, water, or industrial raw materials), there is no assurance that those men charged with utilizing these ideas will do so intelligently—intelligently, that is, not only in the sense of effective exploitation of their productive possibilities but in the larger sense of effective adaptation to the material and human environment so as to minimize waste, pollution, social friction, and other "external" costs. Similarly, there is no assurance that noneconomic exogenous factors—above all, man's incompetence in dealing with his fellow-man—will not reduce the whole magnificent structure to dust.

In the meantime, however, the climb has been spectacular. Improvements in productivity of the order of several thousand to one have been achieved in certain sectors—prime movers and spinning for example. In other areas, gains have been less impressive only by comparison: of the order of hundreds to one in weaving, or iron smelting, or shoemaking. Some areas, to be sure, have seen relatively little change: it still takes about as much time to shave a man as it did in the eighteenth century.

Quantitative gains in productivity are, of course, only part of the picture. Modern technology produces not only more, faster; it turns out objects that could not have been produced under any circumstances by the craft methods of yesterday. The best Indian hand spinner could not turn out yarn so fine and regular as that of the mule; all the forges in eighteenth-century Christendom could not have produced steel sheets so large, smooth, and homogeneous as those of a modern strip mill. Most important, modern technology has created things that could scarcely have been conceived in the pre-industrial era: the camera, the motor car, the aeroplane, the whole array of electronic devices from the radio to the high-speed computer, the nuclear power plant, and so on almost *ad infinitum.* Indeed, one of the primary stimuli of modern technology is free-ranging imagination; the increasing autonomy of pure science and the accumulation of a pool of untapped knowledge, in combination with the ramifying stock of established technique, have given ever wider scope to the inventive vision. Finally, to this array of new and better products—introduced, to be sure, at the expense of some of the more artistic results of hand craftsmanship—should be added that great range of exotic commodities, once rarities or luxuries, that are now available at reasonable prices thanks to improved transportation. It took the Industrial Revolution to make tea and coffee, the banana of Central America and the pineapple of Hawaii everyday foods. The result has been an enormous increase in the output and variety of goods and services, and this alone has changed man's way of life more than anything since the discovery of fire: the Englishman of 1750 was closer in material things to Caesar's legionnaires than to his own great-grandchildren.

These material advances in turn have provoked and promoted a large complex of economic, social, political, and cultural changes, which have reciprocally influenced the rate and course of technological development. There is, first, the transformation that we know as *industrialization.* This is the industrial revolution, in the specifically technological sense, plus its economic consequences, in particular the movement of labour and resources from agriculture to industry. The shift reflects the interaction of enduring characteristics of demand with the changing conditions of supply engendered by the industrial revolution. On the demand side, the nature of human wants is such that rises in income increase the appetite for food less than for manufactures. This is not true of people who have been living on the borderline of subsistence; they may use any extra money to eat better. But most Europeans were living about this level on the eve of industrialization; and although they did spend more for food as income went up, their expenditures on manufactures increased even faster. On the supply side, this shift in demand was reinforced by the relatively larger gains in industrial as against agricultural productivity, with a consequent fall in the price of manufactures relative to that of primary products.

Whether this disparity is inherent in the character of the industrial process, in other words, whether manufacture is intrinsically more susceptible of technological improvement than cultivation and husbandry, is an interesting but moot question. The fact remains that in the period of the Industrial Revolution and subsequently, industry moved ahead faster, increased its share of national wealth and product, and drained away the labour of the countryside. The shift varied from one country to another, depending on comparative advantage and institutional resistance. It was most extreme in Britain, where free trade stripped the farmer of protection against overseas competition; by 1912, only 12 per cent of Britain's labour force was employed in agriculture; by 1951, the proportion had fallen to an almost irreducible 5 per cent. And it was slowest in France, a country of small landholders, where a more gradual introduction of the new industrial technology combined with high tariffs on food imports to retard the contraction of the primary sector. Over half the French labour force was in agriculture in 1789 (perhaps 55 per cent or more), and this was still true in 1866, after three quarters of a century of technological change; as recently as 1950, the proportion was still a third.

Industrialization in turn is at the heart of a larger, more complex process often designated as *modernization.* This is that combination of changes—in the mode of production and government, in the social and institutional order, in the corpus of knowledge and in attitudes and values—that makes it possible for a society to hold its own in the twentieth century; that is, to compete on even terms in the generation of material and cultural wealth, to sustain its independence, and to promote and accommodate to further change. Modernization comprises such developments as urbanization (the concentration of the population in cities that serve as nodes of industrial production, administration, and intellectual and artistic activity); a sharp reduction in both death rates and birth rates from traditional levels (the so-called demographic transition); the establishment of an effective, fairly centralized bureaucratic government; the creation of an education system capable of training and socializing the children of the society to a level compatible with their capacities and best contemporary knowledge; and of course, the acquisition of the ability and means to use an up-to-date technology.

All of these elements are interdependent, . . . but each is to some degree autonomous, and it is quite possible to move ahead in some areas while lagging in others—witness some of the so-called developing or emerging nations of today. The one ingredient of modernization that is just about indispensable is technological maturity and the industrialization that goes with it; otherwise one has the trappings without the substance, the pretence without the reality. . . .

William H. Sewell Jr.

Work and Revolution in France

French Industrial Growth

France, like England and most other European nations, experienced wide-ranging changes in its economy during the nineteenth century. Whether these changes amounted to an "industrial revolution" is a matter of some scholarly controversy. J. H. Clapham, in his classic *Economic*

From William H. Sewell Jr., *Work and Revolution in France: The Language of Labor from the Old Regime to 1848* (Cambridge: Cambridge University Press, 1980).

Development of France and Germany, 1815–1914, was the first to raise the question. "It might be said," Clapham wrote, "that France never went through an industrial revolution . . . The transformation accomplished in a century was in many ways less complete than that which Germany experienced in the forty years after 1871." The contrast with England—the homeland of the industrial revolution—was perhaps even more striking. Between about 1780 and 1830, the face of England was transformed by the application of new industrial techniques. By the end of the 1820s, great areas in the North and Midlands of England had become bustling industrial districts with vast factories turning out cotton and woolen cloth or iron and steam engines. France experienced no great spurt of industrial growth comparable to either that of Germany after 1871 or of England in the late eighteenth and early nineteenth centuries. As a result, economic historians have tended to speak of its economy as "retarded" or "stagnant" in the nineteenth century. Indeed, accounting for "stagnation" or "retardation" has become a dominant problem in French economic history, especially in the writings of English and American scholars.

In recent years, however, economic historians have begun to look at the notion of "retardation" more critically, and the result has been a drastic shift in the perception of the nineteenth-century French economy. Detailed quantitative studies, above all those carried out by the Institut de science economique appliquée, have revealed that the French economy grew steadily and quite impressively in the nineteenth century—physical product per capita, for example, more than tripled from 1803–12 to 1905–13—and that nineteenth-century growth was a continuation of sustained economic expansion dating back at least to the middle of the eighteenth century. Although it is true that the French economy never experienced a "spurt" of industrial growth and that no area of France underwent the kind of dramatic and visible transformation from peaceful countryside to smoky and sprawling industrial district that occurred in the Midlands and Lancashire in Britain or in the Ruhr valley in Germany, the overall rate of increase in real output per capita during the nineteenth century was hardly distinguishable from that of Britain. It now appears that the French experience must be seen as one of the earliest and most successful cases of sustained modern industrial and economic growth and not as the anemic and imitative efforts of a late-starting "follower" of Britain.

One of the reasons for this shift in evaluation of the nineteenth-century French economy is a more careful specification of the meaning of "economic growth." Clapham and his successors were concerned chiefly with palpable signs of economic transformation—the rise of factories, the rapid growth of cities, the adoption of new techniques in agriculture, and so on. Their critics have defined economic growth more precisely—and more technically—as a sustained increase in real output per capita. Introducing the factory system was, of course, one important means of raising output per capita: It increased the productivity of labor by using new sources of power and new large-scale mechanical technology. But there were also many other ways in which output could be increased: by other, less spectacular improvements in technology; by better utilization of existing technology; by lowering transportation costs; by improving the scope and efficiency of markets; by utilizing given factors of production more efficiently through increased specialization, an increased division of labor, or improvements in the organization of firms, and so on. Finally, because income per capita is a fraction, with the national product as its numerator and the national population as its denominator, the rate of increase of population also has a direct effect on the rate of economic growth. In both England and France the introduction of factory production, particularly in textiles and metallurgy, was an important source of economic growth. But factories figured much less prominently in the French pattern of growth than in the British.

One important feature of the French economy that allowed a sustained increase in output per capita without a massive growth of factory industry was a relatively slow rate of population growth. The population of Europe as a whole more than doubled in the nineteenth century, whereas British population rose 350 percent over the century as a whole and German population rose 250 percent from 1816 to 1900. French population, by contrast, rose by less than 45 percent in the entire nineteenth century. . . . This slow growth of population—which resulted from a voluntary reduction in birthrates, not from high death rates—meant that the pressure of population on resources was less severe in France during the nineteenth century than in most other European countries. . . .

France's slow rate of population growth and leisurely pace of urbanization are of fundamental importance for understanding the French pattern of economic growth in the nineteenth century. This can be seen most clearly by contrast with Britain, where the development of large-scale, mechanized industry was intimately connected to rapid population growth. Factories, for all their advantages over handicraft methods of production, also had certain limitations, especially in the early decades of factory technology. They were superior at producing vast quantities of standardized goods of modest quality, but in order to be profitable, they also required a very large market for their goods. Otherwise, demand would be insufficient to justify the large and inflexible capital investment that a factory represented. The French market for mass-produced cotton and woolen cloth was far from insignificant, and French entrepreneurs in fact responded to this demand by constructing a large number of textile factories, particularly in such northern cities as Rouen, Elbeuf, Lille, Roubaix, Tourcoing, Mulhouse, Reims, and Saint-Quentin. But the expansion of demand in France was much slower than in England, and this limited the development of the French factory sector. Part of the British advantage in this respect was their domination of overseas markets and particularly of tropical markets, a domination that was secured by their naval victories in the wars of the French Revolution. However, the British home market also expanded much more rapidly than the French. In part this was simply a function of the higher overall rate of population growth. But the market for the kind of goods that could be produced profitably by factories increased even more rapidly than the population as a whole. . . .

All of this is not to say that rapid population growth or any other single factor by itself can "explain" British economic growth in the industrial revolution. The British economy grew as a result of mutually supporting interactions among a large number of factors: population growth, agricultural organization, foreign trade, favorable resource endowment, technological innovation, urbanization, unification of the market, and many others besides. But it is certainly true that the British economy would not have assumed its *particular* shape—with its massive development of factory production in vast industrial districts—had it not been for the rapid growth and rapid urbanization of the British population. And, by the same token, the very different shape of French economic growth was made possible by the slow growth of the French population. In Britain, the rapid increase in population and massive urbanization unified the market, wiped out peasant agriculture, and spurred demand for mass-produced goods. In France, the slow increase in population and gradual urbanization left many regional and local markets intact, allowed peasant agriculture to make piecemeal adjustments to slowly rising demand, and set limits on the market for mass-produced goods. The result was a much less revolutionary pattern of economic growth—but in the long run a no less successful one. Or to put the same point in terms more favorable to the French: Only a revolutionary transformation of the means of production enabled Britain to sustain a rising output per capita in the face of runaway population growth, whereas the French, with their slow population growth, could afford to be much more gradual.

The French pattern of economic growth, which combined substantial industrialization with the continued expansion of handicrafts and of peasant agriculture, should therefore not be seen as a failed effort to imitate British achievements but as an entirely appropriate response to the French situation. With population increasing only slowly, with much of the agricultural population only partially engaged in the cash nexus, and with the national territory divided into only partially integrated regional markets—both for commodities and for labor—there were inherent limits to the possibilities of factory production. In these circumstances, it was economically rational for a large part of the nation's capital to be invested in small-scale artisanal production. This was particularly true because of the market competitive advantage that France already enjoyed over other nations in many highly skilled, high-quality industries in the eighteenth century. Here the opinion of the Parlement of Paris. . . . can stand for that of most contemporaries:

> *Our merchandise has always won out in foreign markets . . . [It] is sought after all over Europe for its taste, its beauty, its finesse, its solidity, the correctness of its design, the perfection of its execution, the quality of its raw materials . . . Our arts, brought to the highest degree of perfection, enrich your capital, of which the entire world has become the tributary.*

For all its hyperbole, this was basically an accurate assessment, and it remained accurate through the nineteenth century as well. The fine furniture, jewelry, tapestries, and countless other luxury productions of Paris; the silk cloth of Lyons and the silk ribbons and trimmings of Saint-Etienne; the porcelains of Limoges; all of these continued to be admired and sought after throughout the world, and all were major nodes of growth in the nineteenth-century French economy. The success of French industrial growth in the nineteenth century was largely a matter of maintaining and developing France's superiority in highly skilled, high-quality handicrafts. Indeed, even factory industry in France tended to be most successful in the finer and more skill-intensive branches of the trade. Both the cotton industry of Mulhouse and the woolen industry of Roubaix-Tourcoing—the fastest growing centers of factory textile production in France in the first two-thirds of the nineteenth century—specialized in the finest grades of cloth.

One of the important consequences of this pattern of economic growth was that the typical French worker of the nineteenth century lived in an old city with long-standing artisan traditions, not in a new factory town. Of the twenty-five largest cities in France in 1851, all but Saint Etienne had been chartered cities and major centers of commerce, administration, and handicrafts for centuries. Moreover, Saint-Etienne was the exception that proved the rule. Although it was a new city that had grown from a mere industrial village in the eighteenth and early nineteenth centuries to become a major metallurgical and mining center, a far larger proportion of Saint-Etienne's labor force was actually employed in the small-scale and highly skilled silk ribbon and trimmings industry than in mining and metallurgy. Even the new industrial city of Saint-Etienne was dominated by highly skilled artisans rather than by factory workers. Once again the contrast with Britain is striking. Of the ten largest cities in Britain in 1851, six—Manchester, Birmingham, Glasgow, Leeds, Sheffield, and Bradford—were essentially factory towns, and the traffic at the port of Liverpool was dominated by the Lancashire cotton trade. Only three of the top ten British cities—London, Edinburgh, and Bristol—had been important urban centers before the eighteenth century, and in legal terms, both Manchester and Birmingham were actually still unincorporated villages until the 1830s.

The Declining Artisan?

Given the nature of French cities and French manufactures, it is quite understandable that small-scale artisan industry retained a clear numerical predominance far past the middle of the nineteenth century. Markovitch estimates that the industrial population employed in artisan industry in France was twice the population employed in large-scale industry even as late as 1876. And the numerical predominance of artisans over factory workers was even greater in the first half of the century. A substantial portion of these craftsmen, of course, worked in industries producing for the national and international market. But by far the largest number of French artisans made products that were consumed locally—food, buildings, clothing, shoes, furniture, tools and utensils of all sorts, and so on. And these trades grew in virtually all cities, in factory towns as well as in centers of commerce, administration, or luxury production.

The fact that handicrafts were eventually supplanted by factories in nearly all branches of manufacture has led historians to think of factory industry and artisan industry as directly antagonistic. Thus, the "declining artisan" has become a stock character of nineteenth-century labor history, with the British handloom weavers, reduced from proud opulence to pathetic misery by the competition of the power loom, as the standard example. But the handloom weaver was actually a very unusual case; generally, the growth of factories tended not to reduce but to multiply the number of artisans, at least in the first two-thirds of the nineteenth century. Until the last decades of the century, textiles were virtually the only industry in which factories competed directly with artisan producers. Otherwise, factory production either developed in industries already manned by unskilled labor—for example, heavy metallurgy or such food-processing industries as sugar refining, flour milling, or oil pressing—or created entirely new industries that had not existed before the industrial revolution, such as heavy chemicals or the construction of steam engines or textile machinery. Thus, the advent of factories increased the number of unskilled or semiskilled workers in the labor force, but it did not supplant artisans. And in the case of machine construction, the result of industrialization was to create a new demand for skilled metalworkers, who, although they worked in factories, were among the most highly skilled and best-paid workers in the economy. These proud craftsmen bore virtually no resemblance to the ill-paid and unorganized factory hands in the textile, chemical, or food-processing factories. In the days before assembly lines and interchangeable parts, machine construction required great intelligence, judgment, dexterity, and finesse—what in the eighteenth century would have been called "art"—on the part of the workers. Moreover, at least in France, many workers in mechanical construction continued to serve their apprenticeships in the traditional metal crafts and continued to call themselves by such titles as *serrurier* (locksmith) or *chaudronnier* (coppersmith), rather than the newer *mécanicien* (machinist). They also tended to form the same kind of labor organizations as metalworkers who were employed in small shops; many, for example, were members of compagnonnage. The development of machine-construction factories, in short, did not supplant artisans but rather created a large new category of particularly prosperous artisans who worked in factories.

Meanwhile, the development of factories of any kind necessarily multiplied the demand for artisan-produced goods. Factories had to be built, and the labor force of the factories—together with the workers who transported raw materials and finished goods to and from the factories and the businessmen who bought and sold them—had to be housed, clothed, and supplied with goods of all sorts. Given the technology of the first half of the nineteenth century, virtually all of these needs could be met only by artisans: by stonemasons, carpenters, and joiners; by butchers, bakers, and confectioners; by makers of furniture, cooking pots, carts, coaches, cutlery, and a host of other products. Factories also contributed to the multiplication of certain categories of artisans by reducing the cost of their raw materials and thereby increasing demand for their products. This was most notably true in the clothing trades, where the new lower-priced output of cotton and woolen mills made it possible for people to afford a greater quantity and variety of clothing, and in the metalworking trades, where cheaper iron meant a wider demand for assorted ironwares. In nineteenth-century conditions, then, the expansion of factory industry and the expansion of artisan industry went hand in hand.

The only major exception to this mutually supporting relationship between factory and artisan industry was in textiles, where the new factories supplanted hand spinning and handloom weaving. The main effect of spinning mills was to deprive thousands of rural women of a profitable by-employment, but the loss of employment in spinning was probably counteracted by a large increase in the domestic weaving industry, in which women could either weave themselves or assist their husbands in stringing looms, winding shuttles, and other auxiliary tasks. Later, when power looms were introduced, they displaced many full-time handloom weavers, of whom the majority were probably men. Although no detailed study of French handloom weavers exists, it seems clear that their decline was much less traumatic than in Britain. Of course, the growth of the French cotton industry bore no comparison with the British cotton boom of the late eighteenth century, and having risen less precipitously, French handloom weaving had less far to fall. The fall was also slower because the moderate growth rate of the French textile industry allowed only a gradual introduction of power looms and because power looms were much more difficult to adapt to the production of the fine cloths in which the French specialized. In the silk industry of Lyons, for example, power looms were only introduced in the last quarter of the nineteenth century. It also appears that many French handloom weavers made a successful transition to employment in textile factories and that the familial organization of work that characterized domestic textile production also followed them into the factory.

But in spite of all these attenuating circumstances, the rise of textile factories did pose a direct threat to hand production. The impact was later and more gradual than in Britain, but eventually handloom weavers were eliminated in all branches of the industry.

It is worth noting, however, that the skilled textile workers who were displaced by machines were mainly rural domestic weavers. This, of course, did not make their displacement any less painful, but it does mean that the one category of skilled workers who experienced a direct conflict with factory technology in the first half of the nineteenth century were isolated, both physically and culturally, from urban artisans. Country weavers lived in a different world, one they shared more with peasants than with urban craftsmen. And they continued to be sharply distinct from the artisans when they came to work in the new spinning and weaving factories. They lacked any corporate tradition, and, unlike the urban artisans, they rarely formed structured labor organizations, even in the city. Even their strikes in the first half of the nineteenth century often bore more resemblance to rural grain riots or festival processions than to the disciplined work stoppages of the urban artisan trades. And as late as 1848, workers in textile factories generally remained quite separate from the working-class political movements that attracted masses of artisans. The textile workers' hopes, anxieties, resentments, and sufferings—both in the countryside and in the urban factories—remained distant from most artisans' experiences.

In short, the development of factory industry in France in the first half of the nineteenth century did not send urban artisans into general decline. Although the power loom slowly eliminated rural weavers, the urban trades that had been organized as corporations under the old regime generally experienced a vigorous expansion during the first half of the nineteenth century. In numerical terms, at least, this was an era of rise, rather than of decline, for urban artisans. For the better part of the nineteenth century, artisans remained the dominant sector of the urban working class, numerically, politically, and culturally.

The fact that artisans could coexist with the factory system does not mean that life within the artisan trades went on unaltered; on the contrary, these were years of widespread changes, tensions, and conflicts. Expansion of numbers could itself be a source of tension. In particular, a rapid increase in the number of journeymen working in a trade made it difficult for workers to maintain control of the labor market—to assure that only properly apprenticed men were hired, to maintain surveillance of working conditions in hundreds of workshops, to maintain adequate and uniform wages, and so on. Thus, a rapid increase in numbers could have a major impact on relations between workers and masters. There were also some changes in technology—quite apart from the rise of factories—that had important effects on artisan trades. For example, mechanical saws were introduced in the production of lumber, mechanical presses were introduced in printing, and nails and rivets began to be substituted for stitching in shoemaking. But probably more far-reaching than these technical changes were innovations in the organization of production and of marketing that occurred quite independently of any change in technology. As cities grew and markets expanded, some entrepreneurs in the urban trades responded to rising demand by turning away from the older practice of making items to order for their clients and instead came to specialize in lower-quality, standardized, ready-to-wear or ready-to-use items that could be produced more efficiently and sold at a lower price. This system was known as *confection*. Entrepreneurs who adopted the system of confection were, in the language of economists, exploiting "economies of scale" made possible by rising demand.

Labor in workshops engaged in confection could be organized quite differently from that in traditional workshops. Above all, the division of labor was greatly increased. A pair of shoes made to the specifications of a particular client could probably be produced as efficiently by a single workman as by more than one, because each part had to be made to order. But when a workshop turned out dozens of pairs of shoes made in the same style and in standardized sizes, it was much more profitable to assign a different worker to each step of the manufacturing process. The possibility of more finely divided labor meant that the optimum number of employees per entrepreneur was higher and that workers needed a narrower range of skill—a relatively unskilled man or woman could be taught to cut leather to a preset size and shape, but only a thoroughly trained worker could be trusted to make a pair of shoes to order. Indeed, if the process of manufacture was broken down into sufficiently simple and standardized steps, it did not even require the supervision of the entrepreneur and could be carried out by men, women, and children working in their own rooms or garrets. All of these phenomena—skill dilution, an increase in scale and in the division of labor, domestic production on a putting-out basis—are well attested both in Paris and in the larger provincial cities by the 1840s and probably date back to the twenties and thirties as well. Although research on confection is far too sketchy to determine the precise extent of these practices, they seem to have been particularly common in the shoemaking, tailoring, dressmaking, and furniture industries.

A related set of organizational changes took place in the building industry, particularly in Paris. There a big contractor would undertake to build a number of houses and then would subcontract the actual work to *marchandeurs* (bargainers or hagglers), who in turn would engage their own workers at the lowest rate they could negotiate. This system of marchandage tended to squeeze down wages and made the maintenance of uniform standards of pay and working conditions virtually impossible. It certainly was generally regarded as exploitative by the workers. The abolition of marchandage was one of the first concessions that workers wrung from the Provisional Government after the Revolution of 1848, on the grounds that it was "unjust, vexatory, and contrary to the principle of fraternity." Like confection, marchandage seems to have been connected to an increase in the scale of the undertaking. But in the case of marchandage, the economies appear to have arisen less from an increased division of labor than from intensified exploitation, both of laborers and of the marchandeurs, by the capitalist contractors.

Given the present state of research, it is impossible to say how widespread marchandage and confection were. It would be surprising, however, if these or analogous changes in the organization of production were not taking place in most of the larger French cities in the first half of the nineteenth century. After all, such changes in the organization of firms are precisely what one would expect under the stimulus of broadening markets and rising demand. Indeed, as already noted, chambrelans—that is, domestic producers who fabricated inferior goods and evaded the regulations of the corporations—were already a serious problem in some trades in the eighteenth century. From the economic point of view, the widespread development of confection and marchandage can be seen as an extension of processes already under way during the economic growth of the later eighteenth century. . . .

E. A. Wrigley

Continuity, Chance and Change

. . . Given the continued strength of the presumption that the break with a pre-industrial past began sometime in the middle or later decades of the eighteenth century, it is important to begin by stressing the extent to which economic activity in England had already drifted away from the prevailing norm in continental western Europe during the seventeenth and eighteenth centuries. Indeed, one of the casualties of any informed reassessment of the industrial revolution as an historical phenomenon should be the view that it was a unitary, progressive series of events taking place over a restricted time scale. The transformation that gave rise to the industrial revolution is better regarded as spread over a period lasting more than two centuries, and consisting of two main component types of economic growth so markedly dissimilar in nature and with such different chronology that it is questionable whether their understanding is well served by using a single umbrella term to describe them; perhaps the course of change would be more easily and accurately understood if they were more clearly distinguished and the industrial revolution were regarded as their joint product.

It is implicit in the latter view that it is misleading to suppose that the development of one component type out of the other was in some sense preordained, that the second developed ineluctably out of the first. From a stance in the twentieth century the transition from one to the other may appear smooth and inevitable. It was unanticipated by contemporaries, however, and there is much to be learnt from the arguments that they advanced which imply that what actually occurred was extremely improbable, or even flatly impossible.

The first of the two types of economic growth is associated with what I shall term the advanced organic economy; the second with the mineral-based energy economy. The former precedes the latter in time, though there is overlap between them. Each is a stereotype, of value for

From E. A. Wrigley, *Continuity, Chance and Change: The Character of the Industrial Revolution in England* (Cambridge: Cambridge University Press, 1988).

conceptual clarity, but never encountered in a pure form in the empirical complexity of history. . . .

It is common to all such typologies of transition to regard the change from early Tudor to late Victorian England and beyond as movement along a single spectrum, the working out amid the vagaries of time and place of a continuous and progressive change, in which the later stages in the transformation are implicit in those that had gone before. In some cases the industrial revolution is explicitly regarded as a natural concomitant of the later stages of the transition, requiring no special explanation because it represented the logical culmination of the economic side of modernization, the fruit of the gains in productivity that flowed from changes in the institutional structure of society, in its ethos, in its locus of political power and, more immediately, from the economic benefits of rational conduct leading to such helpful new features as greater specialization of economic function. To eliminate any apparent incongruity between a long process of progressive change in institutional forms and social behaviour on the one hand, and a much briefer period of violent economic transformation on the other, Geertz suggested the existence of a process rather like the heating of water in a kettle, which may culminate suddenly with the lid blowing off but only because the water has reached a critical temperature and turned to steam after a much longer and slower heating process.

In my view this model of the transition in its many variant forms is of dubious validity. There may be no reason to challenge the view that the advent of a system with some or all of the attributes that have been listed will increase both aggregate output and, at least for a time, output per head. If a congeries of the underlying changes can be identified that is most helpfully defined as capitalist, then it is also fair to associate the concept of capitalism with the proximate economic changes. But it is a very large additional step to regard the industrial revolution as a further natural stage in the progressive development of the phenomenon.

Modernization and the Industrial Revolution in England

English history appears at first blush to afford support for the view that the modernization process culminated abruptly in an industrial revolution. It is plausible to suggest that England developed unusually early as a nation-state; that many of the economic and political characteristics of feudalism faded early from the scene; that, especially in agriculture, capitalist organization spread rapidly and met remarkably little resistance; that legal institutions and practice facilitated the replacement of custom by contract; that particularistic attitudes were less prominent and less durable than in many other countries; and, of course, that economic progress was unusually rapid. It is clear that most of these changes were progressive and had reached an advanced stage by the later eighteenth century, and it is not in dispute that the industrial revolution was an English phenomenon in the first instance.

Yet there is strong historical evidence casting doubt on any automatic association of the characteristics often grouped under the descriptive label of modernization with the industrial revolution, and there are also cogent theoretical considerations pointing away from the conclusion so often drawn.

The historical evidence relates to the Dutch Republic. Except that the Dutch provinces retained substantial autonomy, calling in question the cohesiveness of Holland as a nation-state, Holland was perhaps more completely "modern" than England throughout the period from, say, 1550 to 1750. Specialization of economic function was far advanced at an early date in both industry and agriculture. Holland possessed a custom-made internal transport network superior to anything to be found in England, and the envy of those foreigners who made use of it. She was the common carrier of Europe. Her cities were numerous and prosperous, and the percentage of the population living in towns was higher than in England and far higher than in most other countries. The bourgeoisie possessed great political influence. Capitalism was perhaps less impeded by legal and institutional handicaps than anywhere else. Real wages were the highest in Europe throughout the later sixteenth and seventeenth centuries, and for much of the eighteenth century also. And yet there was no early industrial revolution in Holland: indeed it was unusually late in making an appearance there.

This empirical fact is not surprising when set against the theoretical considerations disjoining the modernization process from the industrial revolution. There are few if any features present in modernization theory that are not to be found foreshadowed in the *Wealth of Nations*, allowing for the differing modes of expression, yet neither Adam Smith nor the other classical economists believed the prospects for further economic growth to be very inviting. Both the experience of Holland and general considerations bearing upon the constraints to growth cautioned against supposing growth would continue for very long or that the standard of living of the bulk of the population would rise. A technically perfect capitalism appeared to be as easily consonant with the stationary state as with continuous, rapid growth. Something more than modernization or capitalism in the usual meaning of the term was needed to enable England to escape the same fate as Holland and to become the first country in which the age-old constraints on growth lost their force, the country where in spite of the forebodings of some contemporaries, it became clear that poverty was not the inevitable fate of the bulk of the population, nor a sweating brow the precondition of a daily loaf.

The transition that produced the change in prospects was the move from an advanced organic to a mineral-based energy economy. Such a move was essential if the problems so succinctly analysed by Ricardo were not to put a stop to growth sooner or later; nor could the tension exposed by Malthus's *Essay on Population* be overcome without it. A different sort of capitalism was required, in alliance with the familiar variety, if the limitations inherent in all organic economies were to be overcome. Above all, a source of energy was needed whose scale would make feasible a rise in output per worker which remained beyond reach as long as his own muscles and those of his domesticated animals were almost the sole means of lifting, pulling, moving, beating, stretching and pressing material objects; and as long as he was dependent upon organic raw materials for all purposes, including that of raising heat. Such an energy source was not [to] be found within the confines of an organic economy. . . .

Change: A Unitary Process?

Associated with the investigation of the shift from the advanced organic mode of production to the mineral-based energy economy is the question of whether the transition to the latter was implicit in the nature of the earlier system. If so, the nature of the connection needs to be specified. If not, the supposition that the entire process of change and growth from Tudor to Victorian times is in some sense unitary is further called in question. The relative importance of continuity and chance is an issue that must be faced.

The example of Holland is once more instructive. Holland achieved an exceptional success within the canons of an organic economy at a very early date. As in the case of England a century later, success entailed a demand for better transport and for the deployment of much larger quantities of energy within the productive system. The topography and hydrography of Holland offered the opportunity to solve the first problem. The creation of a passenger canal network during the first half of the seventeenth century showed that Holland possessed the enterprise, capital and technical and organizational skills needed to seize the opportunity. Moreover, Dutch peat provided for a time a source of heat energy, if not mechanical energy, commensurate with the economic opportunities of the time, thus making possible a brief flowering of Dutch industrial supremacy in textiles, shipbuilding, brewing and sugar refining. But, though peat could briefly support vigorous expansion, it could not sustain a prolonged burst of growth.

As a source of energy capital the Dutch peat deposits fell part way between the use of virgin timber stands on the one hand and the opening up of a major coalfield on the other in the size of the stock of energy available, and therefore the scale and duration of the boost to economic growth that they could sustain. An unexploited forest area may provide, say, the charcoal needed for a flourishing iron industry for a few decades, after which the industry must either move on elsewhere, or, if it remains, content itself with turning into charcoal whatever annual volume of wood consumption is consonant with a sustained yield basis of exploitation, which, by definition, means an end to growth. Large peat deposits may allow a more substantial expansion over perhaps a century, but, though the period of growth may be longer, the subsequent contraction must be more painful since energy sources that take the form of a stock rather than a flow cannot be put on a sustained yield basis. With coal the time scale stretches out to several centuries. Individual mines become exhausted, of course, but large coalfield areas contain stores of energy that utterly dwarf those to be found in forests or peat beds, and the higher combustion temperatures of coal enable it to be used in processes for which wood or peat cannot be used, or can be used only far less effectively.

Gaining access to deeper coal measures presented severe problems as drainage and haulage difficulties increased, but the consciousness that great riches were available as a tangible reward for success provided a very powerful incentive to the ingenious and persistent. The exhaustion of peat beds, preceded by rising extraction costs, presented different problems. Digging deeper was no solution. English or Scottish coal could be imported but its price to the final consumer in Holland was higher than in more favoured locations in Britain, leaving Dutch industry in a difficult competitive situation. Dutch industries dependent upon cheap heat energy tended to stagnate or decline.

An economy may seize upon a cheap source of energy, exploit it with vigour, develop industries that require heat on a large scale to produce competitively, and yet find itself powerless to prevent their subsequent decline if the energy is drawn from an energy stock rather than an energy flow and the stock becomes exhausted. The existence of a clear need does not imply that the need will be met.

Inasmuch as the growth taking place in some sectors of the English economy was contingent upon the use of cheap energy on a large scale and that energy came from coal, it seems prudent to regard such growth not as a structural feature logically comparable to the benefits derived from specialization of function, or from the development of the landlord, tenant farmer and labourer system in agriculture, but as an uncovenanted blessing. To describe this blessing as the gift of chance rather than the offspring of continuous development may seem an exercise in hyperbole. Coal production grew gradually and continuously over a long period, but in the sense that the presence of a relative abundance of coal in accessible seams is a rare geological feature, unconnected with other resources or with the prevailing economic system; and that the absence of abundant and accessible coal, or an equivalent capital stock of energy, meant that there was no escape from the logical constraints of an organic economy, no matter how successful the economy might be within such bounds, it may not be too great a liberty with language to refer to chance. To succeed in breaking free from the limitations experienced by all organic economies, a country needed not only to be capitalist in the conventional sense, to have become modernized, but also to be capitalist in the sense that its raw materials were drawn increasingly from mineral stocks rather than from the annual flow of agricultural production, and, above all, in the sense that it could tap great stores of energy rather than depend upon the kinds of renewable energy sources that had always previously provided any heat or power needed for production. The English economy was capitalist in both senses of the word, but the connection between the two was initially casual rather than causal. . . .

It is in keeping with the dual nature of the long period of economic growth culminating in the industrial revolution that some attributes of change should be closely related to each other, while others were not. For example, Adam Smith catalogued a series of political, legal, constitutional and social structural features that were conducive to the type of economic progress analysed in the *Wealth of Nations.* Allowing for differences in terminology they are similar to the changes specified in modernization theory, as we have already noted, and are inter-related. Other attributes which Adam Smith did not mention could be added to the list. For example, the very high mobility of the English population, itself closely related to the institution of service and the peculiarities of the English marriage system, made for a flexible response to economic opportunity, while the responsiveness of decisions to marry to prevailing economic circumstances was of crucial importance to preserving a favourable balance between production and reproduction. These were all attributes that assisted in advancing the organic economy in England to an unusually high level of sophistication and achievement. As long as growth was taking place primarily within the context of an organic economy, the possession of this cluster of attributes was important in facilitating growth, and its absence a serious handicap. Many of the attributes of most importance, notably those relating to landholding and to marriage, were deeply rooted in the peculiarities of English society and were not capable of adoption abroad by conscious policy decisions, a fact which helps to explain the length of the period during which the English economy steadily strengthened in comparison to its continental rivals.

When the impetus to further growth began to be derived increasingly from the mineral-based energy sector of the economy, the same considerations no longer applied. The adoption of methods by which heat energy and mechanical energy could be harnessed on a vast scale in the production process, and the increasing substitution of mineral for organic raw materials, were developments which it proved easy to introduce from England into other socio-economic and political contexts. They represented sources of increased productivity that were footloose and exportable in contrast to the position when the organic economy prevailed. Previously the institutional framework of growth had been more important than its material technology and therefore far less easy to transfer.

Thorstein Veblen was grappling with the same general issue when he wrote *Imperial Germany*. It is also a matter that has helped to cause a confusion in Marxist thinking about social change and industrial development. If the sweep of English history during the centuries before and during the industrial revolution represents a unitary and progressive phenomenon it is natural to suppose that the later stages can only be reached after having first traversed the earlier stages. It is reasonable to expect, for example, that a bourgeois state should precede an industrial revolution. But, whereas it may be logical to expect this to be true in relation to the kind of economic growth that characterized the advanced organic economy, it is much less certain that the same should hold true in relation to the mineral-based energy economy. To the degree that the original association between the latter and its predecessor was a matter of coincidence rather than necessity in the land of its origin, its subsequent successful translation to other countries with very different social, political, legal and economic structures is not a matter for great surprise. . . .

Maxine Berg and Pat Hudson

Rehabilitating the Industrial Revolution

. . . Radical change was obvious to contemporaries but it has been obscured in recent historiography, and industrial performance in particular has been viewed as an extension of a pre-industrial traditional past. We argue here that the industrial revolution should be rehabilitated. The national accounts approach to economic growth and productivity change is not a good starting point for the analysis of fundamental economic discontinuity. The measurement of growth using this approach is prone to significant errors of estimation which arise from the restricted definition of economic activity, from the incomplete nature of the available data, and from assumptions embodied in the analysis. We argue that growth and productivity change in the period are currently underestimated. But, much more importantly, we stress that growth rates on their own are inadequate to the task of identifying and comprehending the industrial revolution. The current orthodoxy underplays economic and social transformation because such development is not amenable to study within the frame of reference of national accounts and aggregate statistics. We examine four areas in which fundamental and unique change occurred during the industrial revolution: technical and organizational innovation outside the factory sector, the deployment of female and child labour, regional specialization, and demographic development. For each area we identify both problems of underestimation and of the measurement of fundamental change. We

From Maxine Berg and Pat Hudson, "Rehabilitating the Industrial Revolution," *Economic History Review* 45, no. 1 (1992).

conclude by considering the importance for social and political history of our reassessment of the extent and nature of transformation in these years.

. . . The new interpretations of the industrial revolution rely on an analytical divide between the traditional and modern sectors: mechanized factory industry with high productivity on the one hand, and a widespread traditional industrial and service sector backwater on the other. It is argued that the large size of the traditional sector, combined with primitive technology, made it a drag on productivity growth in the economy as a whole. But it is not clear how helpful this divide is in understanding the economic structure or the dynamism of eighteenth- and early nineteenth-century England. In reality, it is impossible to make clear-cut divisions between the traditional and the modern as there were rarely separate organizational forms, technologies, locations, or firms to be ascribed to either. Eighteenth- and nineteenth-century cotton manufacturers, serving domestic as well as foreign markets, typically combined steam-powered spinning in factories with large scale employment of domestic handloom weavers and often kept a mix of powered and domestic hand weaving long after the powered technology became available. This pattern was a function of risk spreading, the problems of early technology, and the cheap labour supply of women and children in particular. Thus for decades the "modern" sector was actually bolstered by, and derived from the "traditional" sector, and not the reverse.

Artisans in the metal-working sectors of Birmingham and Sheffield frequently combined occupations or changed them over their life cycle in such a way that they too could be classified in both the traditional and modern sectors. Artisan woollen workers in West Yorkshire clubbed together to build mills for certain processes and thus had a foot in both the modern and traditional camps. These so-called "company mills" underpinned the success of the artisan structure. Thus the traditional and the modern were most often inseparable and mutually reinforcing. Firms primarily concerned with metalworking diversified into metal processing ventures as a way of generating steady raw material supplies. This and other cases of vertical integration provide more examples of the tail of "tradition" wagging the dog of "modernity."

The non-factory, supposedly stagnant sector, often working primarily for domestic markets, pioneered extensive and radical technical and organizational change not recognized by the revisionists. The classic textile innovations were all developed within a rural and artisan industry; the artisan metal trades developed skill-intensive hand processes, hand tools, and new malleable alloys. The wool textile sector moved to new products which reduced finishing times and revolutionized marketing. New forms of putting-out, wholesaling, retailing, credit and debt, and artisan co-operation were devised as ways of retaining the essentials of older structures in the face of the new more competitive and innovative environment. Customary practices evolved to match the needs of dynamic and market-orientated production. The result was considerable transformation even within the framework of the so-called traditional sector.

The revisionists argue that most industrial labour was to be found in those occupations which experienced little change. But the food and drink trades, shoemaking, tailoring, blacksmithing, and trades catering for luxury consumption successfully expanded and adapted to provide the essential urban services on which town life, and hence much of centralized industry, was dependent. Furthermore, early industrial capital formation and enterprise typically combined activity in the food and drink or agricultural processing trades with more obviously industrial activities, creating innumerable external economies. This was true in metal manufacture in Birmingham and Sheffield where innkeepers and victuallers were commonly mortgagees and joint owners of metal working enterprises. In the south Lancashire tool trades Peter Stubs was not untypical when he first appeared in 1788 as a tenant of the White Bear Inn in Warrington. Here he combined the activity of innkeeper, malster, and brewer with that of filemaker using the carbon in barm bottoms (barrel dregs) to strengthen the files. There are many examples of this kind of overlap between services, agriculture, and industry. These were the norm in business practice at a time when entrepreneurs' risks were difficult to spread through diversification of portfolios and where so much could be gained from the external economies created by these overlaps.

We do not suggest here that productivity growth at the rate experienced in cotton textiles was achieved elsewhere, but that the success of cotton and other major exports was intimately related to and dependent upon innovations and radical transformations in other branches of the primary, secondary, and tertiary sectors. Dividing off the modern from the traditional sectors is an analytical device which hides more than it reveals in attempting to understand the dynamics of change in the industrial revolution.

. . . [T]he national accounts framework and productivity calculations cannot measure that qualitative improvement in the means of production which can yield shorter working hours or less arduous or monotonous work routines. Clearly, a broader concept of technological change and of innovation is required than can be accommodated by national income accounting. If the most sensible way to view the course of economic change is through the timing and impact of innovation, it is arguable that the use of national accounting has frustrated progress. Emphasis has been placed on saving and capital formation at the expense of science, economic organization, new products and processes, market creativity, skills, dexterity, the knacks and work practices of manufacture, and other aspects of economic life which may be innovative but have no place in the accounting categories.

The problems involved in measuring economy-wide productivity growth, and in regarding it as a reflection of the extent of fundamental economic change, are compounded when one considers the nature both of industrial capital and of industrial labour in the period. Redeployment of labour from agrarian-based and domestic sectors to urban and more centralized manufacturing activity may well have been accompanied by diminishing labour productivity in the short run. Green labour had to learn industrial skills as well as new forms of discipline while, within sectors, labour often shifted into processes which were more rather than less labour-intensive. The same tendency to low returns in the short term can be seen in capital investment in the period. Early steam engines and machinery were imperfect and subject to breakdowns and rapid obsolescence. Gross capital investment figures (which include funds spent on renewals and replacements), when fed into productivity measures, are not a good reflection of the importance and potential of technological change in the period. Rapid technological change is capital hungry as new equipment soon becomes obsolescent and is replaced. Shifts in the aggregate measures of productivity growth are thus actually less likely to show up as significant during periods of rapid and fundamental economic transition than in periods of slower and more piecemeal adjustment.

This point was stressed by Hicks who noted that the long gestation period of technological innovation might yield Ricardo's machinery effect: the returns from major shifts in technology would not be apparent for several decades and, in the short term, innovation would only increase unemployment and put downward pressure on wages. There was such a disjuncture between the wave of innovations surrounding the electric dynamo in the late nineteenth century and an acceleration in the growth of GNP [gross national product]. And the current computer revolution which is transforming production, services, and working lives across a broad front is not accompanied by rapidly rising income, output, or productivity within national economies. Resolving this apparent "productivity paradox" involves recognizing the limited nature of TFP[1] as a measure of economic performance and the long time-frame needed to connect fundamental technological change with productivity growth. Thus, just as it is possible to have growth with little change, it is possible to have radical change with limited growth. In fact the more revolutionary the change technologically, socially, and culturally, the longer this may take to work out in terms of conventional measures of economic performance.

Another striking feature of the new orthodoxy is its restricted definition of the workforce; this in turn has implications for the analysis of productivity change as well as the standard of living debate. . . . It is extremely difficult to quantify the extent of female and child labour as both were largely excluded from official statistics and even from wage books. But analyses based only on adult male labour forces are clearly inadequate and peculiarly distorting for this period. On the supply side the labour of women and children was a vital pillar of household incomes, made more so by the population growth and hence the age structure of the later eighteenth century which substantially reduced the proportion of males of working age in the population. The impact of the high dependency ratio was cushioned by children earning their way at an early age, particularly in domestic manufacturing. On the demand side the need for hand skills, dexterity, and work discipline encouraged the absorption of more and more female and juvenile labour into commercial production. This was further encouraged by sex differentials in wages which may have been increasing under the impact of demographic pressure in these years. Employers were much attracted by low wages and long hours at a time when no attention was yet paid to the incentive effects of payment by results or shorter hours. Thus factors both on the supply and on the demand side of the labour market resulted in a labour force structure with high proportions of child and female workers. They were the key elements in the labour intensity, economic differentiation, and low production costs found in late eighteenth-century industries. And this in turn influenced and was influenced by innovation. New work disciplines, new forms of

[1]TFP [total factor productivity] is a tool some historians have used to argue that technology's impact on productivity was gradual. Calculating TFP entails subtracting changes in the costs of production from changes in gross domestic product.

subcontracting and putting-out networks, new factory organization, and even new technologies were tried out initially on women and children.

The peculiar importance of youth labour in the industrial revolution is highlighted in several instances of textile and other machinery being designed and built to suit the childworker. The spinning jenny was a celebrated case; the original country jenny had a horizontal wheel requiring a posture most comfortable for children aged nine to twelve. Indeed, for a time, in the very early phases of mechanization and factory organization in the woollen and silk industries as well as in cotton, it was generally believed that child labour was integral to textile machine design. This association between child labour and machinery was confined to a fairly brief period of technological change. In the north-eastern United States it appears to have lasted from *c.* 1812 until the 1830s, during which time the proportion of women and children in the entire manufacturing labour force rose from 10 to 40 per cent. This was associated with new large-scale technologies and divisions of labour specifically designed to dispense with more expensive and restrictive skilled adult male labour. Similarly, the employment of an increasing proportion of female labour in English industries was also encouraged by the ready reserves of cheap and skilled female labour which had long been a feature of domestic and workshop production. In addition, in England, many agricultural regions shed female workers first during the process of agricultural change, and much migration within rural areas and from rural to urban areas consisted of young women in search of work.

By mid century female and child labour was declining in importance through a mixture of legislation, the activities of male trade unionists, and the increasingly pervasive ideology of the male breadwinner and of fit and proper female activities. A patriarchal stance was by this time also compatible with the economic aims of a broad spectrum of employers. According to Hobsbawm, larger scale employers (as well as male labour) were learning the "rules of the game" in which higher payments (by results), shorter working hours, and a negotiated terrain of common interests could be substituted for extensive low-wage exploitation with beneficial effects on productivity.

The use of low-cost child and female labour was not, of course, new: it had always been vital in the primary sector and had been integral to the spread of manufacture in the early modern period. What was new in the period of the classic industrial revolution was the extent of its incorporation into rapidly expanding factory and workshop manufacturing and its association with low wages, increased intensification of work, and labour discipline. The female and juvenile workforce undoubtedly had an impact on the output figures per unit of input costs in many industries, but this would not necessarily be reflected in aggregate productivity because some female labour was a substitute for male: it increased at times and in sectors where male wages were low or male unemployment high. The social costs of underutilized male labour (felt in high transfer payments through poor relief) as well as the difficulties of allowing for male unemployment in sectoral weightings are likely to offset gains in the measurable economic indicators of the period. The potential economic performance of the economy as a whole was further limited by the lack of incentive to substitute capital for labour when the labour of women and children was so abundant, cheap, and disciplined through family work groups and in the absence of traditions of solidarity.

The full effects of this expanded role of female and juvenile labour can only be completely understood at a disaggregated level by analysing its impact upon sectors and in regions where it was crucially important. A regional perspective is also uniquely valuable in assessing the extent and nature of economic and social change in the period.

The industrial revolution was a period of great disparity in regional rates of change and economic fortunes. Expanding industrializing regions were matched by regions of declining industry, and chronic underutilization of labour and capital. The story of commercializing agriculture was similarly patchy. Slow-moving aggregate indicators fail to capture these developments, yet the interactions and self-reinforcing drive created by the development of industry in marked regional concentrations gave rise to major innovations. For example, an increase in the output of the British wool textile sector by 150 per cent during the entire eighteenth century seems very modest but this conceals the dramatic relocation taking place in favour of Yorkshire, whose share in national production rose from around 20 per cent to around 60 per cent in the course of the century. If the increase had been uniform in all regions, it could have been achieved simply by the gradual extension of traditional commercial methods and production functions. But Yorkshire's intensive growth necessarily embodied a revolution in organizational patterns, commercial links, credit relationships, the sorts of cloths produced, and production techniques. The external economies achieved when one region took over more than half of the production of the entire sector were also of key importance.

All the expanding industrial regions of the late eighteenth and early nineteenth centuries were, like the West Riding, dominated by particular sectors in a way never experienced before nor to be experienced again after the growth of intra-sectoral spatial hierarchies during the twentieth century. Furthermore, sectoral specialization and regional integrity together help to explain the emergence of regionally distinctive social and class relations which set a pattern in English political life for over a century. These considerations prompt the view that regional studies may be of more value in understanding the process of industrialization than studies of the national economy as a whole.

The main justification which Crafts uses for employing an aggregative approach to identify the nature, causes, and corollaries of industrialization in Britain is that the national economy represented, for many products, a well integrated national goods market by the early nineteenth century. Although the spread of fashionable consumer goods was increasing and national markets for much bulk agricultural produce were established before the mid eighteenth century, it cannot be shown before the second quarter of the nineteenth century that the economy had a "fairly well integrated set of factor markets." The really important spatial unit for production factors, especially capital and labour, and for information flow, commercial contacts, and credit networks in the pre-railway period was the economic region, which was often clearly identifiable. Construction of the improved river and canal systems on which economic growth depended did much to endorse the existence of regional economies, for a time increasing their insularity (in relation to the national economy). Nor were the railways quick to destroy regionally orientated transport systems. Most companies found it in their best interests to structure freight rates so as to encourage the trade of the regions they served, to favour short hauls, and thus to cement regional resource groupings.

Industrialization accentuated the differences between regions by making them more functionally distinct and specialized. Economic and commercial circumstances were thus increasingly experienced regionally and social protest movements with their regional fragmentation can only be understood at that level and in relation to regional employment and social structures. Issues of national political reform also came to be identified with particular regions, for example factory reform with Yorkshire, the anti-poor law campaign with Lancashire and Manchester, or currency reform with Birmingham. Regional identity was encouraged by the links created around the great provincial cities, by the intra-regional nature of the bulk of migration, by the formation of regionally based clubs and societies, trade unions, employers' associations, and newspapers.

In short, dynamic industrial regions generated a social and economic interaction which would have been absent if their component industries had not been spatially concentrated and specialized. Intensive local competition combined with regional intelligence and information networks helped to stimulate region-wide advances in industrial technology and commercial organization. And the growth of specialized financial and mercantile services within the dominant regions served to increase the external economies and reduced both intra-regional and extra-regional transactions costs significantly. Macroeconomic indicators fail to pick up this regional specialization and dynamism which was unique to the period and revolutionary in its impact.

. . . The evolution of social class and of class consciousness has long been integral to popular understanding of what was new in the industrial revolution. Growing occupational concentration, proletarianization, loss of independence, exploitation, deskilling, and urbanization have been central to most analyses of the formation of working-class culture and consciousness, while the ascendancy of Whig laissez-faire political economy has been associated with the new importance of industrialists as a class. But recent economic history has rightly emphasized the complexity of combined and uneven development. Putting-out, workshops, and sweating existed alongside and were complementary to a diverse factory sector. It is no longer possible to speak of a unilinear process of deskilling and loss of workplace control. The diversity of organizational forms of industry, of work experience according to gender and ethnicity, of composite and irregular incomes, and of shifts of employment over the life cycle and through the seasons meant that workers' perceptions of work and of an employing class were varied and contradictory. Nor can one speak of a homogeneous group of industrial employers. There were marked differences between the attitude and outlook of small workshop masters and factory employers. And within these groups there were variations of response to competitive conditions ranging from outright exploitation to paternalism, with many mixtures of the two. There was also a wide range of intermediaries from agents down to foremen and leaders of family work groups to deflect opposition and tension in the workplace. And we now have a much more sophisticated understanding of the complex interplay of customary and market relationships. Any simple notion of the latter replacing the former is to be discarded. In addition, recent writing, including post-structuralist approaches, has questioned any suggestion of deterministic relationships between socio-economic position and political consciousness.

Despite the significance of this work, these interpretations should not be allowed to edge out all idea that the industrial revolution period witnessed radical shifts in social relations and in social consciousness. Much recent social history has been based on an unquestioning acceptance of the new gradualist view of the economic history of the period which, we have argued, severely underplays the extent of radical economic change and of parallel developments affecting the mass of the population. Balanced analyses of the combined and uneven nature of development within industrial capitalism should not obscure the fact that the industrial world of 1850 was vastly different for most workers from that of 1750. There were more large workplaces, more powered machines, and along with these there was more direct managerial involvement in the organization and planning of work. A clearer notion of the separation of work and non-work time was evolving partly out of the decline of family work units and of production in the home. Proletarianization had accelerated and the life chances of a much larger proportion of the population were determined by the market and affected by urban mortality and disease. Capitalist wage labour and the working class developed irregularly and incompletely but with greater speed than in earlier centuries. And the regional concentration of similarities of work experience and of the trade cycle advanced class formation sufficiently to produce social protest and conflict on an unprecedented scale, involving an array of anticapitalist critiques.

While the factory never dominated production or employment nationally, it did so sufficiently in certain regions to create widespread identities of interest and political cohesion. And where it did not exist it exercised enormous influence not only in spawning dispersed production, subcontracting, and sweating, but also as a major feature of the imagery of the age. The factory and the machine as hallmarks of the period may have been myth but they were symbolic of many other changes attendant on the emergence of a more competitive market environment and the greater disciplining and alienation of labour. This symbol provided a focus of protest and opposition and was a powerful element in the formation of social consciousness.

Finally, we must consider the prominence recently given to the economic power and political influence of the landed aristocracy, rentiers, and merchants in the nineteenth century. This prominence is, in part, a response to the new gradualist interpretations of industrial change and industrial accumulation. The major division in the social and political life of nineteenth-century England is argued to have been that between the dominant gentlemanly capitalism of the aristocratic and rentier classes and a subordinate industrial capitalism. But how valid is this? Is it yet another aspect of the current historiography which (while alerting us to the complexity of industrialization) diverts attention unduly from the impact of changes in industry and industrial power in the period?

The gentlemanly capitalism thesis has been shown to have overestimated the dominance of rentier and mercantile capital in elite wealth-holding patterns, and to have overemphasized the separation of interests and cultures between these groups and industrialists. The thesis also exaggerates the internal homogeneity and cohesion of gentleman-capitalists on the one hand and industrial capitalists on the other. Before 1830, or even perhaps before 1850, the economic role of industry and industrialists should not be minimized. The dynamism of industrializing regions, the pattern and finance of their overseas trading, their power in political lobbying, and changes in their local government suggest otherwise. The metropolitan economy may well have become the major locus of service sector growth and of wealth accumulation by the third quarter of the nineteenth century, but in the industrial revolution period itself it is more likely that regional industrial revolutions dictated the course of structural change and colonial expansion.

In short, although industrial transformation gave rise to a complicated mass of differing experiences and social relations, many innovations in the organization and use of labour if not in technology were common to all industries and sectors. Furthermore, changes in markets and in the competitive climate had an impact on all English capitalists whether they were metropolitan or provincial and whether financiers, farmers, small masters, factory employers, or involved in the service sector.

. . . It is time to move on from the macro accounting framework and to rebuild the national picture of economic and social change from new research at regional and local level. We need to adopt a broader concept of innovation, to insist on a greater awareness of female and child labour, and to recognize that the economic, social, and cultural foundations of an industrial capitalist order rest on much more than conventional measures of industrial or economic performance. If this is done it should not be long before the notion of an industrial revolution, occurring in England in the late eighteenth and early nineteenth centuries, is fully rehabilitated.

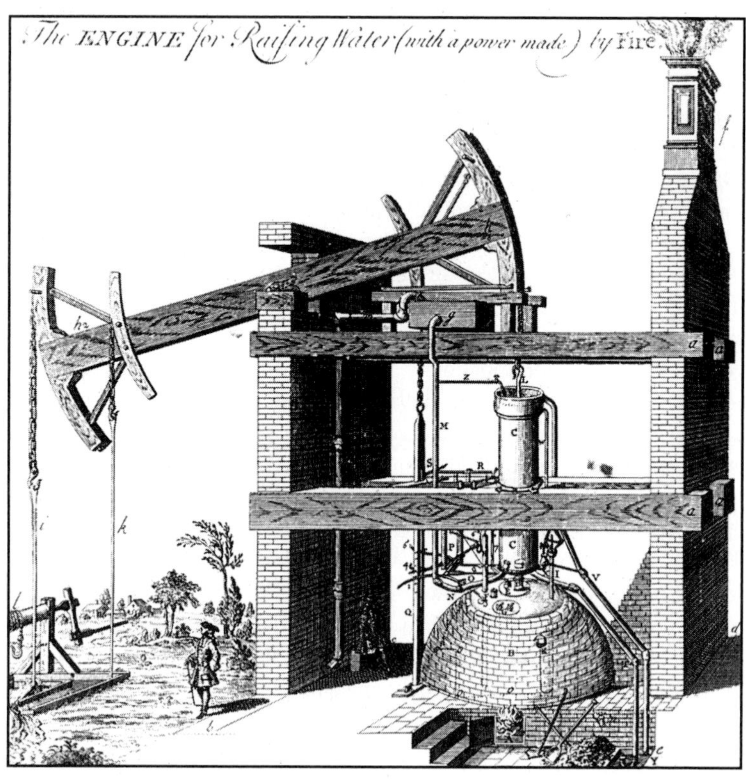

The Newcomen Engine, ca. 1717 The huge steam-filled cylinder (C) was cooled by injecting water from the tank above (G) through a pipe (M). Atmospheric pressure then pushed down the piston, raised the beam, and pumped water from the mine. *(Science Museum/Science & Society Picture Library)*

PART

The Origins and Nature of the Industrial Revolution

The study of the Industrial Revolution's origins reflects the true variety of history, spanning the divides among economic, political, social and even cultural history and incorporating topics as diverse as technological development, state formation, colonialism, and household structure and management. Yet two key questions seem to bind these studies together. The first, inspired by the gradualist approach to defining the Industrial Revolution, concerns temporal scope. How far back should one go to find the true roots of industrialization? While some content themselves with focusing on the eighteenth century and more immediate causes, others argue that historians must cast their gaze even farther back, to the fifteenth century and earlier, when Europe began to develop the institutions necessary to commercial and, later, industrial development. The second question takes an economic bent: which was more important to the rise of industry—supply or demand? Among those who emphasize the former, technology and the conditions that fostered innovation and capital formation capture much of the attention. Those in the latter camp place more weight on population growth and the rise of new markets. Of course, as the following selections demonstrate, the two questions frequently overlap, leading the author of our last selection, Jan de Vries, to attempt a fusion by locating both supply and demand within long- and short-term developments in the European household and economy.

The authors of the first two selections share a supply-side approach to explaining the causes of the Industrial Revolution, but differ in their temporal focus. In his work on the roots of technological creativity, Joel Mokyr addresses two important issues: the nature of technological change and the conditions that foster inventiveness. Mokyr begins by distinguishing between invention, a leap in technological knowledge, and innovation, the process of closing the gap between the best available technology and the techniques most commonly in use. According to Mokyr, industrialization depended upon both; initial strides in technology had to precede the tinkering that adapted inventions to manufacturing. He thus responds to the gradualists, who explain technological change with the concept of "technological drift," by likening the study of technology to evolutionary biology, differentiating "macroinventions," like the first Newcommen steam engine, from the series of "microinventions" that followed James Watt's successful improvements on that engine. Next, Mokyr addresses the causes of both invention and innovation, a topic that necessarily leads him to question why England industrialized first. Among the relevant explanations, which range from serendipity to social ideals that rewarded inventors, Mokyr pays particular attention to political economy. In short, creativity thrived in an environment where government officials guaranteed security and property rights even when popular protest threatened to reverse technological change and its implementation.

In their research, Nathan Rosenberg and L. E. Birdzell Jr. emphasize political economy. Expanding upon Mokyr's concern with the practices that fostered technological creativity, they focus upon the laws and institutions that encouraged commercial ingenuity. This prompts them to locate some of the more basic origins of the Industrial Revolution much farther back in time, as far back as the thirteenth century. This is a period that most historians associate with the rise of capitalism and commerce in Europe. It was Europe's subsequent ability to grow rich, and then put that wealth into the search for innovative, cost-saving production techniques, that best explains the roots of the Industrial Revolution.

For that to occur, European businessmen had to feel secure. The practices and institutions that fostered such sentiments included the legal recognition of private property, the adoption of bills of exchange, and the establishment of banks. These cultivated the growth of both new, purely economic organizations unrelated to strictly family-centered enterprises and an autonomous economic sphere in which merchants could safely earn an income and devote energy to amassing even greater assets. At the same time, however, Rosenberg and Birdzell caution us not to overestimate the capital needs of early industrialization. Clearly, the willingness to experiment and the institutions that permitted and encouraged Europeans to follow those desires remain far more important to explaining the Industrial Revolution.

Robert DuPlessis' work swings attention away from the supply side of economic growth and development and toward the question of demand. If European merchants and engineers helped boost the supply of goods, to whom did they sell their wares? According to DuPlessis, they sold them to Europe's rising population, its colonial possessions, and the expanding states that oversaw and protected these flourishing markets. Together, these offered the incentives that the Industrial Revolution's innovators so feverishly sought to acquire.

By the mid-eighteenth century, Europe's economy seemed poised for a Malthusian disaster. After decades of economic growth thanks to mercantilist policies and a growing population of consumers, inflation threatened to choke the air out of the economy. But two new developments helped maintain an equilibrium that sustained manufacturing and provided the breathing space for technology to revamp the production process. The first was what some scholars label a *consumer revolution,* particularly in Britain, where a rising middle class rivaled the aristocracy for the latest fashions. Eager to cater to the whims of a fickle public, manufacturers like Josiah Wedgewood introduced new techniques, such as advertising, to encourage consumption, and these men amassed huge fortunes in the process. At the same time, Europe's colonies introduced new markets into the economy. While historians previously contended that the colonies' chief contribution to the Industrial Revolution was investment capital, recent interpretations discount this argument and emphasize instead the market they provided for the manufactured items only the metropole could furnish. In this environment, anyone who could increase production while decreasing cost stood to profit handsomely. The race was on.

The first solution to the problem of increasing production was proto-industrialization, or the putting-out industry. While this concept has generated some controversy since Franklin Mendels first introduced it in 1972, it is now firmly entrenched in the historical lexicon. As DuPlessis indicates, many historians now argue that the putting-out system prepared the path for industrialization by promoting an early form of proletarianization while enhancing the skills that industrialization demanded of most merchants and manufacturers. Proto-industrialization has also offered some historians a means of combining both the supply and demand portions of the equation.

Jan de Vries has done just that by introducing the concept of an "industrious revolution" that preceded the Industrial Revolution. Approaching the household as an economic unit, de Vries asserts that during the eighteenth century families broke with traditions of working primarily to subsistence levels and shifted instead to a new form of resource/time allocation that enhanced their connections with markets, both as producers and consumers. So as real wages declined in the latter half of the century, families increased the number of women and children in manufacturing. This maintained the flow of goods to which the entire family had grown accustomed while devoting new energy to the production of marketable goods. By highlighting the household's adaptability within the evolving economy, de Vries adds a striking new dimension to a debate that shows no signs of abating anytime soon.

Joel Mokyr

The Lever of Riches

An essay on the economic history of technological change inevitably contains dates, names, and places. By its nature, the tale of technological creativity requires citing who first came up with an idea and who made the critical revisions and improvements necessary for the idea to work.

From Joel Mokyr, *The Lever of Riches: Technological Creativity and Economic Progress* (New York: Oxford University Press, 1992).

Yet in the past decades, economic historians have not practiced this type of history. As David asks, does technology not simply accumulate continuously from the incremental, almost imperceptible, changes brought about by a large number of anonymous people? Some historians insist that almost all invention consists of this "technological drift" (as Jones has termed it), consisting mostly of anonymous, small, incremental improvements. As a reaction to heroic theories of invention in which all improvements are attributed to individual geniuses, the drift theory has been justly influential. But is it not possible to go too far in the other direction and give too little credit to major inventions made by a vital few? . . . Modern research has shown, to be sure, that most cost savings are achieved through small, invisible, cumulative improvements. But improvements in what? Virtually every major invention was followed by a learning process, during which the production costs using the new technique declined; but for these costs to fall, the novelty had to be invented in the first place. . . .

In discussing the distinction between minor inventions, whose cumulative impact is decisive in productivity growth, and major technological breakthroughs, it may be useful to draw an analogy between the history of technology and the modern theory of evolution. . . . Some biologists distinguish between micromutations, which are small changes in an existing species and which gradually alter its features, and macromutations, which create new species. The distinction between the two could provide a useful analogy for our purposes. I define *microinventions* as the small, incremental steps that improve, adapt, and streamline existing techniques already in use, reducing costs, improving form and function, increasing durability, and reducing energy and raw material requirements. *Macroinventions*, on the other hand, are those inventions in which a radical new idea, without clear precedent, emerges more or less ab nihilo. In terms of sheer numbers, microinventions are far more frequent and account for most gains in productivity. Macroinventions, however, are equally crucial in technological history.

The essential feature of technological progress is that the macroinventions and microinventions are not substitutes but complements. Without subsequent microinventions, most macroinventions would end up as curiosa in musea or sketchbooks. Indeed, in some historical instances the person who came up with the improvement that clinched the case receives more credit than the inventor responsible for the original breakthrough, as is the case of the steam engine, the pneumatic tire, and the bicycle. But without novel and radical departures, the continuous process of improving and refining existing techniques would run into diminishing returns and eventually peter out. Microinventions are more or less understandable with the help of standard economic concepts. They result from search and inventive effort, and respond to prices and incentives. Learning by doing and learning by using increase economic efficiency and are correlated with economic variables such as output and employment. Macroinventions, on the other hand, do not seem to obey obvious laws, do not necessarily respond to incentives, and defy most attempts to relate them to exogenous economic variables. Many of them resulted from strokes of genius, luck, or serendipity. Technological history, therefore, retains an unexplained component that defies explanation in purely economic terms. In other words, luck and inspiration mattered, and thus individuals made a difference. Scholars who cast doubt on the importance of individuals often rely on a dispensability axiom: if an invention had not been made by X it would have been made by Y, a conclusion typically inferred from the large number of simultaneous discoveries. Although this regularity holds true for some inventions, including the telephone and the incandescent lightbulb, it is not applicable to scores of other important inventions.

If there is any area in which a deterministic view that outcomes are shaped inexorably by forces stronger than individuals—be they supply and demand or the class struggle—is oversimplified, it is in the economic history of technology. Asking whether the major breakthroughs are more important than the marginal improvements is like asking whether generals or privates win a battle. Just as in military history we employ shorthand such as "Napoleon defeated the Prussians at Jena in 1806," we may say that a particular invention occurred at this or that time. Such a statement does not imply that individual inventors are credited with all the productivity gains from their invention any more than the statement that Napoleon defeated the Prussians implies that he single-handedly defeated an entire army. It is useful to organize the narrative around the discrete event.

The distinction between micro- and macroinventions is useful because, as historians of technology emphasize, the word *first* is hazardous in this literature. Many technological breakthroughs had a history that began before the event generally regarded as "the invention," and almost all macroinventions required subsequent improvements to make them operational. Yet in a large number of cases, one or two identifiable events *were* crucial. Without such breakthroughs, technological progress would eventually fizzle out. . . .

. . . In what follows, I shall confine myself to the questions of why Britain managed, for about a century, to generate and diffuse superior production techniques at a faster rate than the Continent, and serve as a model that all European nations wished to emulate and how and why it eventually lost its leadership in technology.

Technological success depended on both the presence of positive elements and on the absence of negative ones. Among the positive factors, the generation of technological ideas and the ability to implement them seem a natural enough point from which to start. The generation of ideas . . . was often an international effort. The British, to be sure, were prominent in providing technologically revolutionary ideas: there can hardly be any question that most of the truly crucial inventions in the period were made by Britons. Yet Britain's relative role in invention was smaller than its corresponding role in implementation. Many important inventions that can be attributed to Continental inventors found their successful implementation in Britain. . . . Invention was not equivalent to technological change. More was needed.

One crucial difference between Britain and the Continent that helped Britain to establish its head start was its endowment of skilled labor at the onset of the Industrial Revolution. . . . [B]y the middle of the eighteenth century, Britain had at its disposal a large number of technicians and craftsmen who could carry out the mundane but indispensable construction details of the "new contrivances." These skills rested on an informal and antiquated system of apprenticeship and on-the-job training; they had little to do with schooling. If England led the rest of the world in the Industrial Revolution, it was despite, not because of her formal education system. . . .

Britain had been fortunate. In the late seventeenth century it had taken the lead in clock- and watchmaking. France, its closest competitor, had been "crippled by the exodus of some of its best practitioners fleeing a wave of anti-Protestant bigotry." By contrast, Britain welcomed men of technical ability whatever their religious persuasions. The mechanical skills of clockmakers became one of the cornerstones of the new industrial technology. Another industry that produced skilled artisans was the shipping sector, with its demand for accurate and well-made instruments. . . . A third industry that helped to prepare the skills and dexterity necessary for the Industrial Revolution was mining. . .

The net result of Britain's tradition in high-tech industry was that it could rely on engineers such as Wilkinson, Newcomen, and Smeaton to help build and improve machines conceived by others. Other countries, of course, had some engineers of distinction. But most of these, such as the Swede Christopher Polhem, the Austrian Joseph Karl Hell, and the Frenchman Jacques de Vaucanson, were relatively isolated. In Britain, the number of engineers and mechanics was sufficiently large to allow interaction with each other, through lecturing, spying, copying, and improving. . . . Interaction among engineers, scientists, and businessmen created a total that was larger than the sum of its individual components. . . .

The formation of human capital in Britain before and during the Industrial Revolution depended on a rather unique social environment. By 1750, Britain already had a "middle class" of sorts, that is, people who were literate and well fed, and came from commercial or artisanal backgrounds. This class supplied most of the founders of large industrial undertakings in Britain, and there is no doubt that most of the creative technical minds also came largely from this class. The supply of creativity was channeled into industrial activities, in large part because of the lack of alternatives. Government and military services careers were closed to nonconformists, as they were, for all practical purposes, to anyone not born into a wealthy British family. Members of Parliament and army officers had to buy into their offices and maintain expensive lifestyles. The professional civil service was small, and the imperial bureaucracy was still embryonic in 1800. Moreover, by being exclusive it forced talented men born below it to search for the only key that could open the doors of politics, public schools, and landed estates: money. As far as the social elite is concerned, the landowning elite, which controlled political power before 1850, contributed little to the Industrial Revolution in terms of technology or entrepreneurship. It did not, however, resist it.

One development that may help explain the timing and location of the Industrial Revolution concerns the attitudes of the educated and literate elite toward technological change. MacLeod has recently argued that there was no linear progression from the Baconian notion of technological progress as a means of increasing wealth to the Industrial Revolution. In the late seventeenth century, in her view, attitudes toward inventions regressed, becoming more abstract and detached, and a concern for unemployment coupled with a sense of British inferiority emerges from the writings of economists and philosophers. Technological progress plays a much more modest role in the writings of Hume and

Smith than it did in those of Bacon and Boyle. By 1776, however, the tide was turning again, and Smith's lack of enthusiasm for inventions was exceptional for his time. . . .

Yet advantages in human capital are fragile. With some exceptions, Britain's early inventors tended to be "tinkerers" without much formal technical schooling, whose genius lay primarily in their mechanical ingenuity. As it happened, most of the devices invented between 1750 and 1830 tended to be a type in which mechanically talented amateurs could excel. In many cases British inventors appear simply to have been lucky, although, as Pasteur once remarked, Fortune favors the prepared mind. The cotton, iron, and machine tool industries during the Industrial Revolution lent themselves to technological advances that did not require much scientific understanding of the physical processes involved. When, after 1850, deeper scientific analysis was needed, German and French inventors gradually took the lead, and the breakthroughs in chemistry and material science tended to be more concentrated on the Continent. Bessemer, Perkin, and Gilchrist-Thomas notwithstanding, the "amateur" stage in the history of technology was coming to an end by 1850. But Britain rode the wave high while it lasted.

Another factor in Britain's head start in technology at the beginning of the Industrial Revolution was that Britain alone among the large European economies constituted a comparatively unified market in which goods and people moved easily. Compared to the European Continent, Britain had excellent internal transportation. . . . Moreover, Britain was politically unified and cohesive. No tolls were charged on rivers and no tariffs were levied when crossing man-made lines (unlike France, for example, where before the Revolution internal tariffs were levied on goods moving within the country). As the technology of building roads and canals improved in the eighteenth century, Britain became an integrated market system.

Why did market integration matter to technological progress? Market size affected both the generation and the diffusion of new knowledge. . . . Some minimum level of demand was necessary to cover the fixed costs of development and construction. In very small and segmented markets insufficient demand may have impeded the diffusion of certain innovations that involved fixed costs. . . .

Market integration has a more profound effect on the diffusion of new techniques. In a world of high production costs, inefficient and conservative producers are insulated from their more innovative competitors.

A world of high transport costs is described by an economic model of monopolistic competition. One of the characteristics of such a model is that innovator and laggard can coexist side by side. In the region served by the innovator, lower production costs due to technological change meant a combination of higher profits for producers and lower prices for consumers. Nothing could force the laggards to follow suit, however, and the "survival of the cheapest" model so beloved by economists is short-circuited. High transport costs also made local oligopolies possible. A small number of firms in a market could facilitate conspiracies to stop new techniques, but as the market expanded and the number of firms with access to a given market increased, such "antitechnological cartels" became more difficult to organize and enforce without support from the authorities. In Britain, to a far greater extent than on the Continent, good transportation allowed competition to work, and the new technologies superseded the old sooner and faster than elsewhere. . . .

Much has been made of the British political system as a cause of the Industrial Revolution. Perhaps the most distinguishing feature of Britain was that its government was one of, by, and for property owners. Economists have maintained that well-defined property rights were necessary to static efficiency. But what about technological change? The direct links between the British government and the rate of technological progress were few. Some scholars have maintained that government demand for military purposes led to innovation, but such effects were small. More important was the effect of patent laws on inventive activity. North, in particular, argues that patents, which allowed the inventor to capture a larger part of the social benefits of his invention, were as important as a larger market. Here Britain led the Continent by a large margin. British patent law dates from 1624, whereas France did not have a similar law until 1791, and most other European countries established patent laws only in the early nineteenth century. The United States had a rather ineffective patent system from 1790, and the formal Patent Office was established only in 1836.

How decisive was the protection of the inventor's property rights by patents? Economic theory and contemporary empirical research suggest that the effect of a patent system on the rate of technological progress is ambiguous and differs from industry to industry. The ex ante positive incentive effects on inventors have to be weighed against the ex post negative effects on the diffusion of new knowledge, which will slow down as a result of an inventor's monopoly. Moreover, technological progress may be hampered by the closing of avenues in the development of new ideas if a particular ingredient has been patented by someone else. A monopoly position awarded as compensation for inventions might discourage further activity if it led to increased leisure consumption, or if the profits of additional invention had to be weighed against the possible loss of monopoly profits currently enjoyed. Yet patent rights could also lead to further inventions if they were used to finance additional research, a substantial advantage when capital markets were leery of innovators. . . .

Was the patent system a factor in encouraging technological change during the Industrial Revolution? Dutton has argued that an imperfect patent system, such as the British system, represented the best of all possible worlds. Without patents, inventors would be deprived of their financial incentives. But if patent enforcement had been too perfect, the diffusion of inventions might have been slowed down. The patent system appeared to the inventors as providing more protection than it actually did. Such a gap between ex ante and ex post effectiveness may, indeed, have been beneficial. An economist's intuition would perhaps be that here, too, people cannot be fooled in the very long run. By that logic, however, Atlantic City would have gone out of business long ago. Moreover, invention is not exactly like gambling because by definition no two inventions are the same, and hence the information that a potential inventor can derive from the previous experiences of others is limited. It could thus well be that the patent system fooled would-be inventors into exerting more effort than they would have had they known how stacked the deck was against them. If that was indeed the case, it attained its goal.

Another possible reason technological progress was so much faster in Britain than on the Continent between 1760 and 1830 was that the Industrial Revolution happened to coincide with one of the stormiest episodes in the history of Europe. . . .

Quite apart from political events, there is the matter of the social environment in which inventors and innovators operated. In France, for instance, very few inventors did well financially or otherwise. . . . Of course, not all British inventors fared as well as Arkwright or Watt, but there were enough success stories in Britain to preserve a constant interest in inventive activity. The Continent seems to have suffered more from a scarcity of innovative entrepreneurs than from a scarcity of inventors. Manufacturers such as Wedgwood, Crawshay, Boulton, or Strutt, who did not create much new technology but knew a good thing when they saw it and moved rapidly, seem to have been in short supply on the Continent. It is arguable that though Britain may have had an absolute advantage in both inventors and entrepreneurs, it had a comparative advantage in entrepreneurs and skilled workers, and thus imported inventions and inventors and exported entrepreneurs and technicians to the industrializing enclaves of the Continent. . . . The movement of technically skilled and enterprising Britons to the Continent demonstrates not only that a disequilibrium existed in the first half of the nineteenth century, but also that equilibrating forces were at work, spreading technological change from leader to follower. As long as that disequilibrium was maintained, Britain reaped a quasirent derived from a temporary advantage. . . .

How do we explain concentrated clusters of technological successes such as those that comprised the Industrial Revolution? If innovations occurred at random independently of each other, we should expect their time pattern to be distributed more or less uniformly over time. The difference between the Industrial Revolution and previous clusters of technological change was in the extent to which innovations influenced each other. First, there was an imitation effect: James Watt and Richard Arkwright became famous and wealthy men whom many tried to emulate. Invention and improvement became, in some circles at least, respectable. Second, there was a complementarity effect: the successful solution of one problem almost invariably suggested the next step, and so chains of inspiration were created. Many of the most useful inventions were indeed not more than radical modifications of earlier ideas: Cort's puddling-and-rolling process, Watt's and Trevithick's engines, Crompton's mule, all fall under this definition. Neither of these "one-thing-leads-to-another" theories constitutes an *explanation* of the Industrial Revolution. Both merely explain its time pattern, which is that when agents strongly affect each other, it is likely that success will appear in clusters. Clustering can occur when a critical mass is generated by the continuing interaction and cross-fertilization of inventors, scientists, and entrepreneurs. . . .

One avenue that has barely been explored by scholars interested in the question of "why England first" concerns the political economy of technological change. A widespread concern during the Industrial Revolution was that machines would throw people out of work, a misunderstanding that has persisted over the centuries. A more legitimate concern was the fear of loss suffered by established firms in industries that were being mechanized. From hand-loom weavers to wagon drivers to blacksmiths, the Industrial Revolution forced firms to conform or go out of business because of competitive pressure. Resistance to innovation was more likely to come from existing firms than from labor (though in the case of craftsmen and hand-loom weavers that distinction is perhaps not very sharp). Technological progress reduces the wealth of those possessing capital (real or human) specific to the old technology that cannot readily be converted to the new. Resistance was therefore strongest in long-established, skill-intensive industries such as printing and wool finishing.

Resistance to innovation was exacerbated by the fact that the gains from the innovations in the Industrial Revolution were captured by consumers (for whom joint political action is very hard), while the costs tended to be borne by a comparatively small number of people, many of whom may already have been organized, or knew each other and lived in the same regions. The losers could try to use extralegal methods (rioting, machine breaking, personal violence against innovators) or the political system to halt technological progress. Either way, the diffusion of technological progress became at times a social struggle, and politicians and judges became arbiters of decisions that should have been left to market forces. In this regard, technological change was similar to free trade. The benefits being diffuse and the costs concentrated, the survival of free trade has always been in jeopardy, and its lifespan usually short. And although we understand the forces at work, it is difficult to predict outcomes or even fully understand why a particular outcome came about. What is clear is that between 1750 and 1850 the British political system unflinchingly supported the winners over the losers, on both matters of technological progress and, increasingly, free trade. On the eve of the Industrial Revolution the British ruling class had most of its assets in real estate and agriculture; it had no interest in resisting the factory and the machine.

Once again, the difference between Britain and the Continent was one of degree and nuance. Before and during the Industrial Revolution, there were numerous examples of anti-machinery agitation in Britain. . . .

Were things significantly different on the Continent? As in Britain, resistance came from guilds of skilled artisans and from unskilled workers fearful of unemployment. Before the French Revolution, craft guilds, which still existed in most regions, held some new techniques back. In part, this was done by outright banning of inventions when established interests felt threatened. . . . Increasingly, the old urban guilds became a fetter on technological progress, less by outright resistance than through a vast body of regulations and restrictions on inputs and outputs. Under these regulations, for example, it would have been difficult for a barber like Richard Arkwright to set up shop as a cotton spinner. Yet the powers of the guilds were already declining in the eighteenth century. After 1760, guilds came under pressure in France and Germany, and were abolished in 1784 in the southern Netherlands. The French Revolution abolished them in France in 1791 and subsequently in areas that fell under French domination. By 1815 guilds had either been fatally weakened or abolished altogether on the Continent. The political upheaval and disruptions incurred as the price for ridding the economies of obsolete institutions between 1790 and 1815 may in part explain the lag in the adoption of some techniques into Europe. However, the Revolution's long-term effect was to clear up the debris of the ancien régime on the Continent, thus assuring Europe's ability eventually to follow Britain in revolutionizing its production system.

Not that there was a lack of resistance. . . . The need to placate skilled craftsmen may well have steered France into choosing a technology somewhat different from Britain's. The industrial France that emerged in the nineteenth century thus continued to be based on skilled small-scale handicrafts producing for relatively local markets. Some economic historians have attributed this difference between Britain and France to differences in population growth, but there must be limits to the burdens that demography can bear. More so than in Britain, therefore, technological progress in France had to accommodate the artisans and to find compromises between their traditional skills and the needs of modern factories. In Belgium, Switzerland, Bohemia, and the Rhineland, resistance to new cotton-spinning technology crumbled. In the Netherlands, on the other hand, workers repeatedly smashed machines in the textile industries in the south. Though such cases were not numerous, they may well have deterred entrepreneurs from installing such equipment. . . .

Nathan Rosenberg and L. E. Birdzell Jr.

How the West Grew Rich

The growth of European trade from the fifteenth century on was dominated by private traders in shifting and complex relations with their national political authorities. More was needed for the expansion of trade than a simple abandonment of the medieval objection to trading at negotiated prices. Medieval society was not well adapted to even the most essential trade between regions, and the expansion of trade which occurred in the fifteenth and sixteenth centuries required the invention or adoption of new institutional arrangements to supplement or replace the old medieval institutions.

Some of the institutional innovations reduced the risks of trade, either political or commercial. Among them were a legal system designed to give predictable, rather than discretionary, decisions; the introduction of bills of exchange, which facilitated the transfer of money and provided the credit needed for commercial transactions; the rise of an insurance market; and the change of governmental revenue systems from discretionary expropriation to systematic taxation—a change closely linked to the development of the institution of private property.

Large-scale trade outgrew the family firm whose internal loyalties were based on kinship. What was required was a concept of a firm as an entity distinct from its proprietor and from the family—an entity with a continuity of association among those whose working lives were organized around it and with a capacity similar to that of the family enterprise to create feelings of loyalty and duty. Such an entity required a degree of separation of the individual's property and transactions from the property and transactions of the enterprise unknown in the earlier family firms. The invention of double entry bookkeeping supplied the required separation; perhaps even more important, double entry bookkeeping supplied a financial history and financial picture of the enterprise which enabled other traders to deal with it as an entity and with some understanding of its capacity to meet its commitments. . . .

From Nathan Rosenberg and L. E. Birdzell Jr., *How the West Grew Rich: The Economic Transformation of the Industrial World* (New York: Basic Books, 1986).

The Changing Legal Structure

Large-scale commerce ordinarily involves transactions that take place over a considerable period of time. Unlike the everyday cash sale of goods, the medieval trading voyage, even within the Mediterranean, often lasted six months or more, and trading ventures to the East took years. Thus, the merchant who bought timber, wool, wheat, leather, salt, spices, or other commodities in large quantities was engaged in transactions that took time, and that could not be consummated without unreasonable risk in the absence of dependable commitments at the outset from sellers, ship-owners, buyers, and lenders. It was not absolutely essential that these commitments be legally enforceable; reliance could be, and was, placed upon the character and reputation of the other parties to the transaction. But the lack of enforceability added to the risks and thereby raised the cost of trade and limited its volume.

The development of a commercial law and commercial courts was in part a response to the expansion of commerce. A comprehensive and reliable commercial law required judges experienced in adjudicating commercial disputes and the development of a body of precedents for deciding them. Medieval courts could not develop a body of commercial law until the volume of commerce was large enough to generate a regular flow of commercial disputes, and courts were not likely to be presented with commercial disputes so long as their decisions were made unpredictable by lack of precedent, by medieval concepts of discretionary justice, and by possible bias against foreigners. The impasse was broken here and there, in the courts of trading cities, by the late Middle Ages. But it was not until the latter part of the eighteenth century that the royal courts in London had accumulated enough experience in deciding disputes over insurance, bills of exchange, ships' charters, sales contracts, partnership agreements, patents, arbitrations, and other commercial transactions to make English courts and law seem a factor contributing positively to the development of English commerce. The English courts allowed suits by foreign merchants and acquired a reputation for treating foreign litigants with scrupulous fairness. Mercantile transactions, insurance policies, and credit instruments subject to English law seemed more secure, more calculable in their consequences, less subject to the vagaries of sovereigns and changes of heart by one party or the other—advantages reflected in the growth of the British insurance industry, of London as a world financial center, and of British trade generally, as well as in low interest rates. Other Western countries sought to emulate these advantages by adopting commercial codes and establishing commercial courts.

Max Weber emphasized another aspect of European law. The West inherited from Roman law a formal, logical mode of juristic reasoning, ostensibly free from discretionary, ritualistic, religious, or magical considerations. Modern legal thought tends to emphasize and even justify the informal and discretionary aspects of judicial decision, but there remains a striking contrast between a system of law which seeks to make the legal consequences of human action coherent and predictable and the many systems which either have no such objective or allow it to become lost among competing objectives. The Western system lends itself to calculability; the others do not. As Weber put it:

> *In China it may happen that a man who has sold a house to another may later come to him and ask to be taken in because in the meantime he has been impoverished. If the purchaser refuses to heed the ancient Chinese command to help a brother, the spirits will be disturbed; hence the impoverished seller comes into the house as a renter who pays no rent. Capitalism cannot operate on the basis of a law so constituted. What it requires is law which can be counted upon, like a machine; ritualistic-religious and magical considerations must be excluded.*

Thus, systematic law added to the ability to predict the behavior of others, including people of all social ranks, in a wide variety of possible contexts. It thereby reduced the risks of trading and investing with them. This substitution of comparatively dependable rules for the discretionary justice of the manorial courts or the royal father figures, however Solomonic they might be, was an important element in the development of capitalist institutions.

Bills of Exchange

Merchants in Italy began using drafts drawn on their accounts with each other as a substitute for payment in coin during the thirteenth century. The use of bills of exchange permitted merchants to transfer the amounts they owed each other in the same way that we now transfer bank balances—by drawing a check, which is itself a bill of exchange drawn on a bank. In Antwerp, and later in Amsterdam, markets developed for the buying and selling of bills of exchange. In effect, these markets supplied, at low cost, the short-term credit needed to finance a growing commerce.

Deposit banking developed in a somewhat circuitous way, concurrently with the market for bills of exchange. Trading in bills of exchange circumvented the Church's prohibition of the payment of interest, since the purchase of a bill at a discount from its face value was treated as reflecting the risk that the bill might not be honored when it was presented, rather than as a payment of interest. As bills of exchange came into wide use, lesser-known merchants began to deposit funds with more widely known merchants, in order to place themselves in a position to pay by bills of exchange drawn on the more widely known merchants. It did not take long for the merchants who accumulated these deposits to discover that only a small portion of the deposits needed to be kept on hand to cover withdrawals, and that the balance could safely be used to buy bills of exchange at a discount—that is, for lending money at interest despite the prohibition of usury. They thus introduced deposit banking as a profitable and growing business in a society which prohibited the payment of interest.

Substitution of Taxation for Confiscation

Familiar as we are with constitutional systems that deny governments the power to seize the property of their citizens without compensation, most of us find it difficult to visualize societies in which governments had and commonly exercised exactly that power. Feudal sovereigns might have protected individuals' property against the depredations of other individuals, or even of other sovereigns, as a shepherd protects his sheep from shearing by others. But against their own sovereign lord, individuals of all social classes had to protect their accumulated capital and savings as best they could. Arbitrary assessments were always possible, and even some of the established feudal dues were unpredictable in timing and amount. The chronic threat of such assessments made it prudent for any considerable accumulation of assets of the subject to be held in mobile and concealable form.

Mobility and concealment were not, however, devices available to the barons whose accumulated wealth was in land, stored crops, farm animals, farm buildings and dwellings. The alternative was resort to force, and it was with force that the English barons confronted King John at Runnymede in 1215, long before their military power had been lost to professional armies. The result of the confrontation was Magna Carta, the great charter accepted conventionally as establishing the right of subjects to the enjoyment of their property without arbitrary expropriation by the Crown. Although it was a feudal document, sometimes deprecated as overstressing the rights of the great landowners who exacted it of the king, it contained a number of provisions guaranteeing rights to merchants (including foreign merchants), and merchants benefited from the property rights it established as part of English law and political tradition. The establishment of the right to hold property free of the risk of arbitrary seizure was important to the expansion of commerce, and Magna Carta gave the English a considerable lead on their neighbors.

In the fifteenth century, as professional armies, paid and supplied by money, replaced the self-sustaining feudal militias that fought in exchange for land tenure, the new central monarchies required regular and dependable sources of money. The traditional emergency levies might do once in a while, but as regular sources of revenue they could not be depended upon, partly because of cumulative public resistance and partly because of their disruptive effect, likewise cumulative, on economic activity. The upshot was that rulers were encouraged to give up the power to deal with the property of their subjects in an arbitrary way in exchange for the substitution of the power to levy regular taxes at stipulated rates.

This change had an effect whose significance can be appreciated only by contrast to the Asian and Islamic empires, which never adopted it. Arbitrary levies on the property of a subject were a ready means of political reprisal and social control, preventing successful merchants from accumulating wealth on a scale judged inappropriate to mere subjects. The abandonment of arbitrary levies was thus a major step toward allowing those in the economic sphere to develop their own ways of creating and accumulating wealth. Landes describes the change in this way:

> *[T]he ruler learned that it was easier and in the long run more profitable to expropriate with indemnification rather than confiscate, to take by law or judicial proceedings rather than by seizure. Above all, he came to rely on regular taxes at stipulated rates rather than on emergency exactions of indefinite amount. The revenue raised by the older method was almost surely less than that yielded by the new; over time, therefore, it constituted a smaller burden on the subject. But the effect of this uncertainty was to encourage concealment of wealth (hence discourage spending and promote hoarding) and to divert investment into those activities which lent themselves to this concealment. This seems to have been a particularly serious handicap to the economies of the great Asian empires and the Muslim states of the Middle East, where fines and extortions were not only a source of quick revenues but a means of social control—a device for curbing the pretensions of nouveaux riches and foreigners and blunting their challenge to the established power structure.*

The result was not entirely a substitution of concealment of assets from the tax collector for concealment of assets from the sovereign's bailiffs. So long as taxes were levied at known rates at known times, a merchant could calculate the prospective profits from investment in goods or real estate too visible and immobile to escape taxation, deduct the prospective taxes, and at least occasionally make a decision in favor of investment in taxable wealth.

The distinction between confiscation and taxation made the greatest difference in England and Holland, where the royal governments lost the power to impose arbitrary levies without gaining the power to impose arbitrary taxes. In both countries, the power to impose taxes resided in parliaments in which the merchant class was strongly represented, and the two countries were the leaders in the accumulation of visible forms of mercantile wealth.

In retrospect, it is difficult to see how even modest amounts of trade could have been carried on except where merchants had a measure of immunity from arbitrary seizure. Substantial commerce required a tangible apparatus scarcely less visible than real estate, though for the most part much more mobile: ships, stocks of goods, and warehouses in quantities roughly proportional to the volume of trade. Both commerce and its tangible apparatus were bound to grow more rapidly where the apparatus enjoyed security from arbitrary expropriation—that is, in England, Holland, and the trading cities that had gained similar immunities through feudal charters.

Economic Association Without Kinship

. . . Apart from the family, the Middle Ages offered no satisfactory models for mercantile enterprises. The two great hierarchies were the feudal system itself and the Church, and both embodied the obligations of subordinate to hierarchical superior in elaborate ritual and oath. Solemn though they were, neither produced, in the practice of the later Middle Ages, the practical relationships of trust and confidence needed for long-term economic association.

Yet, where the required scale of trading exceeded the capacity of family firms and of ad hoc joint ventures, private firms could conduct trade and investment only if there existed some basis, beyond kinship, for mutual trust. The expansion of nongovernmental, secular trade and investment after the sixteenth century would simply not have been possible without the creation of a purely economic form of organization, capable of producing the necessary equivalent of family ties. Without it, some solution like the Venetian oligarchy, with the state financing projects too large for families and joint ventures, would have been unavoidable. . . .

Double Entry Bookkeeping

In order to create an economic enterprise distinct from the family, it was necessary first to conceive of an enterprise distinct from the family, and second to establish some way of distinguishing the affairs of the enterprise from the family and household affairs of its principals. This was not easy to do in an age when the members of the family and the members of the enterprise were one and the same, when the enterprise and its owners dwelt in the same premises, and when all the members of the family traded for the joint account of the family.

In a world of family enterprises, the need for a distinction between family and individual assets must have arisen from the desire of individual members of the family to trade for their own account or to distinguish between their own assets and the assets of the family, at least sometimes. It was necessary to do more than simply list the assets of the enterprise separately from the assets of the individual owners. The record of the enterprise's transactions had to be separated from the record of individual transactions, and it had to be related to the assets of the enterprise rather than of the individual. The successes of the enterprise had to be recorded as enhancing its assets, the failures as diminishing them.

The most obvious reason for merchants to adopt double entry bookkeeping was that it provided a check on the clerical accuracy of the entries for each transaction. The general principle behind the complex rules of the system was that one member of each pair of entries recorded a change in assets (or income) and the other an equal change in liabilities (or expenses). Entries of the two types could be separately totaled, and if the totals did not match, an error must have occurred. Neither the principle nor the merchants' interest in clerical accuracy carried any hint that double entry bookkeeping might be the source of the idea of the continuing enterprise as an entity separate from its owners, except for one point: for liabilities to equal assets, the liability accounts had to include both liabilities to third persons and the liability of the enterprise to its owners—its net worth.

Thus a bookkeeping system whose practical appeal lay in its ability to detect errors compelled the merchants and bookkeepers who used it to acquire the habit of thinking of the enterprise, either as a debtor to its owners or as itself the owner of its own net worth. Either way, it was an abstraction created by its own books of account. Sombart went so far as to say that "One cannot imagine what capitalism would be without double-entry bookkeeping." For double entry bookkeeping is an actualization of the profit-seeking firm as a truly autonomous (indeed, one might add, as did Sombart, an abstract) unit, the property of which is no longer mixed up with that of the family, the seigneury, or other social units.

There was another reason for developing a formal record of the assets and transactions of the enterprise, going much beyond the need to distinguish the enterprise from its individual owners. It was indispensable to the growing use of credit to find an objective, quantitative method for evaluating the financial status and prospects of the firm. The needed method eventually emerged from double entry bookkeeping as a set of rules for expressing all economic transactions in numerical terms. It grew into an agreed-upon procedure for recording all economic events in a measurable and therefore calculable way. In a very real sense, economic reality became that which could be expressed in numerical terms in the books: *Quod non est in libris, non est in mundo.*

It was not, in other words, so much the initial advance represented by double entry over single entry bookkeeping that made the great difference in the development of Western capitalist institutions, as it was the impetus which that advance gave to the development of financial accounting and the practice of evaluating the credit of the enterprise by viewing its status in terms of its balance sheet and its activities in terms of its statement of profit and loss.

Meeting the Capital Requirements of Factories

A number of historical arguments have been built on the assumption that the Industrial Revolution, with its shift to factory production, required the accumulation of great quantities of capital. Indeed, if the simple arithmetic of the formula, Consumption = Output – Capital Accumulation, really captured the process of the accumulation of capital, it would mean that many people must have sacrificed current consumption in the interest of accumulating capital. Marx took the sacrificial burden of accumulation for granted but argued that the capitalists had managed to shift it from themselves to labor. Others attributed the accumulation to the

Calvinist principles of the capitalists themselves. To this day, the leaders of the U.S.S.R. use the need to accumulate capital, in the form of industrial facilities, to explain their neglect of the production of consumer goods. Third World as well as socialist countries have assumed burdensome debts in order to provide capital for new industries, and orthodox Western bankers have supposed that such loans serve a useful economic purpose. There may be some truth to all this, but it has to be supported by evidence other than the history of the Industrial Revolution in England.

To begin with, the historical evidence suggests that the capital required for the early factories was modest. Arkwright's first Cromford mill was insured for 1,500, and his second for 3,000 pounds. The introduction of steam power and multistory plants, near the close of the eighteenth century, pushed the cost of a spinning mill as high as 15,000 pounds; but by then the early factory owners had behind them twenty years of operations, sometimes highly profitable. There is some suggestion of a need for outside funds in the fact that factory owners often joined banking partnerships, but these affiliations may have indicated that the factory owners had surplus funds to invest or that they needed close banking ties to provide working capital.

Of course, the capital that supplied the Industrial Revolution was not created out of thin air. But neither was it painfully accumulated by the frugal habits of Protestant burghers, expropriated from labor by massive reductions of wages, or squeezed out of reduced consumption. No reduction in the real income of workers or landowners nor in their rate of consumption, no national resolve to increase the rate of saving, was needed to fund the new machines and the new forms of factory organization. Rather, the increase in output that was generated by the factories was more than sufficient to pay their capital costs over a short period of time, for the increase was large and the capital costs were modest.

The funding of the factories was facilitated by the English system of country banks which, by the usual effects of deposit banking, created the money supply needed for their factory customers' working capital—which roughly equaled the fixed capital embodied in the new factories. Undoubtedly, both the inventories and sales financed by working capital and the underlying plant financed by fixed capital were real assets which had to be drawn off the real stream of production somehow, perhaps by the inflationary effect of the increase in money supply created by this deposit banking. But since the period was one of stable or declining prices, the inflationary effects must have been offset by other factors. One such factor was the improved productivity of the new factories and the resultant downward pressure on prices. To put the same point in terms of the "real" economy rather than the "financial" economy, if the real stream of production was constantly expanded by a continuing stream of more productive capital investments, there need not have been any time at which consumers experienced a reduction in the consumption goods portion of the stream, for no such reduction need have occurred.

It is too late to reconstruct the process in detail, but it is quite clear that the capital financing of the Industrial Revolution required little or no lowering of the existing standards of consumption in the interests of accumulating capital. According to Feinstein's authoritative estimates, overall consumption per capita in Great Britain did not decline between 1760 and 1800, and it rose dramatically thereafter. Moreover, the share of gross investment in British gross national product remained basically constant from the 1780s to the 1850s.

Another indication that the Industrial Revolution did not impose important strains on the ability of Western nations to generate capital is that corporations, the traditional institutional tools for assembling large amounts of capital, played only a limited and specialized part until quite late in the nineteenth century. Corporations were formed for the building of turnpikes, railroads, and canals, but, by and large, widespread adoption of corporate forms of organization in industry came after factory production had become the dominant mode of industrial output. In both Europe and the United States, the entrepreneurial capitalists of the early and middle period of the Industrial Revolution were merchants, bankers, and inventors, operating in partnerships and only rarely making use of joint-stock corporations for manufacturing firms.

The claim that a decline in income among handweavers paid for the new factories is, at best, a metaphor. Economic change implies a relative or absolute reduction in both the value of the resources devoted to, and the income derived from, activities which become partially or wholly obsolete, whether handweaving, sailmaking, hostling, glassblowing, or steelmaking. A reduction in the value of human skills committed to handweaving, because of a decline in demand for handweaving, did not create a fund of resources transferable to the purchase of power looms. The weavers' loss was a consequence of change, not a source of capital for change. The old activity was in no position to finance its successor.

It would be wrong to leave a sense of paradox about the failure of the Industrial Revolution to create painful problems of capital creation. The reason the formula, Consumption = Output – Capital Accumulation, presents a misleading picture of the process of economic growth is that it misses the effect of time. One may readily concede that an increase in output implies an increase in working capital and fixed capital, or else in productivity. But the causal link is between the *present* rate of production and the *past* rate of capital accumulation. It is entirely possible that over a period of time, whether a year or a long period such as 1750 to 1880, output, capital accumulation, and consumption could each increase at the same rate, or with differences in rates which nevertheless allowed a continuous rise in consumption throughout the period. All that is required is that the *current rise* in capital accumulation absorb less than all of the *current rise* in output. In the West, increases in productivity have tended to make this condition easy to meet. . . .

Robert S. DuPlessis

Transitions to Capitalism in Early Modern Europe

. . . Both because food remained the largest category of expenditure in popular budgets, and because farming remained far and away Europeans' single biggest occupation, the state of agriculture significantly shaped the state of industry. Well into the first half of the eighteenth century, stagnant or falling foodstuff prices—of cereals most of all—in a context of sticky or even slightly rising pay levels boosted real wages and, in particular, enhanced the share of urban and rural wage-earners' income available for discretionary spending. It appears that they disbursed about half the gain on manufactures. At the same time, the ongoing expansion of market-oriented agriculture obliged more farmers to buy items they previously had made or which they now needed to stay abreast of their fellows.

Urbanization disproportionately boosted demand. Although the proportion of citydwellers in the population as a whole only inched up from

From Robert S. DuPlessis, *Transitions to Capitalism in Early Modern Europe* (Cambridge: Cambridge University Press, 1997).

8 percent (1650) to 10 percent (1800), their absolute numbers nearly doubled in a time of accelerating demographic advance that saw the 75 million Europeans of 1650 become 123 million by 1800. Even more important, the number of cities with 80,000 or more people, and the number of people living in them, increased more than twofold over that century and a half; Atlantic ports, naval stations, capitals, and new industrial centers also burgeoned. These large cities required heavy infrastructural investment, providing extra stimulus to iron and other metallurgical trades. They also fostered the improvement of commercial structures and means of transportation, and even though these were constructed primarily to move grain and bulky energy sources more efficiently, they widely lowered industry's transactions costs. Spreading networks of canals and canalized rivers brought the advantages of cheap internal transport that the Dutch Republic had long enjoyed to other areas, for example, helping to integrate regional and inter-regional markets.

Capital cities also attracted fashion-conscious elites that consumed disproportionate amounts of luxury goods. On a bigger scale than in the long sixteenth century, the level of demand often became great enough to warrant introducing cost-reducing specializations and divisions of labor that by lowering prices contributed to ongoing market growth. Correlatively, the diffusion of urban styles powerfully molded demand over broad areas. London remained the extreme example of this kind of cultural authority. By the early eighteenth century, 11 percent of all English people lived there and many more directly experienced London life, whether as temporary migrants or as visitors on political, commercial, legal, or social business. Their exposure to the great city helped dissolve traditional consumption patterns and generate new ones as former luxuries became necessities. No other city was nearly so dominant demographically. Yet Continental capitals, too, tended to serve as tastemakers once the consumer society pioneered in England began to appear elsewhere in Europe. Paris housed at most 3 percent of French people, yet it boasted numerous artisans who made fine goods or put the finishing touches to merchandise that provincial workers had roughed out. Specializing in ornamentation, the Paris clothing trades depended on and thus strongly encouraged constant fashion changes and their widespread adoption well beyond its borders. Paris also turned out a proliferating array of cheap knockoffs of upper-class luxury items—umbrellas, canes, watches, fans, and other "populuxe" goods, as one historian has termed them.

Some of the most influential consumption innovations travelled upward rather than percolating down. In later seventeenth-century England, the rage for clothing made of calico emerged first in the urban middling strata, who used it as a cheap substitute for brocade and silk. Only after the directors of the East India Company consciously mounted a publicity campaign—among other things, they gave King Charles II large monetary "gifts" so he would wear a calico waistcoat—was aristocratic disdain overcome. Once it was, a more casual upper-class style that originated in England became a foundation of the calico industry throughout Europe.

New means of cultural diffusion nurtured new habits of consumption. Printed advertisements were being posted in London in the seventeenth century; by the eighteenth, they had appeared in Paris and elsewhere on the Continent. Newspapers, which from the start prominently featured advertisements for all sorts of commodities, were founded first in metropolitan centers and then, beginning in the early eighteenth century, in the provinces and colonies. Around 1753, when Europe's population was no more than 100 million, annual newspaper circulation is thought to have surpassed 7 million. An increasing number of magazines that prominently featured fashion plates and reports also appeared. Printed matter circulated more expeditiously thanks to the organization of regular postal services among many more cities than ever before. From 1660, for instance, mail boats shuttled between Amsterdam and London twice a week and riders joined Amsterdam with Hamburg, while Paris already had a semi-weekly service to several major provincial towns. Ideas and goods were sped on their way by road improvements that on main routes cut travel time in half between the later seventeenth and later eighteenth centuries.

The desires thereby conveyed could more readily be satisfied now that itinerant pedlars were being supplemented by a thickening network of retail shops: in England they trebled in number across the first half of the eighteenth century. Making an ever-widening range of goods available on a permanent basis—and providing an even more sublime abundance by special order to their wholesalers in the big cities—and engaging in competitive pricing, they were critical to both the quantitative and qualitative growth of consumption. . . .

Finally, government spending—most of it, as in the past, devoted to the military—enhanced demand for a parade of goods from bricks to boots. Navies had particularly important effects in this era of colonial empire-building. Employment at English naval shipyards rose at least fourfold from 1650 to 1750, while the complete overhaul of the Spanish navy in the eighteenth century led to the opening of new armaments plants and encouraged Basque iron founders to adopt improved bloomeries that raised output and quality.

Despite all these stimuli, growth of domestic European markets was slowed by several substantial obstacles. On much of the Continent, to begin with, interstate and internal levies impeded the movement of goods, increasing costs and prices. Products travelling on the Rhine, for instance, owed numerous tolls to the many states lining the riverbanks. At several sovereign cities they had to be unloaded and offered for sale; only then could they be shipped on, and only in boats operated by members of the towns' guilds. Again, several of France's peripheral provinces, including rich industrialized parts of Flanders conquered in the later seventeenth century, were deemed "foreign" for fiscal purposes. Upon entering the central "Five Great Farms" provinces, goods made in these reputedly foreign parts had to pay duties similar to those imposed on manufactures from lands outside His Majesty's dominions. To be sure, in some lands internal tolls were reduced or eliminated in the course of the eighteenth century. At almost the same stroke, however, high tariffs or outright prohibitions were instituted on interstate imports of manufactures. Although customs duties between Hungary and the rest of the Habsburg Empire were cut drastically in 1754, for example, and two decades later nearly all internal duties were abolished among the various Austrian provinces, tariffs on foreign manufactures jumped so much that many items were effectively excluded.

In the second half of the eighteenth century, moreover, the limits of agricultural growth began to be felt once again. Even in England, farm output began to trail behind demographic increase, pushing up prices and thus dampening demand among wage-earners and others dependent on food purchases; this was only partly offset by healthier incomes among landlords and market-oriented farmers able to stay ahead of rent increases. For the most important crimp on demand across Europe as a whole remained the levies on the majority of the population that tilled the land. Albeit in varying proportions, taxes, rents, dues, and tithes encumbered popular consumption. The weakness of "mass" demand was a persistent problem in eighteenth-century Europe, threatening to abort eighteenth-century expansion just as it had in the long sixteenth century. But this time another factor was at play—substantial overseas demand—that helped sustain European producers.

So although Europeans remained the paramount customers for each other's manufactures—as late as the 1790s, three-quarters of all European exports went to other Europeans—non-European markets were becoming ever more significant to European industry. . . .

But just what and how much did they contribute? More generally, how valuable were colonial empires to European industrialization? According to one prominent view, rooted ultimately in Marx, gains from exploitative slave-based agriculture and colonial trade were central to the process of original accumulation that provided the funds needed for the triumph of capitalism and, eventually, mechanized factories within Europe.

Although this interpretation has sustained heavy attack, much evidence can be adduced to support it. Admittedly, voyages often ended in shipwreck or capture by pirates or privateers, and plantation agriculture proved risky enough to bankrupt many owners. But English slavers, at least, averaged profits of 8–10 percent, and booming European demand for colonial products created additional opportunities for ample gain by merchants and plantation owners. As always, much of their revenue found its way into landed estates, conspicuous consumption, and government debt, or, among traders, was plowed back into commerce and allied activities like marine insurance. Nevertheless, some colonial merchants, at least, did put funds into many types of manufacturing, often encouraged by the so-called "store system," in which manufactures were traded directly for colonial raw materials. Around Glasgow, the tobacco entrepôt of Europe, they invested substantially in tanneries, slitting mills, forges, sugar refining, sailcloth making, coal and copper mining, linens, and eventually cottons. Merchants themselves, however, did not become industrialists. Rather, they put money into industry at the behest of entrepreneurs but usually had little to do with the operation of the businesses in which they had invested.

The bulk of industrial capital came, nevertheless, not from colonial but from domestic sources. Even in Great Britain, which captured the lion's share of overseas trade profits, less than a fifth of capital for all types of investment came from gains realized in intercontinental trade. The Atlantic economy mattered most for European industries because of markets and raw materials rather than capital. Africa alone took more than 10 percent of total French exports in the later eighteenth century, and nearly 5 percent of British. Dutch and English records indicate that textiles comprised about half the goods sent to Africa, along with appreciable amounts of metal wares, weapons, and distilled spirits. In the Americas, despite the growth of colonial textile, shipbuilding, and other industries (at times in defiance of laws designed to protect home producers), slaves, Amerindians, and especially free colonists consumed much larger and growing amounts of European manufactures. English exports of manufactures grew ninefold between 1699–1701 and 1772–74. France's exports to her West Indian and North American colonies expanded eightfold across the eighteenth century: in 1787, a third of French manufacturing exports went to the New World, including sizable amounts destined for Spanish colonies.

Colonial demand had a salutary effect on woollens, silk, and cotton trades across Europe. Europe's linen industries were particularly oriented to the colonies. To cite just one example, nine of every ten *bretañas* (linens) from Brittany went to Spain, whence most were re-exported to Spanish America. But the colonies bought much else besides cloth: everything from hats to hoes, paint to pewter, brass buckles to mirrors. The trade with Africa that increasingly accompanied colonial commerce likewise benefited European industries, especially metallurgy and textiles. Already in the early sixteenth century, Portugal had made cheap woollens for sale to African slavers, and from about 1700, on a much larger scale, England wove cottons and other light fabrics for the same market.

For their part, the colonies produced raw materials for extremely profitable and rapidly growing processing industries within Europe, particularly its northwestern quadrant: in England, their value quadrupled between 1699–1701 and 1772–74. By the 1770s, sugar accounted for 60 percent of England's imports from America, perhaps half of France's. The 9 million pounds of tobacco sent to Europe in the 1660s had become at least 220 million pounds in 1775; each year around 1750, English hatters alone took at least 80,000 beaver furs, double the 1700 figure; and from the 1760s, New World cotton output boomed, soon surpassing the Levant and Asia as Europe's main suppliers.

Asia, too, became a market for European goods, albeit never on the scale of the Atlantic. Around 1700, only 3 percent of English exports went to Asia, as against 12 percent to the Americas and Africa; in the early 1770s, the shares were 8 percent and 43 percent, and England ranked ahead of any other European nation. Still, Asia took on the average four and a half times as many English manufactures after 1763 as during the preceding half century. Moreover, the composition of exports dramatically altered. Whereas before 72 percent had consisted of bullion, 28 percent of manufactures, now the proportions were reversed: 27 percent bullion, 73 percent goods.

By the late eighteenth century, European manufactures had penetrated heretofore peripheral or recently created markets from domestic popular strata to overseas colonies. This increasingly broad and global reach lent a growing dynamism to European industries both old and new—to Lyon silk, Flemish linens, and Bohemian glass, as well as to Zurich cottons, Ghent-refined sugar, Swedish iron, and Stockport hats. Not all existing crafts were reborn nor did all new foundations bloom. But across Europe, industrial activity quickened, encouraging experiments with new methods and structures of production. Governments figured prominently among the progenitors of these attempts.

State and Industry

For centuries, political authorities throughout Europe had intervened in many aspects of industry to regulate quality, assure raw materials supplies, help control labor, and occasionally—in strategic sectors—to direct production in state-owned workplaces like the Venetian Arsenal. Before about 1650, most of these activities were undertaken by municipalities (or, in Italy and Germany, by city-states) and the guilds located within them. Central governments might step in with general directives on, say, wages or guild organization, but their attention was sporadic at best. From the mid-seventeenth century, however, states intruded much more systematically. Sometimes they were responding to depressed economic conditions; at times, they acted for reasons of prestige. But with increasing frequency and determination, monarchs and statesmen took on an activist economic role in order to build up the military and financial strength of their regimes. Convinced that national wealth and power were intimately and mutually connected, they sought to promote both by means of economic development. In so doing, they borrowed from—and helped to elaborate—a body of ideas, assumptions, and practices labeled, since the time of Adam Smith (who castigated them for obstructing the free play of market forces), "the mercantile system" or "mercantilism."

Mercantilist measures were designed to help a state capture a larger share of international trade and augment bullion supplies at the expense of its competitors, notably by expanding exports and reducing imports of manufactures. In pursuit of these goals, governments not only raised barriers against foreign finished goods, but aided the development of domestic industries and the formation of protected markets for their products. In these ways, they attempted to create comparative advantages for their own industries or, if nothing else, hinder those of rivals. States also championed industrialization to provide jobs for what elites considered dangerously disorderly throngs of the underemployed—who to boot allegedly wasted, by receiving charity, resources that could better be used for the ends of power and plenty.

Tariffs and outright bans that kept out manufactures from abroad while attempting to enhance the inflow of raw materials and to create captive markets were the most effective and widely adopted mercantilist steps; what constrained inter-European trade fostered industrialization within the market units thereby constituted. England pioneered such policies to the advantage of its own woollens industry . . . ; with the Navigation Acts of 1651 and 1660 and subsequent laws it extended a system of monopolies across industries and across the Atlantic. The empire became an enormous free-trade zone for English manufactures and their prime source of raw materials.

Scotland's experience after its union with England in 1707 gave it equal access to protected markets and raw materials demonstrates the powerful impact of the empire on industries in the metropoles. Previously limited by the poverty and small size (just over 1 million inhabitants) of the domestic market, in the eighteenth century Scottish textile industries throve as the rapidly expanding American colonies became their chief overseas customers. Similarly, the Navigation Acts helped to funnel tobacco to Glasgow, which soon became the tobacco entrepôt and a leading processing center for all Europe. But even on the smaller scale available to other countries, barriers against imports of competing goods proved helpful to home industries. In the mid-eighteenth-century southern Netherlands, for example, duties on Dutch, French, and Prussian goods were instrumental to the flowering of trades such as sugar refining, flannel making, and the weaving of mixed cotton–linen fabrics.

The most successful example of protectionist industrial development was the result of ramparts directed not against other European goods but against an Asian import. In the later seventeenth and early eighteenth centuries, Indian calicoes took European markets by storm: from only a few thousand pieces around 1650, English imports surged to 860,000 pieces in the early eighteenth century, Dutch to 100,000. In the face of this deluge, pressure from European textile producers struck a sympathetic chord among mercantilist-inspired officials concerned by the outflow of silver, since at that time Europe bought much more in Asia (including spices, pepper, tea, and coffee as well as textiles) than it sold there. In response, many countries progressively restricted, or banned outright, imports of calicoes.

The linen industry was a major beneficiary of these acts: shipments of Irish linen rose from virtually nothing in 1700 to 40 million pieces a century later; Scottish output grew from 2 million yards (1728) to 13 million (1770); Galician linen output doubled between 1750 and 1800. Textile printing also blossomed: by the 1760s, Barcelona was the largest center in Europe. Initially, printers used imported plain calicoes, but increasingly they switched to mixed fabrics or pure cottons woven within Europe, for cotton manufacturing throve as an import substitution industry once Indian calicoes had been debarred. Annual imports of raw cotton woven within England grew slowly from 1.1 million pounds around 1700 to 4.2 million in 1772, then exploded to 41.8 million by 1800. French cotton and cotton–linen output rose by an average of 3.8 percent a year between 1700–10 and 1780–89; by 1790, more than 170 places in France made these fabrics. By that date, in fact, few countries in Europe were without a cotton industry. . . .

. . . Those who made government economic policy sought primarily to enhance the military, financial, and political standing of their states. Yet in so doing, they helped to expand the scope of European industrialization beyond what market forces alone could have achieved.

Proto-industry and Proto-factory

. . . At least since Marx, for whom putting-out trades in the countryside during the period of what he called "manufactures" were essential to capitalist industrialization, scholars have recognized the significance of this golden age of rural industry. But during the past several decades, the approach known as "proto-industrialization" has generated a wealth of new insights and interpretations. As initially formulated by the economic historian Franklin Mendels, proto-industrialization was characterized by the production of goods for distant, often international, markets by peasant-manufacturers; it grew out of but was distinct from traditional cottage industries for local consumption. Pursuing agricultural activities that did not fully occupy their time, rural folk formed a cheap and elastic labor supply because they could combine farming with the working up of raw materials put out by merchant entrepreneurs; as economists would say, the "opportunity cost" of their labor was low, for they did not have to abandon other remunerative work to take on industrial employment. As proto-industries spread, some districts came to specialize in manufacturing; others nearby focused on commercial agriculture. Thus developed dynamic and symbiotic regional economies, organized and financed from towns, where rurally made proto-industrial goods were finished and sold. Eventually, rising labor, distribution, and supervisory costs brought growth to a halt, but by then proto-industries had provided capital, technical knowledge, a proletarianized and expanding labor force, entrepreneurs with marketing and managerial skills, and some of the consumer demand required for mechanized factory industrialization.

Every aspect of Mendels' theory has been subject to searching critique, elaboration, and reformulation, from which little has emerged unscathed. Some commentators object to the evolutionary models and teleological premises underlying the concept: proto-industrialization is to be understood, Mendels proclaimed in the subtitle of his germinal 1972 essay, as "the first phase of the industrialization process." More frequently, the hypothesis is faulted for trying to squeeze diverse if related phenomena into too narrow a conceptual mold. It is now clear that while a new departure in many places, rural industrialization elsewhere was the renewal of a centuries-old cycle, albeit on a much bigger scale that drew the populations of entire districts into industrial work. Although the growth of international and interregional trade in manufactures is best documented, proto-industries often produced for nearby consumers as well: the critical issue was not the location of demand but the fact that it was supplied by market-oriented putting-out producers. Similarly, although more pronounced in the countryside, proto-industrialization could be urban, too, for the underlying dynamic was the search for cheap and docile labor, wherever it might be found. Nor did proto-industries reign alone: in countryside as well as in town they co-existed with a variety of industrial structures, including the Kaufsystem and proto-factories. Finally, proto-industrialization bore a contingent rather than a necessary relationship with later industrial development; any specific region was as likely to return to an agricultural vocation as to see the rise of mechanized factories. . . .

Jan De Vries

The Industrial Revolution and the Industrious Revolution

. . . Efforts made over the years to explore the possibilities of demand-initiated economic development during the Industrial Revolution have invariably been beaten back by the exposure of logical and theoretical inconsistency. No one is better at that than Joel Mokyr, and at the end of his article "Demand vs. Supply in the Industrial Revolution," he stepped back, as it were, from his work of demolition and, while wiping the muck of faulty reasoning from his hands, concluded with the words "The . . . notion that supply and demand were somehow symmetric in the industrialization process is unfounded. The determination of 'when,' 'where,' and 'how fast' are to be sought first and foremost in supply, not demand-related processes."

But, the conundrum remained; indeed, the evidence for it grew considerably since the lines just quoted were written. And the interest in a demand-side appreciation of early industrialization, beaten back in economic history, emerged again among social historians, among whom sightings of a "consumer revolution" gained credence, and has now found a comfortable home among cultural historians, where the triumph of the will of the consumer can overcome any scarcity, where budget constraints don't exist (and where love never dies).

Which brings me to my proposal. The twin challenges seem to call for a renewed attention to the economic history of the household or the family unit. The insights of the early modern revisionists play themselves out, nearly all of them, in the context of the household unit. And the solution to the conundrum of the falling purchasing power of labor and increased material possessions is to be found, I am convinced, in the behavior of the household as well.

From Jan De Vries, "The Industrial Revolution and the Industrious Revolution," *Journal of Economic History* 54, no. 2 (June 1994).

Consumer demand grew, even in the face of contrary real wage trends, and the productive achievements of industry and agriculture in the century before the Industrial Revolution could occur because of reallocations of the productive resources of households. In England, but in fact through much of Northwestern Europe and Colonial America, a broad range of households made decisions that increased *both* the supply of marketed commodities and labor *and* the demand for goods offered in the marketplace. This combination of changes in household behavior constituted an "industrious revolution." Driven by a combination of commercial incentives (changes in relative prices, reduced transaction costs) and changes in tastes, this "industrious revolution" emanating to a substantial degree from the aspirations of the family, preceded and prepared the way for the Industrial Revolution. This industrious revolution, a change in household behavior with important demand-side features, began in advance of the Industrial Revolution, an fundamentally supply-side phenomenon.

The household is a unit of coresidence and reproduction, of production and labor power, of consumption and distribution among its members, and of transmission across generations. At the heart of the concept of an industrious revolution is the interaction of these functions and of decision making within the household concerning the optimal allocation of time and other resources of its members. Here I adapt Gary Becker's "Theory of the Allocation of Time" to my purposes, proposing that a household purchases market-supplied goods subject to a resource constraint of money income, and combines these goods with the labor and other resources of the household to produce what Becker called "Z," the more basic commodities that directly enter the household's utility function. The purchased goods *(x)* should be thought of as ranging from items requiring very little household labor before they are transformed to the consumable Z commodities (say tea), to those (say sheep) that require extensive household labor before the transformation (to clothing) is complete. Correspondingly, the Z commodities should be thought of as items of utility, many if not all of which can be satisfied in a variety of ways—through purchased goods requiring little labor or through essentially home-produced goods and services (clothing could be produced from home-grown fiber, from a store-bought length of cloth, or ready-made from a tailor—the domestic "value-added" diminishing with each example).

If this is granted, then changes in tastes (chiefly affecting the desired composition of Z commodities) and supply-side changes affecting relative prices (chiefly influencing the choice of technique to achieve a given Z commodity) will jointly determine the demand for market-supplied goods. And, within the household economy, this demand will shape the disposition of the household's potential productive resources (chiefly time) between home production of Z and income-generating production of marketed commodities and the offer of labor. When the demand for leisure (defined as time devoted to neither income-generating nor consumption-preparing activity) is added to the equation, we have what I believe is a way of formulating the household economy that is sufficiently general to comprehend the proverbial preindustrial peasant household characterized by substantial self-sufficiency, and the modern household, often thought to be simply a unit of consumption.

In this framework the industrious revolution, for which evidence can be found from the mid-seventeenth century into the early nineteenth, consisted of two transformations: the reduction of leisure time as the marginal utility of money income rose, and the reallocation of labor from goods and services for direct consumption to marketed goods—that is, a new strategy for the maximization of household utility. We see it among peasant households concentrating their labor in marketed food production, in cottar households directing underemployed labor to proto-industrial production, in the more extensive market-oriented labor of women and children, and finally, in the pace or intensity of work.

Now, a vast body of opinion held both by contemporaries and by modern historians contradicts the very possibility of an industrious revolution such as I have described. Among eighteenth-century observers no end of colorful denunciations of the sloth, fecklessness, and irresponsibility of working people can be assembled. They stress the limited, and base, wants of the working population and the necessity of low wages to secure an elastic supply of labor. Such commentary is not usually the product of disinterested observation of actual behavior. It functioned as part of an ideology that defined the working population's otherness and incapacity for self-governance. In addition, of course, it had the practical benefit, as the "utility of poverty doctrine," of justifying low wages. It is ironic that many historians who regard themselves as champions of the common man appropriate these claims. What had served the original tellers as a trope to justify the subordination of the lesser orders because of their lack of self-control and weak spirit of improvement came to be used by "moral economy" advocates as evidence of the precapitalist natural innocence of common folk.

Thus, the human raw material for a modern capitalist economy could be described by Sidney Pollard as "Men who were non-accumulative, non-acquisitive, accustomed to work for subsistence, not for maximization of income, [who] had to be made obedient to the cash stimulus, and obedient in such a way as to react precisely to the stimuli provided." The factory master not only had to train his workers, he had to train his consumers at the same time, for nothing came harder than regular and intense labor, which required in E. P. Thompson's words "the supervision of labour; fines; bells and clocks; money incentives; preachings and schooling; the suppression of fairs and sports."

There exists another body of literature consisting primarily of novels, diaries, and essays that evokes a rather different image. From Samuel Pepys through Daniel Defoe to Arthur Young, the concern with material culture in the broadest sense is intense, if not compulsive. Indeed, Defoe might well qualify as the chronicler of the industrious revolution, so frequently does he describe manufacturing counties where "you see the wheel going almost at every door, the wool and the yarn hanging up at every window, the looms, the winders, the combers, the carders, the dyers, the dressers, all busy; and the very children, as well as women constantly employed.

"As is the labour so is the living; for where the poor are full of work, they are never empty of wages; they eat while the others starve, and have a tolerable plenty."

This "tolerable plenty" that filled Defoe with admiration, translated to "luxury" for many other observers, and the bitter debate waged over its pros and cons is itself a sign that target incomes and subsistence norms no longer ruled—for the essayists and poets who waxed eloquent on this theme could hardly have been tilting at wholly fictional windmills.

The starting point of this debate might be set at the publication of the poem "Fable of the Bees" by the Dutch immigrant to England, Bernard de Mandeville. Its first version, published in 1705, immediately created a scandal with its argument that the private vices of society—pride, vanity, envy—accounted for the public benefits of industry and prosperity.

> *"Thus every Part was full of Vice,*
> *Yet the whole Mass a Paradise. . . ."*

It did not take long for the point to be made by writers less intent on scandal and publicity than Mandeville, that incentive goods and market access would unleash a beneficial industriousness. It became a hallmark of the Scottish Enlightenment, from Hume through Steuart to Smith, all of whom found occasion to argue, in effect, that the new demand patterns were in place, so that the carrot rather than the stick would suffice to elicit greater effort. "Furnish him [the laborer] with the manufactures and commodities and he will do it [toil to produce a marketable surplus] himself," wrote Hume. Steuart was more blunt: workers had once been forced to work out of poverty or coercion but "Men are forced to labour now because they are slaves to their own wants."

Not everyone was charmed by this prospect. One could cite the poems of Alexander Pope and Oliver Goldsmith, both dubious of the supposed benefits to be gained by redefining ancient vices as new civic virtues. And who can say they were entirely wrong? The "industrious revolution" has an appealing ring to it. To quote an 1802 description of Cornish miners who had found by-employments to fill the hours and seasons between stints in the mines:

> *Instead of being as before, idle, careless, indolent, envious, dissatisfied and disaffected, the fruits of their former depraved, helpless and wretched condition, they become careful and thrifty both of their money and time, and soon begin to imbibe fresh notions respecting themselves and others and are happily found to be better fathers, better husbands and more respected members of the community than they had even been before.*

But the industrious revolution is not altogether an admirable thing. The intensification of work and suppression of leisure was associated with the (self) exploitation of family members—wives and children, the neglect of what we now call human capital formation (literacy rates stagnated in the eighteenth century), and greater recourse to binge drinking and binge leisure (the famous "Saint Monday" was no ancient practice of precapitalist "moral" workmen, it appears to have emerged after 1780). Finally, and more speculatively, the new pressures and possibilities to which the industrious household economy were exposed made courtship and marriage a process of less settled rules, giving rise to a great wave of illegitimacy and child abandonment in the period 1750 to 1820. The social ills of the industrious revolution were not the same as earlier times, but they were disturbing, nonetheless.

I have by no means exhausted the objections to the industrious revolution as a characterization of behavior and motivation; but I will now turn to another category of objection, one that focuses on the very concept of the household economy. The last point about social pathologies already foreshadows what is at issue here: Is it valid to treat the household as an economic unit akin to a firm? In Becker's original time-allocation article he cited approvingly Alex Cairncross's analogy of the household with "a small factory." But, if this is so, who is its "owner"? The household's members are differentiated by relationship, sex, and age, and the interests of these individuals in the operation of the household were rarely identical.

In his recent study of a Württemberg peasant community experiencing an "industrious revolution" in the century after 1750, David Sabean objects to a substantialist concept of the household that treats it as a total unity. The household is permeable, being the locus of complex alliances and reciprocities with external agents; it is fit into hierarchical dependencies; and internally it consists of an alliance between husband and wife and implicit contracts between parents and children. Thus, to be historically useful, the economics of the household must capture the differences in household organization among classes and over time.

If the household's permeability yields to utter porosity, and if the internal decision making is the product of naked struggle among self-interested individuals, then, indeed, we had best abandon this project altogether. But even household realists such as Sabean do not go that far, although they may be skeptical of Paul Samuelson's influential approach to the problem of group utility maximization that treats the household as a "realm of altruism" (where each family member includes the utility of the other members—as defined by that member—in his or her own utility function). Still, this approach has the virtue of focusing attention on a process of negotiation among persons with an affective as well as a material stake in a joint enterprise. It allows for change in the relations among family members without dissolving the essential integrity of the household as an economic unit.

When the notion of the household as a small factory or a patriarchal monolith requiring no internal examination is abandoned, the historical evolution of this unit becomes a proper object of study. And here, the industrious revolution seems to have brought with it two important innovations: the first, foreshadowed in my litany of growing social ills of the eighteenth century, was a growing permeability, the result of the greater labor force participation of household members, whereby economic alliances with outsiders became more important, leading to greater individuation, default of implicit contract, and a shift of demand away from capital-forming consumption (an inelegant term) toward the consumption of nondurables. The second was an augmentation of the decision-making centrality of the wife. A shift from relative self-sufficiency toward market-oriented production by all or most household members necessarily involves a reduction of typically female-supplied home-produced goods and their replacement by commercially produced goods. At the same time, the wife was likely to become an autonomous earner. . . .

The industrious revolution was no sudden thing. Even less than the Industrial Revolution does it warrant that overused yet seemingly indispensable moniker. Perhaps one should speak of the industrious disposition. The concept is not intended simply as a means of injecting the role of demand into the story of early economic growth. Rather, it is a means by which attention can be shifted from the site of new technologies to the site of new supplies of labor, of new aspirations, and of new forms of behavior in which the special contribution of the Industrial Revolution inserted itself.

The industrious revolution was no sudden thing, but neither was it eternal. The tool kit of middle-level generalizations I have assembled to study its emergence allows us also to study its demise—or better its replacement by another mode of household negotiation with the larger economy. The breadwinner-homemaker household, sometimes known as capitalist patriarchy, emerged in the first half of the nineteenth century in the most advanced sectors but became a widespread household norm in the century after 1850. Its defining feature is the withdrawal of wives and children from the paid labor force and the ideal of an adult male wage sufficient to support the household (the ideology of the family wage). As a despairing critic of this regime put it, "By the First World War, this conception had become a pervasive and fervently held proletarian ideal throughout the developed capitalist world." . . .

A Silesian Ironworks, 1841 This plant is using the new British method of smelting iron with coke. Silesia and the Ruhr region emerged as the main centers of German heavy industry in the nineteenth century, but that development was only beginning when this picture was painted. (*Deutsches Museum Munich*)

PART

Sites of Industrialization

In recent years, historians have demonstrated renewed vigor in the search to understand why the Industrial Revolution occurred where and when it did, and they have done so chiefly by widening the scope of their concerns. Traditionally, one simple question has dominated this topic: why was Britain first? While that problem remains pivotal in many studies, the answer has shifted as historians have placed the English example against various backdrops, from the rest of western Europe to China. At the same time, studies of other nonwestern regions, such as Russia, have generated new questions concerning what is often labeled *latecomer industrialization*—industrialization after Britain had acquired a commanding lead. All of this has resulted in significant reevaluations of earlier analyses and conclusions.

To a certain extent, we have seen such reappraisals in earlier selections. William Sewell, for example, uses the French experience to sever the traditional link between technology and the socioeconomic conditions that followed in industrialization's wake. In the selections that follow, however, the question of geographic context serves three different purposes. First, it places the genesis of industrialization into sharper relief, allowing historians to distinguish between those factors that were truly causal and those that merely promoted the process. Historians who have followed this approach concentrate on discovering the most significant origins of British industry's rise—that is, those factors that Britain did not share with the rest of western Europe or the world, such as accessible coal deposits, a state that guaranteed the rights of private property in the face of popular apprehension of new technology, and a set of social values that rewarded innovation. Earlier selections by E. A. Wrigley and Joel Mokyr have already addressed these issues; the following selections by Mokyr and Kenneth Pomerantz focus on those factors that may not have caused the Industrial Revolution, but privileged Britain and western Europe, offering further explanation for why industrialization developed there first.

Second, historians of industrialization outside of Britain have posited the existence of new "engines" of industrial development in different contexts. As Alexander Gerschenkron illustrates, diverse environments often led to specific requirements for industrialization, from dynamic new institutions like investment banks, to motivating ideologies powerful enough to overcome the tensions of industrial transformation.

Third, in addition to questions of place that address specific countries where industrialization occurred, other historians have approached the geographic context of the Industrial Revolution from a completely different vantage point: the industrial city. In their writing, Paul Hohenberg and Lynn Hollen Lees analyze the complex relationship between industrialization and urbanization, tackling such issues as the social consequences of increasing population density and the slow development of institutions and practices designed to manage Europe's burgeoning urban industrial centers.

In the first selection, Joel Mokyr addresses the arguments traditionally offered to explain the causes of the Industrial Revolution, but he finds that many do not hold up to close scrutiny. Agricultural development, population growth, and foreign trade, for example, all helped British industry, according to Mokyr, but none truly caused it. Instead, Mokyr remains true to the supply-side approach he adopts in his previous selection—invention and innovation (and the conditions that fostered them) were the true causes of the Industrial Revolution. Nevertheless, he acknowledges that many other factors promoted industrialization and favored England in the process, among them natural resources, the state, and social ideals. Natural resources entered into the equation primarily by determining where creative energies would flow. Problems with mining, for example, led to the invention of the steam engine. As for the state, it acted as guarantor over a de facto laissez-faire economy that placed few obstacles in the way of business activity. In addition, Mokyr credits England's Poor Laws with maintaining a secure and reliable labor force for both agriculture and industry. Finally, among the social ideals he recognizes as promoting the Industrial Revolution was the religious intolerance that pushed many nonconforming Protestants into business, where they were driven to prove their worth through success.

Kenneth Pomerantz offers a different perspective by placing the Industrial Revolution into a global context, and here the comparison of western Europe and China is particularly interesting. Both early-modern Europe and late-imperial China shared many telling similarities in relation to the Industrial Revolution. Chief among these was the development of rural manufacturing, or proto-industrialization. Pomerantz argues that in western Europe rural manufacturing "grew up" into an industrialized economy because western Europe broke through several important ecological bottlenecks that threatened to choke off its further development. Proto-industrialization by itself, however, did not cause the Industrial Revolution, for parts of Imperial China demonstrated the same characteristics but never developed further. Instead, western Europe's ready supply of coal and other "land-intensive" raw materials and its profitable market in the New World allowed it to overcome the Malthusian constraints that weighed China and the rest of Eurasia down into the twentieth century. It was the New World and its integration into Europe's economy that made all the difference.

Shifting gears to examine alterations in the process of industrialization itself in different contexts, Alexander Gerschenkron notes key differences among the French, German, and Russian industrial transformations. Germany and Russia in particular serve as prime examples for his argument that regions suffering from "economic backwardness" required a new institutional framework in order to undergo industrialization. In Germany, large investment banks played that role by forwarding the tremendous outlays of capital necessitated by the purchase of existing technology (unlike the British experience, which required little capital and derived from the tinkering of individual engineers and manufacturers). In Russia, the state took the lead, from developing a labor force to generating investment capital. In addition, Gerschenkron argues that industrialization in economically backward regions required ideologies that justified hardship and sacrifice for later gains in the new economy. For France and Germany, he believes that a Saint-Simonian faith in a future made brighter and more rational by technology provided that creed, which was further infused with high doses of nationalist competition in Germany. In Russia, Marxism and the belief in the necessity of industrialization on the road to socialism fulfilled a similar function. For Gerschenkron, this has significant policy ramifications for those nations that hope to foster their own Industrial Revolution.

Finally, Paul Hohenberg and Lynn Hollen Lees address the complex relationship between industrialization and urbanization. In short, these two life-altering processes did not significantly overlap in Europe until the last decades of the nineteenth century, during a period we most associate with the Second Industrial Revolution. Before then, industrial development frequently took place outside of existing urban centers, partly because natural resources, such as coal deposits, demanded it, but also because early entrepreneurs hoped to avoid the expense of locating in well-established cities. Nevertheless, it was not uncommon for those former small villages and towns to grow into large urban centers in their own right thanks to the in-migration of industrial workers. In England, for example, the village of Manchester grew from 25,000 inhabitants in 1772 to 367,000 by 1850, while Saint-Etienne in France witnessed a population "boom" from 16,000 in 1801 to 56,000 in 1851.[1]

Such growth had enormous impacts, which scholars have debated since the nineteenth century. The most significant of these was the alteration in personal relationships that resulted from higher population density. Some scholars have linked urban growth to the development of a soul-numbing "anomie," as new urban residents lost their traditional identity in the rush of the city's social complexity. Hohenberg and Lees question this assertion, claiming instead that a whole host of subcultures arose to meet the needs of urban residents

[1]John Merriman, *A History of Modern Europe* (New York: W. W. Norton and Company, 1996), p. 693.

as their traditional identities fractured. These subcultures, rooted in the neighborhood and the workplace, helped residents maintain a sense of connection as their new environments brought them into contact with an ever-increasing and intricate range of social networks. Subcultures eased not just the psychological tensions of relocation, but also the physical hardships of urban life, for as Hohenberg and Lees also argue, city leaders were slow to adapt technology to the new environment of the industrial city. Until well into the second half of the nineteenth century, cities remained dark, dank, and unsanitary, where misery in the factory met only more misery at home.

Joel Mokyr

The Industrial Revolution and the New Economic History

. . . It is not clear that the question "Why Britain?" is necessarily a good way to make sense of the Industrial Revolution. . . . The Industrial Revolution was not an affair that took place in certain national economies, it was primarily a regional affair. To be sure, Britain had a relatively large endowment of regions favorable to industrialization, but by no means all or even most of Britain was in an advantageous position. Some areas in Continental economies such as the provinces of Liège and East Flanders in Belgium, the northern *départements* of France, Alsace, parts of Switzerland, the Rhineland in Germany, and the industrialized region in the eastern United States lagged only a little behind Britain in industrial development, although the surrounding economies (with the possible exception of Belgium) were *on average* less developed than Britain.

From Joel Mokyr, "The Industrial Revolution and the New Economic History," in Joel Mokyr, ed., *The Economics of the Industrial Revolution* (Totowa, NJ: Rowman and Allanheld, 1985).

A different criticism of the "Why was Britain first" question is expressed by Crafts. . . . Crafts maintains that there is a strong element of randomness in Britain's supremacy, and that conditions in France on the eve of the Industrial Revolution were as favorable as they were in Britain. The ultimate success of Britain is thus largely inexplicable. . . . The "randomness" which exasperates Crafts is in part a reflection of the inability of economists to build models which explain big events like the Industrial Revolution. Nevertheless, we have to ask how Britain differed from Continental economies so as to gain a headstart in the race for industrial leadership.

Geographical Factors

The availability of mineral wealth, particularly coal and iron, has traditionally been a popular and seemingly persuasive explanation of Britain's success, as well as the failure of some tardy industrializers like the Netherlands or Ireland. The importance of coal and iron location is logically correct but of a secondary importance. Coal, although it eventually became the main source of energy in Europe, had good substitutes in peat and timber (for thermal energy) and water power (for kinetic energy). Iron was much less easy to replace, but it was already an internationally traded good before steam power reduced the costs of ocean shipping to a fraction. . . . The most dynamic industry in Britain (cotton) was wholly dependent on imports for its raw materials. Switzerland, Flanders, and Alsace are examples of regions which were not abundantly endowed with coal and iron yet were successful in modernizing their industries.

Such criticisms of the geographical explanation should not be exaggerated. A region or an economy had to have *something* going for it to produce goods and services at competitive costs. Surely geography cannot be absolved for the lack of industrial development in, say, Greenland. In a static analysis, however, the importance of raw materials and fuel cannot exceed its share in total manufacturing costs times the extra cost involved in shipping in a substitute. When more dynamic models are considered, the importance of mineral wealth is less easy to assess. . . . Wrigley has emphasized the importance of coal mines in the development of coastal shipping, canals, and later the railroads. Furthermore, coal mining generated more technical innovation than any other industry before the Industrial Revolution. Problems encountered in mining led to the development of the steam engine, as well as pumps, iron rails and other inventions in hydraulic and civil engineering. Natural resources not only supplied cheap fuel and raw materials, but also created technological externalities which affected other activities that were not dependent on location. Britain enjoyed an additional advantage thanks to the availability of coastal shipping, although this form of transportation eventually was found to be inadequate and was supplemented, by canals and highways and later by railroads.

Another way in which geography singled out Britain to become the first workshop of the world was by virtue of being an island and thus a natural fortress. . . . Although some of the ravages caused by civil wars were severe, Britain was never as abused by incessant warfare as Belgium, Poland, northern Italy, and large portions of Germany. Consequently, it never had to spend exorbitant sums to protect itself from foreign invaders, and a comparatively small proportion of Britain's best and brightest citizens wasted their talents and energies on unproductive military careers. Above all, Britain managed to remain insulated from the actual fighting during the crucial years between 1792 and 1814. True, the French and Napoleonic Wars proved expensive to Britain in that they slowed down the rate of capital accumulation compared to what it could have been. Nevertheless, the gap between Britain and the Continent widened during these years. . . . Taxation, conscription, direct war damages, trade disruptions, and the siphoning off of energy and talent into the military and politics cost the Continent at least a quarter century of industrial development despite Napoleon's attempts to encourage the modernization of French industry. Britain escaped this quite simply because Napoleon's army at Boulogne never managed to cross the channel. . . .

Politics and the State

. . . Recent thinking by economists has tended to place considerable emphasis on political elements. Douglass C. North has argued that the British Industrial Revolution was facilitated by better specified property rights, which led to more efficient economic organization in Britain. The link between property rights and economic growth consists of the greater efficiency in the allocation of resources resulting from the equalization of private and social rates of return and costs. Property rights in innovation (patents and trademarks), better courts and police protection, and the absence of confiscatory taxation are examples of how the same phenomenon could raise the rate of innovative activity and capital accumulation. . . .

. . . Different in emphasis but equally unequivocal in its certainty about the role of politics in Britain's Industrial Revolution is the view advanced by Mancur Olson. Olson's theory of economic growth is based on the idea that political bodies are subject to pressure groups who are pursuing the economic interests of their members, even if it comes at the expense of society as a whole. Olson is thus led to associate periods of economic success such as the Industrial Revolution with the comparative weakness of such pressure groups. Britain during the Industrial Revolution, maintains Olson, was relatively free of class differences, and by comparison a socially mobile society, so that loyalty to a particular pressure group was not yet very strong. The Civil Wars of the seventeenth century, moreover, had created a stable nationwide government, which made Britain into a larger jurisdictional unit, in which it was more difficult to organize pernicious pressure groups.

Was Britain a laissez-faire economy, and does the Industrial Revolution therefore stand as a monument to the economic potential of free enterprise? Perhaps, but some qualifications should be kept in mind. In absolute terms Britain was not a pure laissez-faire economy. But absolutes are not very useful here. Compared with Prussia, Spain, or the Habsburg Empire, Britain's government generally left its businessmen in peace to pursue their affairs, and rarely ventured itself into commercial and industrial enterprises. Mercantilism in Britain never took the extreme forms it took in France under Colbert and in Prussia under Frederick the Great, where the State simply deemed private enterprise to be incompetent and stepped in to do its job—usually without success. . . . Turnpikes, canals, and railroads were built in Britain without direct state support and schools were private. . . .

Regulations and rules, most of them relics from Tudor and Stuart times, remained on the books, but the general consensus among historians today is that the regulations were rarely enforced. As the economy became more sophisticated and markets more complex, the ability of the government to regulate and control such matters as the quality of bread or the length of apprentice contracts effectively vanished. The central government was left to control foreign trade, but most other internal administration was left to local authorities. Internal trade, the regulation of markets in labor and land, justice, police, county road maintenance, and poor relief were all administered by local magistrates. While in principle these authorities could exercise considerable power, they usually elected not to. This *de facto* laissez-faire policy derived not so much from any libertarian principles as from the pure self-interest of people who already had wealth and who were making more. By ignoring and evading rather than abolishing regulations, Britain moved toward a free market society. Except for its strictures against the State's intervention in foreign trade, *The Wealth of Nations* was a century out of date when it was published: what it advocated had already largely been accomplished. . . .

Another area in which government intervention was important and the law far from a dead letter was poor relief. Here the difference between Britain and the Continent is striking. Nowhere in the world can one find a well-organized, mandatory poor relief system like the English one. 'The Old Poor Law, sometimes erroneously referred to as "Speenhamland" (in fact, the Speenhamland System of allowances in aid of wages was used in a minority of counties) has had a notably bad press. Two major criticisms have been raised against it. One was the Malthusian complaint that outdoor relief reduced the incentive to work and increased the birth rate. The other criticism, already mentioned by Adam Smith, was that the Old Poor Law (and particularly the Settlement Acts) encumbered the free movement of labor and thus hindered its allocation in a society in which labor markets played an ever increasing role.

These criticisms have not fared well in recent years. Indeed, it seems likely that the effects of the Poor Laws on the Industrial Revolution were not nearly as negative as used to be thought. . . . Indeed, it could be maintained that the Poor Laws, despite their obvious flaws (in particular their non-uniformity), may have had some overall positive effects on the Industrial Revolution. A comparison with Ireland, which had no formal system of poor relief prior to 1838, bears this out. The social safety net provided by the Poor Laws allowed English individuals to take risks that would have been imprudent in Ireland where starvation was still very much a possibility. In societies without such laws, self-insurance in the form of large families and liquid assets were widely held, whereas in England even the "worst case" rarely implied actual starvation. The Speenhamland system assured a regular labor force during the busy seasons in agriculture. A similar argument may be made for manufacturing: workers could be laid off during periods of business slumps without fear of having the labor force emigrate or starve. Irish employers, on the other hand, complained about having to continue to pay their workers during slumps or risk losing them. In addition, the practice of pauper apprenticeships and the recruitment of factory workers from workhouses run by local Poor Law Guardians provided an important source of labor to the factories, especially in rural and small-town mills before 1800. All this is not to argue, of course, that the Poor Laws somehow "caused" the Industrial Revolution. But it seems that a case can be made that their net effect was not nearly as negative as has been maintained, and that they may have had hitherto unsuspected beneficial effects.

Another political difference between Britain and most other European countries was the lack of centralization of political power. Britain's system of government left most of the power of the day-to-day management of affairs to local magistrates, most of whom were respectable residents for whom administration was a form of leisure activity. Whether this government by amateurs was an effective way of providing government services is another matter, but one effect was the relative unimportance of London as an administrative and cultural center when compared to Madrid, Paris or Vienna. . . . This rural-urban brain drain would not have mattered, of course, if industrialization could have been concentrated near the capital of the country. Interestingly, this seems to have happened nowhere. . . . Wrigley has argued more or less the opposite, ascribing to London a major role in creating the conditions leading to the Industrial Revolution. The size of London relative to England's population and its enormous needs in terms of food, fuel, and other products seem to support his claim. Sheer size, however, is not necessarily an advantage. A top-heavy capital might just as well be viewed as imposing a major cost on the country. Wrigley's argument seems better suited to explain commercial development before 1750 than industrial development thereafter. During the Industrial Revolution, indeed, the demographic predominance of London declined somewhat. Between 1650 and 1750 London's share of English population rose from about 7 percent to 11.8 percent. By 1800 this percentage had declined to 10.5 percent.

Some historians have argued that the British government stimulated the Industrial Revolution by creating a demand for military products which led to rapid technological change in some industries. It is true that some of these externalities can be identified. Cort's rolling and puddling technique was completed when its inventor was working on a contract for the Admiralty. Wilkinson's lathe, which bored the accurate cylinders needed for Watt's steam engines, was originally destined for cannon. Nevertheless, most scholars seem to agree that these effects were relatively small, and the effects of the Wars between 1756 and 1815 were negative on balance. Not only that the evidence for the hypothesis is not strong, it also runs into the dilemma that if military efforts created major technological externalities, why did France and other continental countries not benefit from them in the same degree that Britain did?

To summarize, most economic historians would agree that politics was a positive factor working in Britain's favor, although the exact magnitude of the effect as well as its *modus operandi* is still in dispute. The appropriate standard of judgment should be a comparative one, and it seems hard to disagree with the proposition that the form of government in Britain created an environment which was more conducive to economic development than elsewhere. Some oppressive mercantilist laws were on the books, but most were successfully evaded. Britons were heavily taxed, but taxation was never allowed to become arbitrary and confiscatory. Most important, the right to own and manage property was truly sacrosanct, contrasting sharply with the confiscations and conscriptions of the French Revolution and the Napoleonic era. Personal freedom—with some exceptions—was widely accepted in Britain. True, the Acts of Settlement remained on the books until 1834, but they were by no means as restrictive as the harsh requirements on the books in France and in Prussia, where workers were required to have "cahiers" or "Wanderbücher" in which their employment was recorded and which required them to ask for passes for journeys within the country. Serfdom was still very much in existence east of the Elbe in 1815. Only the cathartic revolutionary medicine administered to the Continent between 1789 and 1815 by the French prepared the rest of Europe for the modern age. But the medicine's immediate side-effects were so painful that most of the Continent required many years and maybe decades to recover from the treatment and start to threaten Britain's lead. Britain did not need this harsh shock treatment, since it alone had learned to adapt its institutions to changing needs by more peaceful means, and the channel sheltered it from undesirable political imports.

Britain's political stability contrasts sharply with the history of France, with its four major revolutions in the eight decades following 1789. But was political stability always an asset in the path toward modernization? Common sense suggests that investors will be wary of investment in politically unstable environments. It is likely that political stability was an asset and that its absence had a negative effect on industrialization. But how important was that effect? And how do we judge the economic performance of powerful autocratic regimes in Russia and Prussia? Moreover, Olson has insisted that political stability is in fact a rather mixed blessing , because it permits the crystallization of pressure groups whose activities are, in Olson's view, the archenemy of economic development. It is thus unclear how much of the difference in economic development can be attributed to this difference. Still, it is no exaggeration to say that nowhere in the world was property *perceived* to be more secure than in Britain.

Society and Entrepreneurship

Perhaps the most controversial hypothesis is that England's miraculous performance resulted from the special features of British society, which were conducive to economic growth. Invention, capital accumulation, the sacrosanct nature of private property, the willingness of the regime to alter the environment to adapt to changing needs, and the interest of scientists and engineers in applications of science to industry, are all considered "endogenous to the system," that is, consequences of deeper social conditions. In the center of the stage, in this view, stands that controversial figure, hero in some opinions, sidekick in others: the entrepreneur. . . .

Persuasive explanations of long-run economic change require some causal element which is exogenous, i.e., does not need an economic explanation itself. It is thought that differences in the quality of entrepreneurship is a weak explanation of economic differences between nations because economic conditions determine the quality of entrepreneurship. Therefore it is necessary to discover whether there were noneconomic determinants behind differences in such entrepreneurial qualities as willingness to bear risk, resourcefulness, initiative, perseverance, and similar elements thought to be part of successful entrepreneurship.

A well-known and highly controversial theory of entrepreneurship is the one somehow linking businessmen to religion. Originally proposed by Weber, the argument is more successful in explaining the differences between Western Christianity and the rest of the world than in explaining differences within the West. Some modern social scientists have nonetheless displayed considerable ingenuity in an attempt to explicate and justify the link between religion and economic development. Thus McClelland defines the personal need for success, or n-Achievement as the prime mover of development. The nonconformists in England, because of their higher n-Achievement, were "more responsible for the increased entrepreneurial activity that sparked the Industrial Revolution from around 1770 on." In particular, McClelland points to the Wesleyan Church as placing much stress on personal excellence and success, and thus promoting the type of motivation which led to entrepreneurial behavior. Unfortunately for this thesis, however, few entrepreneurs belonging to the Wesleyan Church can be found. Wider definitions of non-conformism are more promising. Everett Hagen has shown that non-conformist entrepreneurs did indeed play a disproportionate role in the Industrial Revolution. Whereas they constituted 7 percent of total population, they provided almost half of the major innovators in manufacturing. Hagen rejects Weber's thesis that the causal link operated through dogma, and instead focuses on a psychological model of entrepreneurial behavior. In this model entrepreneurship was facilitated by a reaction of children to "retreatist" fathers who had been rejected by society because of their dissent. While Hagen's theory has not gained many adherents, it is a bold attempt to infuse the question with original interdisciplinary thinking, and it is a pity that no further attempts have been made to apply psychological theory toward a deeper understanding of the men who made the Industrial Revolution.

The most complete and persuasive attempt to provide a social explanation of the Industrial Revolution had been provided by Perkin. Perkin dates the creation of the type of society which was most amenable to an Industrial Revolution to the Restoration of 1660 and the social and political changes accompanying it. He points out that the principle upon which society was established following the Civil War was the link between wealth and status. Status means here not only political influence and indirect control over the lives of one's neighbors, but also to which houses one was invited, what partners were eligible for one's children to marry, which rank one could attain (that is, purchase) in the army, where one lived, and how one's children were educated. In Perkin's view, the quality of life was determined not just by "consumption" as usually defined by economists, but by the relative standing of the individual in the social hierarchy. Whether this social relativity hypothesis is still a good description of society is an open question, but a case can be made, as Perkin does, that it is an apt description of Britain in the eighteenth century. . . .

In Perkin's own words, "To the perennial desire for wealth, the old society, [i.e., Britain after 1660] added more motivation which gave point and purpose to the pursuit of riches. Compared with neighbouring and more traditional societies it offered both a greater challenge and a greater reward to successful enterprise. . . . [T]he pursuit of wealth *was* the pursuit of social status, not merely for oneself but for one's family." Perkin's insight is important because it underlines a basic point often overlooked by economists trying to understand entrepreneurial behavior. It is almost always true that an easy opportunity to earn money will not be passed over by a rational individual. Moreover, if there is a divergence of opinion about the expected profitability of an opportunity, one should expect the optimists to replace the pessimists. Unexploited opportunities to quick gains will rapidly disappear. There were opportunities to make money during the Industrial Revolution, but few were quick and easy. Almost all major entrepreneurial figures took enormous risks, worked long and hard hours, and rarely enjoyed the fruits of their efforts until late in life or enjoyed them vicariously through their descendants. Entrepreneurship will be more forthcoming if the rewards of money exceed the costs of risk-bearing, hard work, and postponed gratification. Perkin's thesis stresses the benefit side in this equation: in Britain money bought more than just comfort. It is perfectly consistent with economic logic and should be regarded as complementary to the New Economic History.

Still, some empirical questions have to be answered before it can be accepted as one explanation of England's success. Was the correlation between wealth and social status stronger in Britain than elsewhere? At least in one case, Holland, this is probably false, and this case indicates that having the "right kind of society" is not a sufficient condition for a successful Industrial Revolution. But what about France? In the eighteenth century aristocratic titles could be bought, and much of the nobility was *a noblesse de robe*, i.e., of bourgeois origins. Was the aversion to parvenus among the upper class stronger in France than in England? While the latter question cannot readily be answered, there were two important differences between the two countries in this respect. First, in France money could enhance social status, but the respectable local country gentleman who ran the affairs of the parish was a wholly British institution. Secondly, in France social status was often literally bought. The price of a noble title reflected a tax-exemption, so that the sale of titles was not a one-way street in which the crown soaked up wealth. But nobility implied high standards of consumption in the noblesse oblige tradition. In England, by contrast, wealth was correlated with influence and respect, but one did not have necessarily to part with the former to attain the latter. . . .

Kenneth Pomeranz

The Great Divergence

. . . It is true, as Eric Jones has argued, that not just any group of people stumbling on the New World (and depopulating it, as any people bearing Old World diseases would have done) could have used these continents as Europe did; but the European entrepreneurship Jones points to was not the *unique* part of the equation, or one in which western Europe had surpassed developments in other densely settled parts of the globe. Western Europeans' innovations in organizing for exploration and durable conquest and in creating institutions that combined entrepreneurship with intense coercion—plus favorable global conjunctures shaped by everything from Amerindians' vulnerability to smallpox to the massive supplies of New World silver and the equally massive project of Chinese remonetization—gave them much of their edge. This, in turn, gave western Europeans a privileged position from which to endure the last century of the "biological old regime," with its multiple ecological challenges, and even continue expanding industries (from textiles to brewing to iron) that made great demands on the products of the land.

Last Comparisons: Labor Intensity, Resources, and Industrial "Growing Up"

Thus when coal, steam, and mechanization opened up vast new technical possibilities, western Europeans (especially in England) were in a unique position to capitalize on them. Vast untapped New World resources (and underground resources) still lay before them, essentially abolishing the land constraint. Moreover, what they had already gained in the New World meant they entered the nineteenth century with a higher standard of living than they would otherwise have had, enlarged military capabilities (which could force open markets in some cases and impose monopolies in others), and far more extensive handicraft industries than they could otherwise have maintained. And it was from these

From Kenneth Pomeranz, *The Great Divergence: China, Europe, and the Making of the Modern World Economy* (Princeton: Princeton University Press, 2000).

proto-industrial workers, not directly from the peasantry, that most early factory workers came.

The importance of a factory workforce drawn heavily from people already working in proto-industry is brought out very clearly in Joel Mokyr's "growing up" model of European industrialization. First, despite numerous attempts to find "surplus labor" in agriculture—i.e., workers who could be removed from that sector without appreciably affecting production—such cases seem rare, even in today's Third World; and none of our cores could afford to have their agricultural output fall very much circa 1800. Second, factories employing former proto-industrial workers have a distinct advantage. If factory workers were drawn out of agriculture, then even if demand for them did not raise wages (in other words, if there *was* surplus labor in agriculture), there would be no reason for that wage to fall; and as the diffusion of mass-production techniques caused the price of the product made by a factory to fall, the firm would encounter declining profits and might have difficulty expanding. (Mokyr assumes that the fixed capital needed is fairly cheap, as is common in early industrialization; and since the raw materials cost roughly the same regardless of the production process, the factory's wage bill is the most important variable cost.) But if the nascent industry can draw on proto-industrial workers who made the same product as the factory did, then the same technological diffusion that places downward pressure on the factory's prices also depresses workers' alternate earnings possibilities. Thus the factory can reduce wages and still attract recruits from this sector; this allows it to maintain higher profits for longer.

Thus, in this scenario, industry can result from the "growing up" of proto-industry; it does not require a *simultaneous* social and technological transformation that enables agriculture to maintain or increase output from about the same amount of land while releasing a huge number of workers. Moreover, proto-industrial workers often moved to the factory with some relevant skills and/or knowledge useful for making further innovations. All this suggests that the continued growth of proto-industry in the decades preceding and overlapping the growth of mechanized industry left Europe in a far better position than if it had been compelled to keep more people in agriculture and forestry.

To put things slightly differently: Europe's expansion of both proto-industry and many early mechanized industries required more agricultural output. Quite aside from whether Britain (or even Europe more generally) could have found enough land at home to resolve these problems, putting large additional amounts of labor into supplying these farm goods directly would have created further problems later on. But instead, Europe acquired many of these supplies by having others grow them, while putting its own labor into additional soldiers, sailors, traders, and producers of manufactured goods. As factories at home needed more labor, they could draw on proto-industrial workers, with the advantages discussed above.

Over time, soldiers and sailors became more effective per capita thanks to technological change (e.g., better guns and ships) and were increasingly supplemented or replaced by "natives" hired with the proceeds of colonial taxation. Thus the overseas sector went through a sort of "growing up" of its own, which meant that this way of obtaining primary products did not absorb increasing amounts of European labor. The massive expansion of agriculture at home, which would have been needed otherwise, would have been not only ecologically difficult, but hard to reconcile with the expansion of the industrial workforce. When Britain's agricultural workforce finally began to decline in absolute numbers after 1850, it was tied both to technologies that had been unavailable earlier in the century and to massive increases in agricultural imports; production held steady as labor inputs declined, but did not rise much. The contrast to the atypical (for Europe) case of Denmark . . . is striking. There, a near-stabilization of the ecology through labor-intensive methods seems to have been inconsistent with industrialization for many decades, even though the marginal returns to much of this work—and the real wages of both urban and rural laborers—were low and falling further.

For a long time China and Japan, like Europe as a whole, also found ways to keep expanding their proto-industrial sectors, even without a New World to supply the needed fiber and other land-intensive inputs. These processes also involved some expansion of trade (and of fishing) to relieve local pressure on the land in cores; but compared to the European solution, they involved a greater intensification and expansion of their own agricultural sectors, particularly for fiber production. And by the end of the eighteenth century, that process seems to have been proceeding at diminishing rates and at considerable ecological cost. Japan's population stopped growing by 1750, and while China's continued growing for another century, the percentage of the population in proto-industry likely stagnated or even declined. In all probability, few areas in China that had extensive proto-industry actually underwent significant deindustrialization. What happened instead was that the heavily agricultural areas of China came to make up a much larger percentage of the population by 1850 than they had in 1750.

The most advanced prefectures of the Yangzi Delta, which had roughly 16–21 percent of China's population in 1750, were barely 9 percent of the empire by 1850, and about 6 percent by 1950. As we shall see shortly, the percentage of these prefectures' population that worked in proto-industry may have fallen slightly, but whether or not that happened, the empire's most proto-industrial region simply ceased to have the same weight in aggregate figures. In Lingnan, the second most proto-industrial macro-region, population growth between 1750 and 1850 was about 75 percent, but China as a whole grew about 100 percent; moreover, a disproportionate share of Lingnan's growth was in Guangxi, a province largely limited to agriculture and forestry.

Thus, even though some of the heavily agricultural macro-regions were becoming more proto-industrial, their very large share in post-1750 population growth meant that China as a whole was at least as agrarian in 1850 as in 1750 and not much less so in 1950. Moreover, proto-industrial workers scattered across the farmsteads of the interior and often seen as part of an ideal agrarian household were not as easily available to move into hypothetical factories as true proletarians with no ties to the land might have been. Thus, during the two centuries or so after 1750, China became less well positioned for industrializing along the relatively easy path of "growing up" and has instead had to deal with all the problems of drawing most of its factory workers directly out of agriculture.

The United States, however, is an important reminder that not all early industrializers had large proto-industrial sectors. In fact, Kenneth Sokoloff and David Dollar, comparing the United States and England in the nineteenth century, have emphasized that the much greater seasonality of agricultural work in England slowed the development of factory-based industry. With large numbers of workers available only part of the year, but at wages far lower than what they would have required to leave the land completely, handicraft industry proved a tenacious competitor for factories, and investment in centralized plants, equipment, and supervision was less advantageous than it would have been had the agricultural and industrial workforces been more completely separate. In the United States, by contrast, very favorable land-to-labor ratios meant that farmers could supplement their grain-growing with other activities—animal husbandry, wood-cutting, fruit-raising and land-clearing, for instance—which yielded less per acre but paid well per hour; thus the rural labor force was occupied full-time without much resort to handicraft industries. Thus when factories were built, they could grow still more rapidly than in England (especially grain-growing, handicraft-producing south England).

This argument is persuasive for the two cases of England and the United States. But the American case was radically different from anything in our Eurasian cores. The very favorable land-to-labor ratios meant that American farms could easily feed a separate industrial workforce as that group emerged (whether from immigration or from rapid natural increase and rural-urban migration). It also meant that these farmers were sufficiently prosperous, even without industrial by-employments, to buy factory goods, even if those goods were made with fairly expensive labor. Long distances and tariffs, meanwhile, helped ensure that European manufactures made with what was often cheaper labor did not capture all of the United States market.

Under those special circumstances, American factories that had to find their laborers among ex-farmers (whether from Massachusetts, Ireland, or Germany) might still, contrary to the "growing up" model, expand more rapidly than English factories. But very few places in the eighteenth-century Old World could have accommodated a huge increase in population that neither raised local farm output nor brought in primary products by producing industrial *exports*; and where rural populations in Old World cores were not available for proto-industry, this was more likely due to very labor-intensive year-round multi-cropping (e.g., in parts in Lingnan) or enormous amounts of work to preserve a fragile ecology (e.g., marling, ditch-digging, and so on in Denmark) than to the sorts of lucrative but land-intensive by-employments that one finds on nineteenth-century U.S. farms.

Thus, Old World cores could not create a factory labor force in the way the United States did. For them, the choice was between pulling people out of full-time proto-industry or out of at least part-time farming. Given that, being able to draw on proto-industrial workers would still seem the most advantageous way to create Old World industrial workforces. This left England far better-off than places like the Yangzi Delta, which lacked peripheral trading partners that would complement it in the way that England's did.

This argument can also be expressed in terms of another feature of Mokyr's "growing up" model of European industrialization. The model assumes that people turn to proto-industrial activities in the first place when the marginal productivity of their labor in agriculture falls below that of proto-industry. (The former starts off higher than the latter, but falls much more rapidly, largely because the supply of land is limited.) Thus, the extra labor beyond a certain point will all go into proto-industry, as long as the area in question can continue exporting proto-industrial products in exchange for food (and, we might add, fiber and timber) without affecting the relative prices of food and handicrafts in the "world" market where it makes these exchanges.

This condition, usually called the "small-country assumption," makes perfect sense for the Netherlands and Belgium, the cases for which Mokyr developed this model—and at one point it also made sense for the Lower Yangzi and Lingnan, and the Kantō and Kinai regions. Although, as we have seen, the Yangzi Delta prefectures imported huge amounts of primary products—36,000,000 people importing 15–22 percent of their food, plus timber, beancake fertilizer, and so on—the hinterlands and marketing networks they drew on were so vast that the small country assumption still makes sense as a way of looking at the region's trade in the mid-eighteenth century. But as some of these hinterlands, such as the Middle and Upper Yangzi and North China, grew more populous, experienced diminishing returns in agriculture and developed more of their own proto-industry, the terms of trade did shift, to the marked disadvantage of proto-industrial producers.

Though silver-denominated cotton cloth prices fluctuated from year to year, there seems to have been no trend in nominal cloth prices from 1750 to 1850. Raw cotton prices in Canton, for which we have relatively good data, also show no clear trend, though short-term fluctuations were often violent. But silver-denominated rice prices in the Lower Yangzi rose by 40 percent over that same century. That increase alone would have cut the spinning and weaving income of [a] wom[a]m . . . by about 30 percent, from 7.2 *shi* of rice in 1750 to 5.0 *shi* in 1850.

Moreover, fragmentary data collected by Kishimoto Mio suggest that in the Lower Yangzi itself, raw cotton prices did rise substantially between 1750 and 1800. Such a finding is consistent with trendless prices near Canton, since transport costs between these two areas fell sharply in the late eighteenth and early nineteenth centuries. It would also be consistent with seventeenth-century patterns, in which the price of raw cotton in the Yangzi Delta seems to have roughly tracked that of rice. If Kishimoto's data are roughly representative for Jiangnan, then the fall in spinners' and weavers' earnings would be roughly 50 percent just between 1750 and 1794 (when her data stop), though they would be falling from a higher starting point. And if we guess that the trend in raw cotton prices followed that of rice over the long haul, the rice-buying power of [a] weaver/spinner would fall 25 percent between 1750 and 1800, and 37 percent by 1840. Measured in salt or probably firewood, they fell further still.

Even these depreciated earnings could still meet the subsistence needs of the woman herself and would be close enough to male agricultural wages (which were also falling in real terms) that China's "gender gap" remained less severe than that in Europe. But they do show a substantial decline in earnings from home-based textile production, even before any competition from machine-made cloth. A woman weaving very high-grade cotton cloth would have escaped these pressures, since its prices nearly doubled over this same century, but these were atypical women who had unusual skills and probably produced fewer pieces each year.

In Mokyr's model, such a fall in returns to proto-industrial labor in the Lower Yangzi should have led to at least some labor shifting back into agriculture at what would previously have been unacceptably low returns, and thus to a combination of further agricultural intensification and some measure of deindustrialization. Though any such shift would have been modest, we have one possible indication of it. Raw cotton from the Lower Yangzi seems to have become cheaper and more plentiful in Guangzhou (Canton) in the early nineteenth century, much to the dismay of foreign merchants bringing Indian cotton to sell. Though the fall in price may have been largely a matter of improved transportation, the growth in quantity suggests that perhaps less Yangzi Delta cotton was being spun and woven locally; it seems unlikely that Lower Yangzi raw cotton output rose much in this period, and imports from North China were almost certainly falling.

And yet, most Yangzi Delta women continued to spin and weave, even at lower returns; in fact, as we saw earlier, it is precisely in the nineteenth century that references to women of that region working with men in the fields finally disappear completely. If some families were unwilling to move their wives and daughters back into the fields where they would be more visible—and perhaps even tried to increase cloth output to maintain income—the situation might have come to resemble the quasi-involuntary situation described by Goldstone, in which women "stuck" in very low-wage home-based spinning and weaving made it much less profitable to contemplate factory-based textile production. Any such pattern emerging in this period would be the result of a temporary conjuncture, rather than a fundamental feature of long-term Chinese development based on timeless norms (as Huang suggests) and it would be too late appearing to be the basic explanation of the nondevelopment of factories, as Goldstone proposes. Nonetheless it might have helped slow the replacement of domestic textile production by factory production, even once the technology became available, as Goldstone suggests later in his essay. Either way, these women remained part of households in which the men (and to some extent children) were driven to increasingly labor-intensive strategies of farming, fuel-gathering, and land-management—not a promising precursor to industrialization.

Japan's response to similar pressures remained within the same basic framework as China's, but with some differences that may have had long-term implications. First of all, Japan's population broke through its historic ceiling, never to return, earlier than that in either China or Europe. Population reached new heights in the late seventeenth century, when both Europe and China experienced downturns, and by about 1720 it had reached a plateau that would last until about 1860. This long period of zero population growth may represent a more rapid and thorough demographic adjustment to ecological constraints than the slowing, but still positive population growth of early nineteenth century China, but it could also be argued that the adjustment was sharper because the situation was even worse: after all, overall population density in Japan even circa 1860 was still much higher than it was in China. And while the enormous increase in Japanese ocean fishing offered a kind of relief much less used in China (it provided both food and fertilizer), and the early development of systematic silviculture was also an important adjustment, Japan, too, faced serious barriers to further expansion of proto-industry in its core regions.

Agricultural prices rose sharply relative to those of industrial goods during the 1730s, then showed no trend until the late 1820s, when they began another steep climb; the average prevailing level for the 1735–1825 period was about 20 percent above the mid-1720s peak and almost 50 percent above the 1730 trough. I know of no signs of deindustrialization in either the Kantō or the Kinai in response to changing relative prices, but these regions did decline in population: 16 percent for the Kantō between 1751 and 1821 and perhaps 5 percent for the Kinai, while the prefectures with impressive population growth were mostly in areas that were still relatively sparsely populated in 1870 and also still well below the national average on Saito's index of rural industrialization. (By contrast, the Kinai region had both a population density and a rural industrialization index that doubled the national averages.) We have already seen that the major growth of both industry and population was in poor domains such as Tosa, where old monopolies were being relaxed; but many such monopolies persisted, as did barriers to migration. These barriers to growth in the peripheries may have spread pressure for family limitation into more peripheries than in China (though any comparison is speculative with current data), ultimately preserving some of the same sort of slack capacity that much of continental Europe had but China lacked. To put it another way, the share of Japan's most advanced regions in national aggregates declined, as it did in China, but much more gently, since peripheral growth was more modest. Labor intensity increased, but this was due almost entirely to increased hours per worker, not to population growth. And though cities and towns lost ground relative to the countryside, the country's still relatively high urbanization rate also suggests that more of what Mokyr calls "pseudo-surplus" labor was stored in handicrafts (as opposed to agriculture) than was the case in China.

As we would expect, the Indian story is different again, but it still fits within the same general framework. Moreover, India's differences from China point in the opposite direction from Japan's differences and suggest more serious long-term obstacles to industrialization. India . . . began its population boom later than China or western Europe did, and much later than Japan: probably after 1830, and almost certainly after 1800. The nineteenth century saw an enormous increase in cultivated land in India and few signs of serious overall shortages of food, fuel, fiber, or building materials. (Distribution was, of course, quite another matter: India exported large amounts of grain in the late nineteenth century, for instance, while it had serious hunger at home.) But despite a continuation of late precolonial commercialization, the share of India's population in non-farming occupations probably fell during early British rule. The subcontinent underwent what Bayly calls "peasantization," as both formerly migratory peoples and former handicraft workers were increasingly drawn—and pushed—into sedentary farming. The process appears to have begun before colonialism, in part because the competing successor states to the Mughal empire hoped that settling migratory peoples on the land would increase state control, public security, and state revenues; it accelerated under the British and touched increasing numbers of former urbanites as well.

An intense debate has been waged about whether India deindustrialized in the nineteenth century; with inadequate data, it is unlikely to be settled. However, it does seem fairly well established that the number of full-time weavers and spinners (especially those based in towns) decreased significantly beginning in the late eighteenth century. This seems to have been due at first to measures taken (especially in Bengal) by the East India Company and some other merchants who increasingly bound weavers to a single potential buyer; as this depressed earnings, many artisans fled their occupation. Later, earnings came under intense further pressure from competition with Lancashire. And the percentage of the Indian population living in cities declined significantly over the long term—from 13–15 percent in the late seventeenth century to 9.3 percent in 1881—though it is currently impossible to date the decline much more precisely. Deindustrialization is also suggested by Habib's finding that the value of sugar, cotton, and indigo grown in India quite likely fell in absolute terms (not to mention per capita terms) between 1595 and the 1870s.

While total yarn and cloth output in India may have held their own, thanks to an increase in part-time rural spinning and weaving, this would not have had the same significance for future industrialization as would the growth of a full-time proto-industrial workforce. These were not people who could later be moved into factories with no cost to agricultural output; nor were they workers whose cost to a potential factory owner would fall together with the unit price of his product, since much of their income came from farming.

Thus, it could be argued, though India began the nineteenth century with a less-monetized economy than that found in China, Japan, or western Europe, it was moving in similar directions and had more ecological room for increasing population and per capita consumption than they did. But by the early twentieth century it had lost that advantage and had both the disadvantages of a densely populated zone and those of a zone with limited proto-industrial development and a limited internal market. This combination of problems had occurred not so much through the sort of (largely) market-driven regional development that seems to have led to China's cul de sac, but through the preferences of colonial (and, to some extent, indigenous) authorities for settled populations, "customary" law, agricultural and forest exports, and a captive market for the mother country's industrial goods. The result was an *increasing* emphasis on primary-product exports even amid great population growth—primary products often produced with labor that was no less coerced (and maybe more so) than in the least free areas of eighteenth-century India.

Thus, despite considerable growth in agriculture and commerce, India may have become less well positioned for industrial-led transformative growth. Compared to what at least might have happened had eighteenth-century social trends continued a bit longer while population grew and competition from mechanized goods stayed away a little bit longer, colonial India's form of "peasantization" might reasonably be labeled a "development of underdevelopment." The British probably did not frustrate an industrial breakthrough that was otherwise highly likely, as some nationalist scholars claim, but nineteenth-century changes may have made such a breakthrough even more difficult than it would have been otherwise and more difficult than the transition faced by either western European economies or east Asian ones. To put it another way, Japanese and especially Chinese cores may have faced bottlenecks due to the convergence of their peripheries toward "core" profiles, but Indian cores suffered the worse fate of converging toward a more peripheral profile.

The wonder then is that at roughly the same time that the "small-country assumption" became less applicable to east Asian cores—largely because the growth of population and proto-industry in their peripheries was making the quantity of primary products available on their "world" markets smaller relative to their needs—that same assumption remained applicable to Britain even though its population soared and its per capita demand grew (first slowly, then very rapidly after about 1840). Moreover, it remained applicable over the next century, not only to Britain, but to an ever-larger "industrial Europe." Without that wonder the combination of a much larger population, higher per capita consumption, and far *less* labor-intensive land management—all central to the "European miracle"—was not possible. Without that wonder, the achievements in Europe's preindustrial market economy—impressive though they were—could have led in the same direction as the also impressive market economies of other regions. Even that other wonder—the string of technological innovations that makes up the original history of the "Industrial Revolution"—might well have slowed to a crawl without this one.

The wonder can be partly explained by western Europe's own "advantages of backwardness" . . . : domestic resources left unexploited because of institutional blockages that were only relieved in the nineteenth century and that, at that point, kept the import needs of some industrializing areas from being even larger. But as we have seen, this argument has little applicability to Britain, and little to fiber and wood.

Technological catching up—e.g., in per-acre yields—also helped, but that alone can hardly explain Europe's surge ahead of the rest of the globe. Europe's wood problem was of course substantially eased by coal, but for quite a while this applied only in Britain and a few other places. Furthermore, overall timber demand kept rising even where coal was used heavily, since wood had many other uses: timber imports continued to rise throughout the late eighteenth century and at an unprecedented rate in the nineteenth century. (Though coal, as we saw, also had other dimensions, through its links to steam power, railroads, and so on.)

Thus, for a more complete explanation of what occurred in Europe's core, we must also look at its peripheries and understand why they became growing rather than shrinking suppliers of primary products to the "world" market. Part of the answer lies in institutional arrangements in eastern Europe and Russia that long inhibited population growth and proto-industrialization of the sort that occurred relatively rapidly in the Chinese interior and Japan's Region II—more "advantages of backwardness," but ones that could not be reaped on a large scale until after 1860. Much of the rest of the answer—and the bridge that got Europe through the first century of the proto-industrial to industrial transition—lay . . . in the New World: not just in its natural bounty, but in the unique institutions and conjunctures that brought far more of its bounty to Europe far earlier than purely Smithian trade could have.

The institutional factors include some—like the slave trade and the mine labor systems—whose departure from market principles are obvious and which we often consign too quickly to a "premodern" world, forgetting their role in making our world possible. Others, like the corporation, are familiar, "modern," and clearly European in origin. Consequently, we tend to forget that they were created by and for extracontinental encounters and that for a long time they may have been most significant as a method of underwriting the huge fixed costs of violence: a method that then forced these enterprises to increase *volumes* of "exotic" imports (rather than focusing exclusively on profit margins, as the Venetians and Portuguese had tended to do) and thus to expand the European presence abroad. Still others, like the specialized slave plantation, are well known, but their role in creating a new kind of periphery for Europe is here placed in a new light. And beyond these institutions lie various global conjunctures that favored the expansion of the European presence in the New World: from wind patterns and disease gradients to European state competition and Chinese silver demand.

Together, these largely extra-European and nonmarket factors were essential in making transatlantic trade a uniquely self-expanding route by which Europe (especially Britain) could use its labor and capital to relieve its hard-pressed land and thus turn even a demographic and proto-industrial expansion that (unlike in east Asia) far outpaced advances in agriculture into an asset for further development. Without those factors, this demographic and proto-industrial expansion could have been the basis for a later catastrophe; or it could have been stopped by rising primary-product prices in the nineteenth century; or it could have been severely constrained by a need for much more labor-intensive approaches to exploiting and conserving a limited land base.

Thus, forces outside the market and conjunctures beyond Europe deserve a central place in explaining why western Europe's otherwise largely unexceptional core achieved unique breakthroughs and wound up as the privileged center of the nineteenth century's new world economy, able to provide a soaring population with an unprecedented standard of living. Our long journey through interregional comparisons has brought us to at least some resolution of the methodological question with which we began: it has shown that rather than pretend we are seeking the differences among truly independent entities on the eve of industrialization, we must acknowledge the importance of preexisting connections in creating those differences.

Alexander Gerschenkron

Economic Backwardness in Historical Perspective

. . . A good deal of our thinking about industrialization of backward countries is dominated—consciously or unconsciously—by the grand Marxian generalization according to which it is the history of advanced or established industrial countries which traces out the road of development for

From Alexander Gerschenkron, *Economic Backwardness in Historical Perspective: A Book of Essays* (Cambridge, Mass.: Belknap Press, 1962).

the more backward countries. "The industrially more developed country presents to the less developed country a picture of the latter's future." There is little doubt that in some broad sense this generalization has validity. It is meaningful to say that Germany, between the middle and the end of the last century, followed the road which England began to tread at an earlier time. But one should beware of accepting such a generalization too wholeheartedly. For the half-truth that it contains is likely to conceal the existence of the other half—that is to say, in several very important respects the development of a backward country may, by the very virtue of its backwardness, tend to differ fundamentally from that of an advanced country.

It is the main proposition of this essay that in a number of important historical instances industrialization processes, when launched at length in a backward country, showed considerable differences, as compared with more advanced countries, not only with regard to the speed of the development (the rate of industrial growth) but also with regard to the productive and organizational structures of industry which emerged from those processes. Furthermore, these differences in the speed and character of industrial development were to a considerable extent the result of application of institutional instruments for which there was little or no counterpart in an established industrial country. In addition, the intellectual climate within which industrialization proceeded, its "spirit" or "ideology," differed considerably among advanced and backward countries. Finally, the extent to which these attributes of backwardness occurred in individual instances appears to have varied directly with the degree of backwardness and the natural industrial potentialities of the countries concerned. . . .

The typical situation in a backward country prior to the initiation of considerable industrialization processes may be described as characterized by the tension between the actual state of economic activities in the country and the existing obstacles to industrial development, on the one hand, and the great promise inherent in such a development, on the other. The extent of opportunities that industrialization presents varied, of course, with the individual country's endowment of natural resources. Furthermore, no industrialization seemed possible, and hence no "tension" existed, as long as certain formidable institutional obstacles (such as the serfdom of the peasantry or the far-reaching absence of political unification) remained. Assuming an adequate endowment of usable resources, and assuming that the great blocks to industrialization had been removed, the opportunities inherent in industrialization may be said to vary directly with the backwardness of the country. Industrialization always seemed the more promising the greater the backlog of technological innovations which the backward country could take over from the more advanced country. Borrowed technology, so much and so rightly stressed by Veblen, was one of the primary factors assuring a high speed of development in a backward country entering the stage of industrialization. . . .

The industrialization prospects of an underdeveloped country are frequently judged, and judged adversely, in terms of cheapness of labor as against capital goods and of the resulting difficulty in substituting scarce capital for abundant labor. Sometimes, on the contrary, the cheapness of labor in a backward country is said to aid greatly in the processes of industrialization. The actual situation, however, is more complex than would appear on the basis of simple models. In reality, conditions will vary from industry to industry and from country to country. But the overriding fact to consider is that industrial labor, in the sense of a stable, reliable, and disciplined group that has cut the umbilical cord connecting it with the land and has become suitable for utilization in factories, is not abundant but extremely scarce in a backward country. Creation of an industrial labor force that really deserves its name is a most difficult and protracted process. . . .

Under these conditions the statement may be hazarded that, to the extent that industrialization took place, it was largely by application of the most modern and efficient techniques that backward countries could hope to achieve success, particularly if their industrialization proceeded in the face of competition from the advanced country. The advantages inherent in the use of technologically superior equipment were not counteracted but reinforced by its labor-saving effect. This seems to explain the tendency on the part of backward countries to concentrate at a relatively early point of their industrialization on promotion of those branches of industrial activities in which recent technological progress had been particularly rapid; while the more advanced countries, either from inertia or from unwillingness to require or impose sacrifices implicit in a large investment program, were more hesitant to carry out continual modernizations of their plant. Clearly, there are limits to such a policy, one of them being the inability of a backward country to extend it to lines of output where very special technological skills are required. Backward countries (although not the United States) were slow to assimilate production of modern machine tools. But a branch like iron and steel production does provide a good example of the tendency to introduce most modern innovations, and it is instructive to see, for example, how German blast furnaces so very soon become superior to the English ones, while in the early years of this century blast furnaces in still more backward southern Russia were in the process of outstripping in equipment their German counterparts. Conversely, in the nineteenth century, England's superiority in cotton textile output was challenged neither by Germany nor by any other country.

To a considerable extent (as in the case of blast furnaces just cited), utilization of modern techniques required, in nineteenth-century conditions, increases in the average size of plant. Stress on bigness in this sense can be found in the history of most countries on the European continent. But industrialization of backward countries in Europe reveals a tendency toward bigness in another sense. The use of the term "industrial revolution" has been exposed to a good many justifiable strictures. But, if industrial revolution is conceived as denoting no more than cases of sudden considerable increases in the rate of industrial growth, there is little doubt that in several important instances industrial development began in such a sudden, eruptive, that is, "revolutionary," way.

The discontinuity was not accidental. As likely as not the period of stagnation (in the "physiocratic" sense of a period of low rate of growth) can be terminated and industrialization processes begun only if the industrialization movement can proceed, as it were, along a broad front, starting simultaneously along many lines of economic activities. This is partly the result of the existence of complementarity and indivisibilities in economic processes. Railroads cannot be built unless coal mines are opened up at the same time; building half a railroad will not do if an inland center is to be connected with a port city. Fruits of industrial progress in certain lines are received as external economies by other branches of industry whose progress in turn accords benefits to the former. In viewing the economic history of Europe in the nineteenth century, the impression is very strong that only when industrial development could commence on a large scale did the tension between the preindustrialization conditions and the benefits expected from industrialization become sufficiently strong to overcome the existing obstacles and to liberate the forces that made for industrial progress.

This aspect of the development may be conceived in terms of Toynbee's relation between challenge and response. His general observation that very frequently small challenges do not produce any responses and that the volume of response begins to grow very rapidly (at least up to a point) as the volume of the challenge increases seems to be quite applicable here. The challenge, that is to say, the "tension," must be considerable before a response in terms of industrial development will materialize.

The foregoing sketch purported to list a number of basic factors which historically were peculiar to economic situations in backward countries and made for higher speed of growth and different productive structure of industries. The effect of these basic factors was, however, greatly reinforced by the use in backward countries of certain institutional instruments and the acceptance of specific industrialization ideologies. Some of these specific factors and their mode of operation on various levels of backwardness are discussed in the following sections.

The Banks

. . . The industrialization of England had proceeded without any substantial utilization of banking for long-term investment purposes. The more gradual character of the industrialization process and the more considerable accumulation of capital, first from earnings in trade and modernized agriculture and later from industry itself, obviated the pressure for developing any special institutional devices for provision of long-term capital to industry. By contrast, in a relatively backward country capital is scarce and diffused, the distrust of industrial activities is considerable, and, finally, there is greater pressure for bigness because of the scope of the industrialization movement, the larger average size of plant, and the concentration of industrialization processes on branches of relatively high ratios of capital to output. To these should be added the scarcity of entrepreneurial talent in the backward country.

It is the pressure of these circumstances which essentially gave rise to the divergent development in banking over large portions of the Continent as against England. The continental practices in the field of industrial investment banking must be conceived as specific instruments of industrialization in a backward country. It is here essentially that lies the historical and geographic locus of theories of economic development that assign a central role to processes of forced saving by the money-creating activities of banks. As will be shown presently, however, use of such instruments must be regarded as specific, not to backward countries in general, but rather to countries whose backwardness does not exceed certain limits. And even within the latter for a rather long time it was mere collection and distribution of available funds in which the banks were primarily engaged. This circumstance, of course, did not detract from the paramount importance of such activities on the part of the banks during the earlier industrialization periods with their desperate shortages of capital for industrial ventures.

The effects of these policies were far-reaching. All the basic tendencies inherent in industrial development in backward countries were greatly emphasized and magnified by deliberate attitudes on the part of the banks. From the outset of this evolution the banks were primarily attracted to certain lines of production to the neglect, if not virtual exclusion, of others. To consider Germany until the outbreak of World War I, it was essentially coal mining, iron- and steelmaking, electrical and general engineering, and heavy chemical output which became the primary sphere of activities of German banks. The textile industry, the leather industry, and the foodstuff-producing industries remained on the fringes of the banks' interest. To use modern terminology, it was heavy rather than light industry to which the attention was devoted.

Furthermore, the effects were not confined to the productive structure of industry. They extended to its organizational structure. The last three decades of the nineteenth century were marked by a rapid concentration movement in banking. This process indeed went on in very much the same way on the other side of the English Channel. But in Britain, because of the different nature of relations between banks and industry, the process was not paralleled by a similar development in industry.

It was different in Germany. The momentum shown by the cartelization movement of German industry cannot be fully explained, except as the natural result of the amalgamation of German banks. It was the mergers in the field of banking that kept placing banks in the positions of controlling competing enterprises. The banks refused to tolerate fratricidal struggles among their children. From the vantage point of centralized control, they were at all times quick to perceive profitable opportunities of cartelization and amalgamation of industrial enterprises. In the process, the average size of plant kept growing, and at the same time the interests of the banks and their assistance were even more than before devoted to those branches of industry where cartelization opportunities were rife.

Germany thus had derived full advantages from being a relatively late arrival in the field of industrial development, that is to say, from having been preceded by England. But, as a result, German industrial economy, because of specific methods used in the catching-up process, developed along lines not insignificantly different from those in England.

The State

The German experience can be generalized. Similar developments took place in Austria, or rather in the western sections of the Austrian-Hungarian Empire, in Italy, in Switzerland, in France, in Belgium, and in other countries, even though there were differences among the individual countries. But it certainly cannot be generalized for the European continent as a whole, and this for two reasons: (1) because of the existence of certain backward countries where no comparable features of industrial development can be discovered and (2) because of the existence of countries where the basic elements of backwardness appear in such an accentuated form as to lead to the use of essentially different institutional instruments of industrialization.

Little need be said with reference to the first type of country. The industrial development of Denmark may serve as an appropriate illustration. Surely, that country was still very backward as the nineteenth century entered upon its second half. Yet no comparable sudden spurts of industrialization and no peculiar emphasis on heavy industries could be observed. The reasons must be sought, on the one hand, in the paucity of the country's natural resources and, on the other hand, in the great opportunities for agricultural improvement that were inherent in the proximity of the English market. The peculiar response did not materialize because of the absence of the challenge.

Russia may be considered as the clearest instance of the second type of country. The characteristic feature of economic conditions in Russia was not only that the great spurt of modern industrialization came in the middle of the 1880s, that is to say, more than three decades after the beginning of rapid industrialization in Germany; even more important was the fact that at the starting point the level of economic development in Russia had been incomparably lower than that of countries such as Germany and Austria.

The main reason for the abysmal economic backwardness of Russia was the preservation of serfdom until the emancipation of 1861. In a certain sense, this very fact may be attributed to the play of a curious mechanism of economic backwardness, and a few words of explanation may be in order. In the course of its process of territorial expansion, which over a few centuries transferred the small duchy of Moscow into the huge land mass of modern Russia, the country became increasingly involved in military conflicts with the West. This involvement revealed a curious internal conflict between the tasks of the Russian government that were "modern" in the contemporaneous sense of the word and the hopelessly backward economy of the country on which the military policies had to be based. As a result, the economic development in Russia at several important junctures assumed the form of a peculiar series of sequences: (1) Basic was the fact that the state, moved by its military interest, assumed the role of the primary agent propelling the economic progress in the country. (2) The fact that economic development thus became a function of military exigencies imparted a peculiarly jerky character to the course of that development; it proceeded fast whenever military necessities were pressing and subsided as the military pressures relaxed. (3) This mode of economic progress by fits and starts implied that, whenever a considerable upsurge of economic activities was required, a very formidable burden was placed on the shoulders of the generations whose lifespan happened to coincide with the period of intensified development. (4) In order to exact effectively the great sacrifices it required, the government had to subject the reluctant population to a number of severe measures of oppression lest the burdens imposed be evaded by escape to the frontier regions in the southeast and east. (5) Precisely because of the magnitude of the governmental exactions, a period of rapid development was very likely to give way to prolonged stagnation, because the great effort had been pushed beyond the limits of physical endurance of the population and long periods of economic stagnation were the inevitable consequences. The sequences just mentioned present in a schematic way a pattern of Russian economic development in past centuries which fits best the period of the reforms under Peter the Great, but its applicability is by no means confined to that period. . . .

[Of] Russian industrialization in the eighties and the nineties of the past century, it may be said that in one sense it can be viewed as a recurrence of a previous pattern of economic development in the country. The role of the state distinguishes rather clearly the type of Russian industrialization from its German or Austrian counterpart.

Emancipation of the peasants, despite its manifold deficiencies, was an absolute prerequisite for industrialization. As such it was a negative action of the state designed to remove obstacles that had been earlier created by the state itself and in this sense was fully comparable to acts such as the agrarian reforms in Germany or the policies of Napoleon III. . . . Similarly, the great judicial and administrative reforms of the sixties were in the nature of creating a suitable framework for industrial development rather than promoting it directly.

The main point of interest here is that, unlike the case of Western Europe, actions of this sort did not per se lead to an upsurge of individual activities in the country; and for almost a quarter of a century after the emancipation the rate of industrial growth remained relatively low. The great industrial upswing came when, from the middle of the eighties on, the railroad building of the state assumed unprecedented proportions and became the main lever of a rapid industrialization policy. Through multifarious devices such as preferential orders to domestic producers of railroad materials, high prices, subsidies, credits, and profit guaranties to new industrial enterprises, the government succeeded in maintaining a high and, in fact, increasing rate of growth until the end of the century. Concomitantly, the Russian taxation system was reorganized, and the financing of industrialization policies was thus provided for, while the stabilization of the ruble and the introduction of the gold standard assured foreign participation in the development of Russian industry.

The basic elements of a backward economy were, on the whole, the same in Russia of the nineties and in Germany of the fifties. But quantitatively the differences were formidable. The scarcity of capital in Russia was such that no banking system could conceivably succeed in attracting sufficient funds to finance a large-scale industrialization; the standards of honesty in business were so disastrously low, the general distrust of the public so great, that no bank could have hoped to attract even such small capital funds as were available, and no bank could have successfully engaged in long-term credit policies in an economy where fraudulent bankruptcy had been almost elevated to the rank of a general business practice. Supply of capital for the needs of industrialization required the compulsory machinery of the government, which, through its taxation policies, succeeded in directing incomes from consumption to investment. There is no doubt that the government as an *agens movens* of industrialization discharged its role in a far less than perfectly efficient manner. Incompetence and corruption of bureaucracy were great. The amount of waste that accompanied the process was formidable. But, when all is said and done, the great success of the policies pursued under Vyshnegradski and Witte is undeniable. Not only in their origins but also in their effects, the policies pursued by the Russian government in the nineties resembled closely those of the banks in Central Europe. The Russian state did not evince any interest in "light industry." Its whole attention was centered on output of basic industrial materials and on machinery production; like the banks in Germany, the Russian bureaucracy was primarily interested in large-scale enterprises and in amalgamations and coordinated policies among the industrial enterprises which it favored or had helped to create. Clearly, a good deal of the government's interest in industrialization was predicated upon its military policies. But these policies only reinforced and accentuated the basic tendencies of industrialization in conditions of economic backwardness. . . .

The Gradations of Backwardness

. . . The question remains as to the effects of successful industrializations, that is to say, of the gradual diminution of backwardness. At the turn of the century, if not somewhat earlier, changes became apparent in the relationship between German banks and German industry. As the former industrial infants had grown to strong manhood, the original undisputed ascendancy of the banks over industrial enterprises could no longer be maintained. This process of liberation of industry from the decades of tutelage expressed itself in a variety of ways. Increasingly, industrial enterprises transformed connection with a single bank into cooperation with several banks. As the former industrial protectorates became economically sovereign, they embarked upon the policy of changing alliances with regard to the banks. Many an industrial giant, such as the electrical engineering industry, which could not have developed without the aid and entrepreneurial daring of the banks, began to establish its own banks. The conditions of capital scarcity to which the German banks owed their historical position were no longer present. Germany had become a developed industrial country. But the specific features engendered by a process of industrialization in conditions of backwardness were to remain, and so was the close relation between banks and industry, even though the master-servant relation gave way to cooperation among equals and sometimes was even reversed.

In Russia the magnificent period of industrial development of the nineties was cut short by the 1900 depression and the following years of war and civil strife. But, when Russia emerged from the revolutionary years 1905–1906 and again achieved a high rate of industrial growth in the years 1907–1914, the character of the industrialization processes had changed greatly. Railroad construction by the government continued but on a much smaller scale both absolutely and even more so relatively to the increased industrial output. Certain increases in military expenditures that took place could not begin to compensate for the reduced significance of railroad-building. The conclusion is inescapable that, in that last period of industrialization under a prerevolutionary government, the significance of the state was very greatly reduced.

At the same time, the traditional pattern of Russian economic development happily failed to work itself out. The retrenchment of government activities led not to stagnation but to a continuation of industrial growth. Russian industry had reached a stage where it could throw away the crutches of government support and begin to walk independently—and, yet, very much less independently than industry in contemporaneous Germany, for at least to some extent the role of the retreating government was taken over by the banks.

A great transformation had taken place with regard to the banks during the fifty years that had elapsed since the emancipation. Commercial banks had been founded. Since it was the government that had fulfilled the function of industrial banks, the Russian banks, precisely because of the backwardness of the country, were organized as "deposit banks," thus resembling very much the type of banking in England. But, as industrial development proceeded apace and as capital accumulation increased, the standards of business behavior were growingly Westernized. The paralyzing atmosphere of distrust began to vanish, and the foundation was laid for the emergence of a different type of bank. Gradually, the Moscow deposit banks were overshadowed by the development of the St. Petersburg banks that were conducted upon principles that were characteristic not of English but of German banking. In short, after the economic backwardness of Russia had been reduced by state-sponsored industrialization processes, use of a different instrument of industrialization, suitable to the new "stage of backwardness," became applicable.

Ideologies of Delayed Industrializations

Before drawing some general conclusions, a last differential aspect of industrialization in circumstances of economic backwardness should be mentioned. So far, important differences with regard to the character of industrial developments and its institutional vehicles were related to conditions and degrees of backwardness. A few words remain to be said on the ideological climate within which such industrialization proceeded. . . .

To break through the barriers of stagnation in a backward country, to ignite the imaginations of men, and to place their energies in the service of economic development, a stronger medicine is needed than the promise of better allocation of resources or even of the lower price of bread. Under such conditions even the businessman, even the classical daring and innovating entrepreneur, needs a more powerful stimulus than the prospect of high profits. What is needed to remove the mountains of routine and prejudice is faith—faith, in the words of Saint-Simon, that the golden age lies not behind but ahead of mankind. It was not for nothing that Saint-Simon devoted his last years to the formulation of a new creed, the New Christianity, and suffered Auguste Comte to break with him over this "betrayal of true science." What sufficed in England did not suffice in France. . . .

. . . Friedrich List's industrialization theories may be largely conceived as an attempt, by a man whose personal ties to Saint-Simonians had been very strong, to translate the inspirational message of Saint-Simonism into a language that would be accepted in the German environment, where the lack of both a preceding political revolution and an early national unification rendered nationalist sentiment a much more suitable ideology of industrialization.

After what has been just said it will perhaps not seem astonishing that, in the Russian industrialization of the 1890s, orthodox Marxism can be said to have performed a very similar function. Nothing reconciled the Russian intelligentsia more to the advent of capitalism in the country and to the destruction of its old faith in the mir and the artel than a system of ideas which presented the capitalist industrialization of the country as the result of an iron law of historical development. It is this connection which largely explains the power wielded by Marxist thought in Russia when it extended to men like Struve and in some sense even Milyukov, whose Weltanschauung was altogether alien to the ideas of Marxian socialism. In conditions of Russian "absolute" backwardness, again, a much more powerful ideology was required to grease the intellectual and emotional wheels of industrialization than either in France or in Germany. The institutional gradations of backwardness seem to find their counterpart in men's thinking about backwardness and the way in which it can be abolished.

Conclusions

. . . It is, of course, not suggested here that current policies vis-à-vis backward areas should be formulated on the basis of the general experience of the past century without taking into account, in each individual instance, the degree of endowment with natural resources, the climatic disabilities, the strength of institutional obstacles to industrialization, the pattern of foreign trade, and other pertinent factors. But what is even more important is the fact that, useful as the "lessons" of the nineteenth century may be, they cannot properly be applied without understanding the climate of the present century, which in so many ways has added new and momentous aspects to the problems concerned.

Since the present problem of industrialization of backward areas largely concerns non-European countries, there is the question of the effects of their specific preindustrial cultural development upon their industrialization potentialities. . . . At the same time, past Russian experience does show how quickly in the last decades of the past century a pattern of life that had been so strongly opposed to industrial values, that tended to consider any nonagricultural economic activity as unnatural and sinful, began to give way to very different attitudes. In particular, the rapid emergence of native entrepreneurs with peasant-serf backgrounds should give pause to those who stress so greatly the disabling lack of entrepreneurial qualities in backward civilizations. Yet there are other problems.

In certain extensive backward areas the very fact that industrial development has been so long delayed has created, along with unprecedented opportunities for technological progress, great obstacles to industrialization. Industrial progress is arduous and expensive; medical progress is cheaper and easier of accomplishment. To the extent that the latter has preceded the former by a considerable span of time and has resulted in formidable overpopulation, industrial revolutions may be defeated by Malthusian counterrevolutions.

Closely related to the preceding but enormously more momentous in its effects is the fact that great delays in industrialization tend to allow time for social tensions to develop and to assume sinister proportions. As a mild example, the case of Mexico may be cited, where the established banks have been reluctant to cooperate in industrialization activities that are sponsored by a government whose radical hue they distrust. . . .

Paul M. Hohenberg and Lynn Hollen Lees

The Making of Urban Europe, 1000–1950

Too often the factory town with its smoking chimneys and workers' slums has been used to typify the cities of the industrial age. Indeed, the visible connections between cities and the new units of production have given rise to a picture of the relationship between industrialization and urbanization that is more neat and simple than it is faithful to the realities of history. These two phenomena should be seen as related, but distinct, changes. Their interaction cannot be reduced to a two-way accretion of towns around factories and spread of factories in towns. Remember that in the early and mid-nineteenth centuries, Italy and the Netherlands were sustaining and even increasing their high proportions of urban dwellers with little help from an industrial revolution in the usual sense. Moreover, in Switzerland and in parts of northern France, manufacturing was thriving with only slow urbanization. Even where urban and industrial growth were more nearly congruent, as in Germany and England, regional patterns of change show much variation.

While hundreds of new towns had mushroomed early in the West Midlands, west Yorkshire, and Lancashire, urban growth in the industrializing East Midlands was largely confined to the county capitals and market towns, which had been in existence since at least the eleventh century. Economic development in the Ruhr area produced new settlements; yet in central Germany older cities remained the major sites for economic development. Finally, industrialization could displace employment elsewhere, leading to a restructuring of settlement patterns if not to actual deurbanization in regions of economic decline. No simple, direct relationship between urban and industrial growth can explain the diversity to be found across the European landscape.

At a minimum, understanding the impact of industrialization upon urban networks requires us to examine the settlement patterns produced

From Paul M. Hohenberg and Lynn Hollen Lees, *The Making of Urban Europe, 1000–1950* (Cambridge: Harvard University Press, 1985).

by the three different phases of economic growth in the nineteenth century. By looking first at protoindustrial development, then at coal-based expansion, and finally at the era of the second industrial revolution, we can trace how the linkage of urban and industrial growth changed over time and show that the appearance of new towns was a limited phenomenon closely linked to the exploitation of particular natural resources. . . .

. . . [M]uch industrial production in Europe before 1850 took place in the countryside as part of a complex division of labor with urban production sites and market centers. This interdependence of town and country before the era of the factory often produced a penumbra pattern of new settlement. The need to distribute materials and to collect finished goods in the absence of mechanized transportation limited the radius of development. Villages near a country town or commercial center grew along with protoindustry. In the environs of Ghent, Leicester, and Berlin, urban merchants put out raw materials into the hands of domestic workers. The hinterlands of Abbeville, Saint-Quentin, Amiens, and Nottingham became more densely settled with rural industrial workers; yet burgeoning villages did not turn into cities. They remained dependent upon older central places, as investments in services and administration lagged behind the needs of growing populations.

Despite the amount of growth in production and employment under protoindustrialization, the impact on existing settlement patterns was therefore minor in many regions. In fact, this was a major economic strength of the system. In Marxist terms, the early capitalists were spared the costs of reproducing labor and its living environment. The weavers of western Ireland usually lived in scattered cottages and small villages; cloth production was a common by-occupation of rural women. The early combination of farming with rural spinning and weaving encouraged dispersed settlement, as did the need for wood as fuel for early forges. When the silk industry expanded from the center of Lyon in the early nineteenth century, two sorts of sites were favored. First, suburban weavers' areas were created. Then factories at a greater distance from the city were built along rural streams. But new towns did not result. Units of production were small enough so that factory dormitories could provide housing. Services and supplies came from nearby market towns. Growth of the silk trade in the area was accomplished through existing settlement patterns. Even cities closely involved with protoindustry did not always increase their population, let alone their physical size. Rouen, the center of a thriving cotton region, grew only slightly between 1750 and 1850. Ghent's strong, even if short-lived, textile boom during the Napoleonic period required adding neither people nor buildings. Only high and sustained growth actively modified the settlement pattern, for instance, in the West Riding of Yorkshire and in the Lille region, where Roubaix and Tourcoing became major towns and textile producers.

The dominant influence upon location became physical power, whether available from an adjoining mine, a waterfall, or an accessible transportation artery. Mill villages multiplied along the upland streams of west Yorkshire. Intensified urbanization outside the confines of an older central place array took place primarily where the combination of technology and coal gave rural sites strong production advantages. There, migration and high fertility rates turned hamlets into villages and finally into towns.

Despite the increasing importance of large-scale producing units, the new industry did not quickly seek out existing concentrations of potential workers. There were good reasons why early factories and older cities remained wary of each other. Urban location raised production costs, from land rents to wages reflecting the expense of urban living. Early engines were too inefficient to operate far from cheap coal. Moreover, political fears of large concentrations of workers settling into the urban community made elites reluctant to welcome modern industry. From the point of view of the entrepreneur, a rural or village location was efficient and cheap. The older towns of a region could easily provide marketing, finance, and other services at a distance. As long as employers were willing to build housing, coal-based settlements were able to grow enormously without massive, early investment in urban services. In newly industrialized regions such as South Wales or the Borinage, specialized settlements were grafted onto older urban hierarchies but did not displace them. Eighty percent of the towns in Wales in 1800 dated from medieval times; the economic development of the nineteenth century then doubled the size of the Welsh urban network.

The geographic limits of this paleotechnic expansion can easily be seen with the aid of a French example. In the department of Pas de Calais new towns arose primarily between 1850 and 1900 along the coal fields. Growth of the mines brought an influx of migrants, who settled in villages and hamlets such as Hénin-Liétard, Bailin, or Bruay-en-Artois. Yet in nearby districts, expansion was largely limited to older centers and their suburbs, around Boulogne, Calais, Saint-Omer, and Arras. Away from the coal fields, migrants drifted into existing towns.

Thus, industrial development did not automatically produce an array of new towns. Outside the Alpine regions of adaptable protoindustrial heritage, older towns with their resident labor supplies, markets, and service sectors provided entrepreneurs with decisive advantages. In northern Italy industrial expansion in the later nineteenth and early twentieth century centered upon Milan and two lines of older towns along the railway lines east to Venice and southeast through Bologna to the coast. In the economically dynamic parts of Italy the mid-nineteenth century urban networks constituted a "favorable condition for modern industrialization." In Sweden, too, where economic development in the later nineteenth century did not depend upon coal, 80 percent of the urban growth between 1840 and 1920 took place in existing cities. Only twenty-five new towns were created during this period, and they accounted for less than 10 percent of the increase in urban population. Even where new towns and mill villages had expanded urban networks, development in the longer run concentrated in the larger places, where railway and business services eased both production and distribution. Growth in the Calder valley after 1850 centered in the towns along the railway—Halifax, Elland, and Sowerby Bridge. While outlying mills closed, housing was built and new firms were founded in and near the towns.

The true merger of industrial with urban growth took place during the later part of the nineteenth century in western and central Europe. The second industrial revolution became established in and near major cities. As new industries moved into southeastern England, London and its hinterland leapt ahead of the north in growth rates. Other national capitals such as Vienna, Berlin, and Paris attracted a great deal of industry and consequently exploded in size. In central and eastern Europe, where capital of all kinds was scarce and the rail network more centralized, the concentration of industry in larger cities was particularly strong. There were large, thriving firms not only in St. Petersburg and Budapest, but also in regional capitals such as Leipzig, Prague, and Breslau.

If there is one constant in the complex and changing story, it is that the factory town has never adequately represented the urban dimension of the industrialization process. Rather than seeing nineteenth-century urban growth from the vantage point of Bochum or Le Creusot, we should recognize its true habitat: the teeming streets and spreading suburbs of Berlin, Milan, Lodz, and Leeds. . . .

It is easy to caricature industrial towns. Their sprawling jumble of factories, railroads, and mines conjures up images of visual and social pollution. Charles Dickens's description of Coketown, a place of "unnatural red and black, like the painted face of a savage" gives a common indictment of the structures of industrial urbanism. Patrick Geddes and Lewis Mumford argued that the new technology, largely unrestrained by communal planning or government regulation, turned cities into slums and superslums. Moreover, Coketown stands condemned for its psychological and cultural effects, as well as for its degraded environment. Friedrich Engels, who constructed one of the most powerful critiques of urban life in the nineteenth century, saw in the new cities a suicidal style of social relations: "On the one hand the most barbarous indifference and selfish egotism and on the other, the most distressing scenes of misery and poverty. Signs of social conflict are to be found everywhere." Indeed, Engels anticipated that class warfare would break out after a large proletariat was created and then confined in squalid city housing. Both Engels and Dickens, however, looked at atypical places during the early decades of industrial expansion. The textile towns that sprang up like mushrooms in the English north represented only one facet of industrial urbanization. Much more common in the European setting was the vast array of older cities, linked by their central place functions, into which industry moved slowly as economic development shifted from the countryside to urban settings. In any case, protoindustrial towns like Nuremberg, Geneva, Bologna, and Leiden had long been the sites of extensive manufacturing and the home of a large propertyless worker population. How did advanced technology affect these older settlements? To see industrial urbanization only in terms of Coketown is not only simplistic but misleading.

The biggest changes wrought by the nineteenth-century burst of urban growth can be grouped under two headings: increases in scale and heightened density. Each affected the social as well as the physical shape of the city. Ever greater numbers living in ever closer proximity altered the ways people related to one another: rising density necessitated shifts in housing patterns, and increases in scale altered lines of distribution and circulation. Even more importantly, scale and density changed the nature of personal relationships. Size and social complexity are closely correlated. In larger places people become embedded in more intricate networks. They are more vulnerable to forces beyond their control as they need remote groups and institutions to supply food and other services. At the same time, individuals become more anonymous and are freer to move both geographically and socially from the place and the status in which they were born. In this perspective, many of the excesses and much of the suffering can be ascribed to instances in which urban settlements were too dense and/or too large to manage, particularly when an overly rapid pace of local urbanization overloaded the system. . . .

The argument here is that industrial urbanization restructured social relationships, generally by eroding older, multiple social roles and systems of authority and by creating large, relatively autonomous subcultures. Here again, however, the process was not confined to the cities, nor did it typically begin with the move from county to town. Under the influence of agricultural transformation and protoindustrial growth, large rural proletariats were being created or expanded. For them, and also for many in densely populated peasant areas, the structures of traditional society were either severely threatened or lacking altogether. However hard and unfamiliar the urban environment might be, it offered the chance to construct new lives with new webs of relationships, and multitudes grasped at that chance.

As the scale of social life increased, so necessarily did specialization. Already complex urban societies became more fragmented and highly differentiated, while simpler ones evolved in the same direction. Individuals were unlikely, therefore, to develop multiple, congruent contacts with a given set of neighbors and social elites. Whereas an apprentice in medieval Cologne probably had the same person as employer, landlord, elder of the craft guild, and perhaps town councillor, the worker in late nineteenth-century Cologne would not even know many of the people who separately filled these roles. Although the importance of economic divisions within cities grew over time, so too did distinctions of ethnicity, sex, education, and political allegiance. However, nationality, religion, and neighborhood—to name only a few—also served as integrating forces. Depending upon the extent of cultural sharing and the degree of overlapping among the multiple allegiances acquired by individuals, urban populations in the nineteenth century demonstrated very different amounts of social and political integration. Compare the look of Paris in June 1848, when the haves battled the have-nots over the desired shape of the government, to the temper of Blackburn in the 1850s and 1860s, when crowds of workers and their employers marched together to the polls to vote for the same candidates. Class divisions existed in both places, to be sure, but their effect on the propensity for conflict at the level of both city and neighborhood varied widely. To some extent, this was again an effect of scale, but is also derived from the internal structure of the urban population and its cultural coherence. . . .

The idea that cities affect social relationships is a common one, but debate rages over the results and their moral significance. Disgust with urban social problems has prompted countless critics to link cities to crime, disorder, and deviant behavior. Tennyson, in "Locksley Hall Sixty Years After," charged that "There among the glooming alleys, progress halts on palsied feet / Crime and hunger cast out maidens by the thousands on the street." Louis Wuarin, a French economist, deplored the rush into the city by rural laborers because in front of them lay a "thousand traps set for vanity and sensuality . . . that quietly lead the victim into the abyss." Moreover, he thought that cities, replete with "vagabonds and criminals who form a sort of secret society in order to thwart the power of the law," had a polluted moral atmosphere. Sociologists, too, have joined the chorus of those predicting dire results from urban residence. Park and Wirth both thought that urban life brought with it mental instability, loneliness, and alienation, as well as an increase in pathological behavior. Chevalier in his compelling study of nineteenth-century Paris linked crime, suicide, prostitution, and mental illness to the hordes of people crowding into the capital. High density and poverty, he felt, deformed social life and turned respectable workers into dangerous lunatics. The city became sick because of intensive migration. . . .

Industrial urbanism did change society, but in ways not easily labeled either good or evil. As the size of residential units increases, they become more complex. People in small settlements see one another repeatedly in a variety of roles, whereas in large cities they interact in more superficial, partial ways. Their neighbors might not be their co-workers or members of the same church, union, or club. Each person has multiple contacts, who need not know one another. The networks of social life tend to be fragmented rather than congruent. As a result, individuals are less visible and accountable. Social control becomes more impersonal and bureaucratized, while chances for individual mobility increase. Also, setting aside systemic differences, the larger a city, the more diverse its populations. Vienna had more Poles and Portuguese, Muslims and Jews, musicians and nerve doctors than did Graz. And there were enough of each to create subcultures based on ethnicity, religion, or occupation. Large cities bring together the critical mass of similar people needed to found communities. While the Irish in small Leicestershire villages were forced to blend in with the native English, those in Glasgow began Catholic churches and clubs, building communities around their ethnic loyalties. In fact, Claude Fischer argues that "the more urban a place, the more intense its subcultures." Large cities, in his view, produce strongly articulated value systems rather than isolated individuals. They are not melting pots, but mosaics of disparate groups, each of which fights to maintain its own identity. At first glance, this view of cities is puzzling, for how can a place be both impersonal and culturally intense? How can an individual be both anonymous and closely involved in a specific subculture? The answer is that cities contain both large-scale and small-scale environments. Although in public places—the stores, offices, streets, and large institutions—contacts are relatively brief and anonymous, there is a separate, private social life to be found on the level of family, neighborhood, club, and ethnic group that operates with different rules. There, social identities are personalized and longer lasting—multiple rather than fragmented. Aside from the occasional fair or election-day ritual, urban social life in recent times is not a mass phenomenon. It rests on the smaller social worlds created by citizens around units that matter to them. . . .

Overcrowded London The French artist Gustave Doré depicted the tenements of industrial London where workers and their families lived. This drawing shows crowded and unsanitary row houses, each one room wide, with tiny back yards, and a train steaming across a viaduct overhead. (*Prints Division, New York Public Library, Astor, Lenox, and Tilden Foundations*)

PART

Class Formation and Work Experience

Among the myriad impacts of the Industrial Revolution, perhaps no other topic has attracted more attention from historians than class formation. Few doubt that the creation of a working class, or proletariat, is one of the Industrial Revolution's chief legacies—and one that was perceived as early as the 1840s. Karl Marx, in his life's work on the dynamics of class formation, credited the rise of industrial capitalism with the foundation of a new mass of workers who had nothing to survive on except their labor. According to Marx, once these workers recognized their common plight and indispensability to society, they would usher in a socialist economic system that would acknowledge and reward their centrality to the production of Europe's wealth. Because European history diverged significantly from this model, however, historians have dedicated enormous effort to understanding the process of proletarianization and its impacts. This has led not only to reconsiderations of the very concept of class, but also to detailed examinations of the concrete realities of workers' lives and what role those factors played in the formation of class identities.

In the first selection, Ira Katznelson constructs a multilayered approach to understanding class. Rejecting Marx's "class in itself, for itself" model, which posits the automatic recognition of class identity once the class itself has formed, Katznelson argues instead that working-class formation occurs on four levels: structure, ways of life, dispositions, and collective action. Structure and ways of life correspond most with the traditional Marxist approach, for they refer to the overall configuration of the economy and the workers' lifestyles. Relevant factors at these two levels include the prevalence of factory labor, the retention of traditional craft structures, the extent of urbanization, and the institutions that constitute life outside of the workplace. Dispositions signify the meanings that workers give their lives, the sense that they make of their circumstances. This is the level that is most often associated with the concept of class consciousness, a term Katznelson eschews because it implies a teleological progression to class formation. Finally, collective action entails the translation of belief into deed. While it may be tempting to view this last level as the culmination of class formation, Katznelson argues that the scholar's task is to understand and account for the various connections among these four levels, seeing class formation not as an ideal outcome but as one of a range of possible contingencies that demand explanation.

The long-standing debate over the standard of living of industrial workers figures prominently in the study of those contingencies. For some historians, the pessimists, the deterioration of workers' standards of living precluded revolutionary organization and activity in the short run, but formed an important building block for the socialist politics that developed later in the nineteenth century. The optimists argue, however, that the rising standards of living made possible by industrial capitalism muted fervent calls to the barricades and spelled the ultimate demise of revolutionary politics. In other words, the standard of living is an essential component of the link between ways of life and dispositions. Yet a consensus on the impact the Industrial Revolution had on workers' standards of living remains elusive because the terms of analysis themselves defy easy detection and scrutiny. Among the practitioners of the New Economic History, who privilege economic data concerning real wages above all else, the task of isolating the impacts of the Industrial Revolution in England entails factoring out other significant variables, including the Napoleonic Wars, the poor harvests of the mid-eighteenth century, and population growth. In addition, the data themselves are difficult to interpret, for aggregate data on income and consumption incorporate a population far beyond the workers directly affected by the Industrial Revolution, while wage data frequently overlook hidden contributors to the economy, such as domestic workers and menial laborers. Nonetheless, the prevailing interpretation detects rising real wages after 1819, with some arguing improvement as early as 1780. Given the data and the ideologically charged nature of the debate, however, there is no telling how long that interpretation will stand the test of time.

At this point, the most promising challenges arise from the incorporation of noneconomic data concerning quality of life, such as health and work-discipline. In the selection by Stephen Nicholas and Richard H. Steckel, concern with standard of living extends beyond wages and consumption to include anthropometric data on nutrition and height. Height, they argue, is an excellent measure of standard of living because it reflects the amount of food available for a body's growth after essential maintenance needs are met. In other words, a secure and plentiful supply of food will result in a taller population. If, however, the standard of living does not provide for enough nutrition, that deficiency will be revealed in the data. According to their statistics on the heights of English and Irish male convicts transported to New South Wales, Australia, between 1817 and 1840, the Industrial Revolution did indeed result in lower average heights and delayed growth spurts among English urban men. This, Nicholas and Steckel argue, resulted from lower standards of living in British industrial cities, possibly due to poor housing conditions, the higher cost of food, and the greater work effort required by factory labor. While they concede that poor harvests and the impacts of the Napoleonic Wars may account for some of this decline, the differences between English rural and Irish convicts on one side and English urban convicts on the other belie the detrimental impacts of industrialization on those who lived in the factories' shadows.

E. P. Thompson likewise addresses quality-of-life issues in his essay on the impact of industrial capitalism on workers' conceptualization of time. When an agricultural economy shaped society, most workers based their lives on an organic system of time and work-discipline. Work schedules depended upon seasons and growing cycles. To this, tradition and religion added certain holidays and leisure opportunities. The factory, however, worked according to its own rhythm, based on the clock and the pace of the machinery. Moreover, industrial capitalism incorporated a new logic that equated time with money, making it essential to instill a time-based work-discipline in workers. While the task proved difficult, factory managers accomplished it with the aid of whistles, fine schedules, and even nonwork-related institutions and methods such as schools and moralistic sermons on sloth. In the end, workers incorporated the new system of time so well that it figured into their demands in labor disputes. As Thompson remarks, while the first generation of factory workers resisted time-discipline, the next struck for the ten-hour workday. The selection concludes with a consideration of the price paid for this transition, with Thompson arguing against a value-free assessment of industrialization and its impacts.

In the final selection, Michael B. Miller shifts our focus from England to France, and to a later period in industrial development when modern forms of marketing and economic organization gave rise to the department store, a new arena in which the complex connections between ways of life and dispositions unfolded. Paris's most successful of these new "bazaars" and "emporia" was the Bon Marché, and its owners, the Boucicauts, grew rich by pioneering innovative techniques for promoting consumption. At the same time, however, they helped to create a different type of industrial worker: the white-collar worker. These men and women posed real problems for their bourgeois employers, for they straddled the divide between the middle and working classes; they had attained a certain level of education and sophistication necessary for working in close proximity to the Bon Marché's bourgeois patrons, but their salaries and lack of independence placed a true bourgeois lifestyle far out of reach. Moreover, the pressures of working for commission and the overbearing discipline the Boucicauts demanded made these employees potential devotees of union and socialist "agitators." As Miller indicates, integrating these men and women into the middle class became a chief concern not just for the Boucicauts, but also for all white-collar employers, from banks and insurance companies to railroads and post offices. For the Bon Marché, paternalism forged that bond between employee and "the House." Paternalist policies included provident and pension funds based solely on employer contributions, subsidized meals, social organizations, and free evening classes. By developing programs to tie the workers' private and work lives to the store, and by carefully differentiating between "employees" and "workers," the Boucicaut sought to solidify a middle-class identity among their white-collar workers. Their success allowed them to dominate Parisian retail into the twentieth century, but for many enterprises the problems posed by working-class formation evaded easy solution.

Ira Katznelson

Working-Class Formation

. . . The concept "class" provides the obvious starting point. As a term, "class" has been used too often in a congested way, encompassing meanings and questions that badly need to be distinguished from each other. I suggest that class in capitalist societies be thought of as a concept with four connected layers of theory and history: those of structure, ways of life, dispositions, and collective action.

"It is not against a body of uninterpreted data, radically thinned descriptions that we must measure the cogency of our explications," Clifford Geertz has written, "but against the power of the scientific imagination to bring us into touch with the lives of strangers. It is not worth it, as Thoreau said, to go round the world to count the cats in Zanzibar." The extensive literature on working-class formation has succeeded in achieving much more than counting cats in Zanzibar, but it has not always known how to identify a particular kind of cat or to make crisp distinctions between types. As a contribution to social theory, the effort to distinguish between levels of class is an attempt to provide tools to construct cases of class formation systematically in order to promote comparative historical analysis.

As a concept, class has soaked up so much meaning that it has become bulky to use. Because it is often employed without a clearly specified definition, debates about class often become conversations in which

From Ira Katznelson, "Working-Class Formation: Constructing Cases and Comparisons," in Ira Katznelson and Aristide R. Zolberg, eds., *Working-Class Formation: Nineteenth-Century Patterns in Western Europe and the United States* (Princeton: Princeton University Press, 1986).

people talk past each other because they are talking about different dimensions of class. Without clear analytical distinctions between levels or layers of class, it is hard to improve on the "class in itself–for itself" model. With the specification of different levels it becomes possible to construct the various cases of class formation in their own terms and to explore the competing capacities of various macrohypotheses about linkages between the levels. Above all, the distinctions that follow are meant to be aids to concrete description and explanation.

The *first* level is the structure of capitalist economic development, whose main elements include an economy based on privately owned autonomous firms that seek to make profit-maximizing decisions. These enterprises employ labor for a wage and sell what they produce in the market. This process of economic development contains some elements shared by all capitalist societies and others that are distinctive to each. As Karl Polanyi pointed out, this "great transformation" entailed the commodification of money, land, and labor. Capitalism is unthinkable without proletarianization; and, as Marx observed as the centerpiece of his political economy, capitalism is impossible without a quite specific mechanism of exploitation.

Because these key properties are shared by all capitalisms, it is appropriate at this first level of class analysis to propose such distinctions as collective capital and collective labor, and productive and unproductive labor. And it is at this level that the heuristic model building Marx did in his mature works of political economy must test its mettle against other competing accounts.

Structural analyses of capitalism at this level use class analytically as a construct that is "experience-distant" (that is, as a concept employed by specialists to further scientific, philosophical, or practical aims). Used in this way as a tool to analyze the "motion" of capitalist development, class has no direct or unmediated phenomenological referents.

But economic development, of course, occurs not just in theory or in capitalism in general, but in real places at actual times. If capitalism is structured everywhere in coherent ways, it is also structured in different particular manners. Each specific national history of capitalist development is shaped by the shared impulses and boundaries of all capitalisms; but each national economy is shaped not only by these tendencies. Family patterns, demography, cultural traditions, inherited practices, state organization and policies, geopolitics, and other factors help determine the specific empirical contours of macroscopic economic development at this first level of class.

Even as we pay attention to these variations, however . . . , at this level of economic structure class remains an experience-distant analytical concept, needed to describe and explain what happened because class is a constitutive element of any capitalist structure. Distinctive national histories of capitalist economic development perforce are structural histories of class formation in the sense of Charles Tilly's "thin" definition in his treatment of the demographic origins of the European proletariat: "people who work for wages, using means of production over whose disposition they have little or no control." Proletarianization at this level provides a necessary, indeed the necessary condition for class formation in the more thickly textured senses of ways of life, dispositions, or patterns of collective action. But even when we take variations in macrolevel economic development into account it is not a sufficient condition. It is impossible to infer ways of life, dispositions, or collective action directly from analyses of class at the first level.

Nevertheless, broad patterns of economic development are of central importance in shaping patterns of life and social relations in specific capitalist societies. This *second* level, determined in part by the structure of capitalist development, refers to the social organization of society lived by actual people in real social formations. For this reason, theories that deal with this level of class must be "experience-near."

Because this second level includes such economic phenomena as workplace social relations and labor markets, it is tempting to collapse the first two levels of class into the single category of the "economy." Such a conflation, however, eliminates in one stroke a series of important questions about the connections between key aspects of capitalist accumulation and national economic histories on one side and the organization of labor markets and workplaces on the other. As any student of capitalist industrialization knows, the growth and expansion of capitalism has proved capable of fostering many different kinds of workplaces and work. . . .

Although the second level of class includes work settings and labor markets (here classes can be stacked up and counted according to criteria that distinguish between various active members of the labor force), it is not coextensive with these social relationships. The level of ways of life refers to how actual capitalist societies develop at work *and* away from it.

One of the hallmarks of industrial capitalist societies is that they tend to foster ways of life that differentiate between the location and social organization of these two realms. Over time, this distinction is expressed in the social geography of industrial cities. Work leaves the home. Cross-class households break up. Whole regions of cities come to be defined as areas of residence or of production. Further, residential communities segregate by the class position of their residents (in both the Marxist sense of location in a system of production and the Weberian sense of capacity to consume goods and services in the marketplace). With these separations between work and home and between the social classes in space, class relations are lived and experienced not only at work but also off work in residence communities.

The first two levels of class are closely related, of course, in that it is something of a conceit to separate too starkly the structure of capitalist accumulation and the self-sustaining development of the economy at the first level from how such broad patterns of economic development exist for working people where they labor and where they live at the second level. Moreover, if we understand that neither level of social relations is purely economic, then it makes sense to see the second level as an attribute of the first. But however closely connected, they are separate nonetheless, and many debates, such as the one between Erik Olin Wright and Nicos Poulantzas about mappings of class, suffer from the failure to make this distinction.

At the first two levels of class it is appropriate to construct classifications of class relations, and the literature of social science is full of them. At both levels class is defined, from an orthodox Marxist position, as G. A. Cohen writes, solely "with reference to the position of its members in the economic structure, their effective rights and duties within it. A person's class is established by nothing but his objective place in the network of ownership relations, however difficult it may be to identify such places neatly." Even if the criteria used in such definitions are expanded to other bases of class relations and to patterns of class embedded in residence communities, Cohen is right to stress that at these levels of analysis a person's "consciousness, culture, and politics do not enter the *definition* of his class position. . . . Not even his behavior is an essential part of it." Yet by themselves no such schemata, however compelling, can tell us how class exists distinct from other bases of solidarity and action in specific societies at specific times. This level of analysis may tell us how workers exist and live in certain circumstances, but not how they will think or act in those experienced circumstances.

At a *third* level social classes are not heuristic or analytical constructs nor do they consist of members of this or that cell of a typology. At this level, classes are formed groups, sharing dispositions. Such cognitive constructs map the terrain of lived experience and define the boundaries between the probable and improbable. Note that I am deliberately avoiding the term "class consciousness" in order to make clear my rejection of any notion of degrees of consciousness, with the highest corresponding to the "real" interests of the working class. Further, the scheme of four levels of class does not imply a series of necessary stages or a natural progression (after all, ways of life are not independent of thought or action). It is, rather, a classification that aims to promote the development of theory free from developmental assumptions.

I take it that the third level of class is what Thompson means when he writes:

> *Class is a social and cultural formation (often finding institutional expression) which cannot be defined abstractly, or in isolation, but only in terms of relationship with other classes; and, ultimately, the definition can only be made in the medium of time—that is, action and reaction, change and conflict. When we speak of a class we are thinking of a very loosely-defined body of people who share the same congeries of interests, social experiences, traditions, and value-system, who have a disposition to behave as a class, to define themselves in their actions and in their consciousness in relation to other groups of people in class ways.*

This suggestive formulation condenses a number of significant issues. To say that people share dispositions can mean that they have come to share understandings of the social system or that they have come to share values of justice and goodness. These two kinds of disposition are at least partially independent. Further, whether they are class dispositions is a contingent matter. Members of a class may share dispositions of either kind, but they need not necessarily be class based analytically or normatively. Further, either knowledge- or norm-based dispositions may view the current situation as the outcome of circumstances that cannot be altered or as posing the possibility of something better.

Much of the variation between the French, American, and German cases consists of variations in the ways working people, confronting changes in the conditions of life at the second level of class, mapped and interpreted these changes at the level of dispositions. Most new social history joins the story of class formation here, studying situations from the point of view of a specific working class in a specific place at a specific time. It is at this level that a Geertzian cultural analysis of the ways people construct meaning to make their way through the experienced world is most compelling, especially because shared dispositions are interactive. They are formed by the manner in which people interact with each other. Thus dispositions are transindividual, not merely opinions or views of individual actors. They constitute cultural configurations within which people act. In Bernard Cohn's terms, "[T]here can be no practical realities without the symbolic coding of them as *practical*. . . . People cannot act as maximizers—either out of self interest or out of deep psychological conditionings— . . . without the preexistence of meaning in cultural terms."

The third level of class, that of dispositions, is not coextensive with class structures and class-based ways of life; nor, however, do dispositions simply mirror reality. Rather, they are plausible and meaningful responses to the circumstances workers find themselves in.

A number of important recent discussions in philosophy concern the issue of "correspondence." Analytical philosophers, much like some orthodox Marxists, have taken very seriously the idea that for something to be "right" it must correspond to something "real." Some efforts have recently been made, especially by Hilary Putnam and Nelson Goodman, to transcend this assumption of correspondence. Putnam proposes that the key issue is "how can language or thought connect up to what is outside the mind"; and Goodman insists that "philosophy must take into account all the ways and means of worldmaking." But though such worlds are made, they are not constructed from scratch. Meaning is the result of the interaction between the world and human efforts to signify it. If the construction of meaning is not entirely an open or contingent matter, what are the causes of the construction of different kinds of meaning systems about class? I will return to this question shortly.

Thompson follows his discussion of class dispositions by adding, "[B]ut class itself is not a thing, it is a happening." Here he moves much too quickly from this third level of class to a *fourth*, collective action. Groups of people sharing motivational constructs ("disposition to behave") may or may not act collectively to transform disposition to behavior. Even where workers have close contact at work and in their residential communities; even if this interaction promotes strong collective identities; and even if these workers share common systems of meaning that incline them to act in class ways, they may not necessarily act together to produce collective action. For this reason it is useful to distinguish between class at the third level and at the fourth, which refers to classes that are organized and that act through movements and organizations to affect society and the position of the class within it. This kind of behavior is self-conscious and refers to activity that is more than just the common but unself-conscious shared behavior of members of a class. After all, members of categorical classes must immanently share certain behaviors, but they do not necessarily act consciously and collectively in pursuit of common goals.

The "class in itself–for itself" formulation makes thinking about the links between the social organization of class, class dispositions, and collective action superfluous. But in fact class conflict of any particular kind is not necessarily entailed in the class organization of patterns of social life, nor even in the development of groups of people inclined to act in class ways. The one broad exception to this general rule of contingency is the development of trade unions to fight for better wages and working conditions at the place of work. Although here too there are wide variations between the experiences of different working classes, there are no examples of national histories of class formation utterly lacking in the effort to create trade unions.

There are always impediments to collective action, to those occasions when "sets of people commit pooled resources, including their own efforts, to common ends." A key feature of the historical study of class must consist "of discovering which sets of people, which resources, which common ends, and which forms of commitment were involved in different places and times. Did the configurations change systematically with the advances of capitalism and large organizations?" Both the content and the form of collective action are highly variable, and this variation demands explanation.

Class, Thompson suggestively points out, is a "junction term," which lies at the intersection of structure and process, social being and social consciousness. Structural change gives rise to changed experience: that is, both to a set of subjective perceptions of objectively ordered realities and to a more active process of learning, possibly leading to action to modify the objective realities. I have already noted that Thompson, in my view, makes the movement from class structure to class action too certain a passage, but this teleological element can be extruded from his formulation.

The distinctions drawn here between the four levels of class may be read as an elaboration of Thompson's insight that class is a junction term.

They allow us to specify more precisely the points of connection *between* the structure of class relations at the macroeconomic level; the lived experience of class in the workplace and in the residence community; groups of people disposed to act in class ways; and class-based collective action. These points of contact specify the possibility of alternative kinds of relationships between the levels, a problem best approached by asking what we mean by class formation after moving beyond "class in itself–for itself" formulations.

It is possible, of course, to continue to define class formation in terms of specific outcomes, rather than to leave open the content of class formation. We might say that class formation has occurred only when class exists at all four levels of structure, patterns of life, dispositions, and action simultaneously. This would have a number of advantages. It would turn our attention to the links between class levels, and it would treat class formation as only one of a number of possible outcomes. It would dispose of the Hobson's choice between structuralist formulations that claim, at least implicitly, that experience is ideology, and culturalist stances fashionable in much current linguistic and semiotic theory in which class society is said to exist only when it is signified.

But despite these advantages, such a definition would be unsatisfactory. An outcome approach hinging on the appearance of class at each of the four levels without specifying the components of class and the range of both class and nonclass possibilities at each of the levels too starkly posits a dichotomous outcome (and in this way resembles the tradition of "revolutionary consciousness"): class either exists or does not as the basis of social solidarity and action. This distinction does not appear to be terribly helpful in explicating the puzzles posed by our three cases. Further, such an approach fails to answer the question, class formation with respect to what content?

Class formation may be thought of more fully and more variably as concerned with the conditional (but not random) process of connection between the four levels of class. The specification of four levels of class allows us to keep the advantages of defining class formation in terms of outcomes while providing a more elaborated and variable object of comparative historical analysis. The content of each of the four levels of necessity will vary from society to society; no level need be understood or analyzed exclusively in class terms; and the connections between the levels are problematical and conditional.

Questions about the content of each level and about the connections between the levels of class constitute the very heart of the analysis of class formation. A precise (but not too narrow) charting of class formation, based on a contingent but not undetermined approach to the relationship between these levels, and the attempt to develop macrocausal hypotheses about variations in class formation are the interrelated tasks that follow from this approach. . . .

Stephen Nicholas and Richard H. Steckel

Heights and Living Standards of English Workers During the Early Years of Industrialization, 1770–1815

The last decade has seen a substantial research effort directed toward measuring the trend in real wages and living standards during the British Industrial Revolution. Although most historians agree that workers received real-wage improvements from the 1820s on, controversy still surrounds the changes in English workers' living standards before that decade. Advising the standard-of-living pessimists to retreat to the pre-1820 era, Peter Lindert and Jeffrey Williamson argued that their data on male earnings pointed to real-wage stability between 1755 and 1797, then falling real wages until 1819, broken only by a brief rise between 1810 and 1815. Taking issue with Lindert and Williamson's cost-of-living index, N. F. R. Crafts thought that pre-1820 real wages of all blue-collar

From Stephen Nicholas and Richard H. Steckel, "Heights and Living Standards of English Workers During the Early Years of Industrialization, 1770–1815," *Journal of Economic History* 51, no. 4 (December 1991).

workers possibly grew somewhat faster than consumption per head. But consumption expenditures showed retarded growth during this period, and per capita levels of food consumption actually fell. The emerging "consensus" view is that real-wage growth for all blue-collar workers increased in line with overall personal consumption, which grew only very slowly. The pessimists' case, if there is one, can be found between 1770 and 1825.

Among regional studies, L. D. Schwarz discovered falling real wages in London between 1750 and 1770 and between 1780 and 1800, and generalized London's experience to those regions of England that shared a similar pattern of handicraft production. The regional character of industrialization was also identified in Nicholas von Tunzelmann's measures of the differential impact of Lancashire and the south on the national real-wage trend, and Crafts as well as Lindert and Williamson cautioned that industrialization was geographically uneven and that regional consumption patterns differed greatly across England. Not only did living standards vary regionally, but wage rates and living standards varied between sections of the working class, creating working-class winners as well as losers even during periods of falling real wages.

Since then E. H. Hunt and W. Botham have taken issue with Schwarz's, Lindert and Williamson's, and Crafts's claim that wages fell "everywhere" between 1755 and 1810 and that slow growth meant that the Industrial Revolution marked no real "discontinuity" in the late eighteenth century. Using a series of north Staffordshire male wages, Hunt and Botham found that real wages increased before 1820 and speculated that those real-wage gains were typical of much of the north and midlands, as those regions experienced the stimulus of rapid industrialization even more strongly than did north Staffordshire. Accepting that Schwarz's estimates of London's wage movements held for the south, Hunt and Botham's wage data support E. W. Gilboy's conclusion that regional divergence, especially the north-south divide, was the outstanding characteristic of movements in money wages and the standard of living of the working classes in eighteenth-century England. However, though they underscore the importance of regional variations in living standards, the north Staffordshire wage series do not reinstate the old view of marked discontinuity in British growth.

After a decade of research on real-wage trends, our knowledge of pre-1820 living standards can at best be termed "tentative," leading Crafts to call for "a substantial effort to augment the existing database on wages and prices." Anthropometrics offers an alternative to real wages as a method for assessing changes in living standards in the 1770-to-1820 period. Roderick Floud, Kenneth Wachter, and Annabel Gregory have led the way in the analysis of British height data, collecting information on 108,000 army recruits between 1750 and 1880 and similar data on adolescent boys from the Marine Society of London and the Royal Military Academy at Sandhurst. Correcting for the truncation problem associated with minimum height requirements that varied by regiment, birth cohort, and age group, Floud and his colleagues found that the long-term or secular trend in average height of 24- to 29-year-old military recruits was upward for birth cohorts of 1750 to 1840, then downward until the 1870s before turning upward again. For birth cohorts of the 1760-to-1820 period, the army data show a downward trend from a 1760s peak to a 1790s trough, then a strong upward trend until the 1820s, when average height once again fell. This pattern of mean height also held for 18-year-old recruits, 21- to 23-year-old recruits, and for poor London boys recruited into the Marine Society. The average height of 24- to 29-year-old army recruits increased over 2 inches (from 65.84 to 68.02 inches) for soldiers born between 1792 and 1822 and by up to 4 inches for Marine Society recruits born after 1800, pointing to rapidly rising living standards. Army recruits born in 1810, for example, were the tallest men in the sample, almost an inch taller than early twentieth-century soldiers. Early industrialization was not simply benign: by this measure of stature it brought widespread improvements in workers' living standards.

This article provides an alternative interpretation of living standards for English workers during the early (1770 to 1815) industrialization period, using data on the height of 11,303 men tried in English courts and transported to the penal colony of New South Wales, Australia, between 1817 and 1840. We first briefly outline our methodology and survey our data source. In the second section we provide descriptive measures of the height profile of English workers and a measure of changes in English workers' living standards during the crucial period (1770 to 1815). . . .

Methodology and Data

Research on height by economic historians has proliferated in the past 15 years. The common motivation that binds together this growing field of work is the need for improved measures of living standards in the past. Underpinning this line of investigation are studies by human biologists, anthropologists, and nutritionists that establish the reliability of anthropometric measures as indexes of health and nutrition. Height for age, the change in height between successive ages (velocity or rate of growth), the age at which final height is reached, and final adult height "reflect accurately the state of a nation's public health and the average nutritional status of its citizens." Although genetic conditions could also affect growth, the common genetic pool of our English and Irish convicts means that environmental factors were dominant in our questions of changes in stature.

In interpreting stature as a measure of living standards, it is important to recognize that height is a net rather than a gross measure of nutrition. Height depends on the nutrition available for physical growth after the claims made by body maintenance needs, illness, and work. An individual's ability to generate a surplus for growth depends on the body's efficiency at nutrient utilization, on the intensity of work performed, on the disease environment, and on the state of public health. Despite the large number of factors that may influence stature, average height has been found to be highly correlated with the log of per capita income in a sample of developed and developing countries.

Our sample comprised 11,303 English and, for comparative purposes, 5,005 Irish male convicts transported to New South Wales between 1817 and 1840. In all, some 160,000 convicts were sent to Australia (of whom about 16 percent were female), including roughly 80,000 men transported to New South Wales from the First Fleet in 1788 to the end of transport in 1840. Accompanying each convict ship was an indent, a document that contained complete information on each convict, including age, gender, occupation, conjugal status, literacy status, town and county of birth, crime and previous convictions, as well as height. The fine grid of height measurements and the accompanying detailed information bolster our confidence in the accuracy and reliability of the convict records. A survey of the trial records of 596 of our transported convicts tried in the London Central Court revealed that over 98 percent of the sentences and crimes recorded there corresponded with those in the indents. Although the court records only listed information on occupations for 3.5 percent of the 596 men surveyed, all of that fraction agreed with those in the indents. The indents recorded over 1,000 separate occupations, with a level of accuracy and detail far superior to that in the contemporary census. Cross-tabulations of county of trial with occupations were consistent with a priori expectations: most cutlery makers were tried in Sheffield, knitters and stocking makers in Nottingham, and potters in Staffordshire. There were no significant changes in the proportion of convicts born in the various counties of England between 1817 and 1840. Comparing the distribution of the convicts' origins with that of the English population in 1831 and 1841 showed that most convicts came from the heartland of England. Cornwall, Devon, and Dorset in the south and Northumberland, Cumberland, Westmoreland, Yorkshire, and Durham in the north were underrepresented relative to the whole population, whereas Middlesex and Warwick were overrepresented.

Height was typically recorded to the nearest quarter-inch, and the frequency distribution shows little sign of "heaping," which would indicate careless procedures or a disinterest in accuracy. . . . The absence of truncation bias is a desirable feature of our height data, given that the alternative source of English male heights, the British army records, is contaminated by minimum-height standards that erode the lower tail of the distribution and complicate the interpretation of the data.

Before attempting to interpret average heights, we must consider the possibility that the individuals measured did not represent the entire population about which we would like to draw inferences. For example, data based on army volunteers are biased because they typically included proportionately more individuals from the lower classes. One way to address this problem of selectivity is to compare characteristics of the sample with those of the entire population. Having done so, we can assert that the convict sample was broadly representative of the English working classes. First we coded the occupational structure of the convict sample and the 1841 English census, using Armstrong's skill–social class scheme: (1) professional, (2) intermediate, (3) skilled, (4) semiskilled, and (5) unskilled. As shown in [the] table, the major difference between the English work force and the convict sample was that over three times as many English workers as convicts fell into Armstrong's classes 1 and 2. However, the proportion of skilled and semiskilled convicts corresponds very closely to that in the English population. A Spearman's rank correlation between 83 occupations identified in both the 1841 census and the convict indents was 0.714, suggesting a close match between the sample occupations and those of the English work force. . . .

We also assessed the representativeness of the convict sample by comparing the transported convicts with offenders left at home. Recent work by historians of crime has rejected the idea of a separate nineteenth-century criminal or dangerous class, born and bred to a life of crime and

Skill Classification of English Work Force and English Transported Convicts (in percentages)

Armstrong Classification	*English 1841 Census (Male Only)*	*English Convicts (Male Only)*
1. Professional	1.7	0.3
2. Intermediate	9.2	3.1
3. Skilled	47.9	45.6
4. Semiskilled	25.7	26.3
5. Unskilled	15.5	24.7

Sources: Great Britain, *1841 Census;* and *Convict Indents.*

operating as organized gangs. These studies argue that the great majority of crime was committed by ordinary men who worked at jobs in the normal fashion but who also stole articles on occasion. Though not "honest men," the convicts were employed people who supplemented their income by theft in times of distress. There can be little doubt that our transportees were typical of such British criminals. Compared with offenders in Warwickshire, transported convict workers had a similar occupational breakdown: 58.8 and 53.4 percent unskilled and semiskilled, 38.4 and 43.6 percent skilled, and 2.8 and 2.9 percent middle and upper class, respectively. They had committed the same types of offences: less than 3 percent were against persons; the rest were property offences, the great majority of them larceny. The rank correlation between the occupations of the transported male convicts and the male prisoners held in British jails in 1841 was 0.908. On the basis of these tests, it seems fair to argue that the convicts transported to Australia were coincident with the broad skill–social class mix of the English working class.

Profile and Timing of Changes in Height

The growth spurt, final attained height, and age at terminal height presented in [the] table are sensitive measures of the environmental impact on individuals' well-being. Both terminal height and the peak in the growth spurt occurred at about the same age for English rural and urban workers, but it was more vigorous for rural workers. This rural-urban differential for the whole period reflected in [the] table was also present

Terminal Height and *t*-Test of Differences in Terminal Heights of Convicts

	English	*Rural English*	*Urban English*	*Irish*	*Rural Irish*	*Urban Irish*
Height (in inches)	65.76	65.96	65.44	66.03	66.10	65.82
English		3.61*	4.82*	5.25*	5.20*	0.63
Rural English			7.12*	1.07	1.94	1.39
Urban English				7.87*	8.16*	3.57*

* = significant at the 5 percent level

Source: Convict Indents.

when the sample was broken into pre-1790 and post-1790 subsamples. Our rural-urban distinction was based on whether a man gave his birthplace as a city or a town; it is a measure of birth location superior to that employed by Floud, Wachter, and Gregory, who used whether a recruit came from an urban or a rural county. The rural advantage was most pronounced between the ages of about 14.5 to 17, and at maturation the rural-born were 0.5 inch taller than their urban counterparts, a statistically significant difference. The peak in the growth spurt between the ages of 14 and 15 for both groups was a year later than that for well-nourished children today. Because the adolescent growth spurt requires large additional nutritional requirements, the one-year delay in adolescent growth may imply some measure of early childhood malnutrition, retarded food intake, or increased work loads relative to dietary allotments for Industrial Revolution children. In addition, male workers continued to grow until they were 23, well beyond the modern standard, in which final height is attained by about 18. The centiles of modern growth attained by the convict workers, shown in [the] table, suggest that a catch-up occurred during the last four years of growth for urban and rural workers alike.

In terms of international comparisons, English workers were better nourished than German peasants of the late 1700s, the poor in Italy in the 1870s, and nineteenth-century American slaves during adolescence (but not at maturity). Although the average English Industrial Revolution worker was shorter than white Americans and Stuttgart aristocrats

Convict Workers' Centiles of Modern Height

Rural English				
Age	*Height*	*Number*	*Standard Deviation*	*Centile*
13	53.94	4	2.79	
14	56.94	16	2.19	1.0
15	61.56	61	3.04	3.4
16	61.61	48	2.72	0.6
17	63.52	75	3.08	2.4
18	63.87	209	2.25	3.0
19	64.78	342	2.16	6.3
20	65.43	431	2.44	10.0
21	65.67	417	2.42	11.7
22	65.67	453	2.53	11.7
23	65.96	3,133	2.50	14.1
Urban English				
Age	*Height*	*Number*	*Standard Deviation*	*Centile*
13	55.17	19	3.66	2.0
14	56.60	53	2.88	0.7
15	60.25	155	3.06	1.2
16	60.62	199	2.71	0.2
17	62.68	254	2.46	1.1
18	63.47	390	2.32	1.8
19	64.39	516	2.22	4.7
20	64.60	505	2.24	5.0
21	65.17	448	2.59	8.4
22	65.19	408	2.53	8.5
23	65.44	1,966	2.56	10.1

Source: Convict Indents; and Tanner, Whitehouse, and Takaishi, "Standards."

in 1800, rural workers were about as well off as the Stuttgart middle class at the end of the eighteenth century. The height of English workers, then, compared favorably with other eighteenth- and nineteenth-century workers. But their lower achievement relative to modern height standards and the later maturation of males during the Industrial Revolution confirms hard times during early childhood or adolescence or both for rural and urban workers. The significantly shorter stature of urban males meant that Englishmen born in the country were taller, fitter, and probably (all else being equal) more productive than those born in the city. Besides using the standards of modern populations—that is, continental Europeans and North Americans in the eighteenth and nineteenth centuries—the height of English Industrial Revolution workers can be compared with that of men born in Ireland. Ireland, predominantly rural and agricultural, was a part of the British economy that remained relatively untouched by the forces transforming the industrializing regions in England. Using a subjective index of impoverishment, Mokyr and Ó Gráda found that the Irish poor became poorer before 1850, yet the average height of Irish recruits into the Royal Navy and the East India Company army who were born before 1815 was about half an inch greater than British recruits. Our data show that Irish convicts were approximately a quarter-inch taller than English convicts, a statistically significant difference consistent with Mokyr and Ó Gráda's results on stature.

These data provide new insights into English as well as Irish economic progress. Final heights of English workers, either rural or urban, were not significantly different from those of rural Irish workers, but their growth profiles were. Although the sample sizes for convicts under 16 years of age were small, it seems that the Irish had a head start on the timing of the growth spurt and a more vigorous spurt than the English from about the age of 15. During their whole adolescent growth period, rural Englishmen were considerably shorter (more than an inch at 16) than rural Irishmen, a gap not significantly narrowed until the age of 19. The comparison for urban Englishmen is even more dramatic. At 16, English urban workers were 2.5 inches shorter than rural Irishmen, and their final attained height was significantly less than that of Irish workers.

This suggests that, during the vital growth spurt years, rural Irishmen were either better nourished than Englishmen or faced different work demands and environmental conditions than did urban English workers. Insofar as Ireland serves as a useful "control" economy, rural

Englishmen were much better insulated from industrial changes than were urban British workers, who bore more of the brunt of industrialization than did their rural countrymen.

The Irish height advantage appears inconsistent with evidence that per capita income was lower in Ireland than in England. Because comparisons of many countries indicate that income is one of the important determinants of stature, an interesting research problem arises whenever these measures disagree to a substantial extent. However, per capita income is merely an approach to living standards—as are stature, real wages, literacy, and life expectation at birth. Obviously, care should be taken in using any one of these as an index of the other. The problem illustrated by this case is that income is not the only determinant of average height; others are exposure to infectious diseases (and therefore public health measures, population density, and standards of personal hygiene), the distribution of income, work effort, and the quality of the diet. Therefore the evaluation of the possible explanations will require a thorough study of the social and economic history of both regions.

It was in the cities and towns, the pessimists argued, that the living standards of ordinary working-class Britons fell most sharply during the early years of the Industrial Revolution. Moving averages of final attained urban and rural height by year of birth provide a sensitive indicator of the changing living standards of urban and rural workers. The five-year moving average of final attained height shown in [the] figure is based on between 22 and 357 observations for each year between 1780 and 1815, but far fewer (an average of 12) observations in the 1770s. The figure displays the different pattern in the time trends of urban and rural heights, with urban height falling more steeply than rural heights—a pattern Floud and his colleagues also discovered in their data.

Although the heights of both rural and urban birth cohorts declined after 1780, rural height remained fairly stable between 1790 and 1804, averaging 66 inches before deteriorating during the last years of the Napoleonic Wars. Meanwhile, urban height fell continually, except for a weak comeback in the early 1790s and a somewhat stronger comeback between 1803 and 1811. The time profile of attained final height shows a fall in living standards for urban workers, who in 1802 were more than 1.25 inches shorter than birth cohorts born in 1780. As can be seen in the centiles on the right-hand scale of [the] figure, urban workers born in the 1770s were near centile 19, which corresponded to the Stuttgart aristocracy (at the 18.7 centile), but those born in 1800

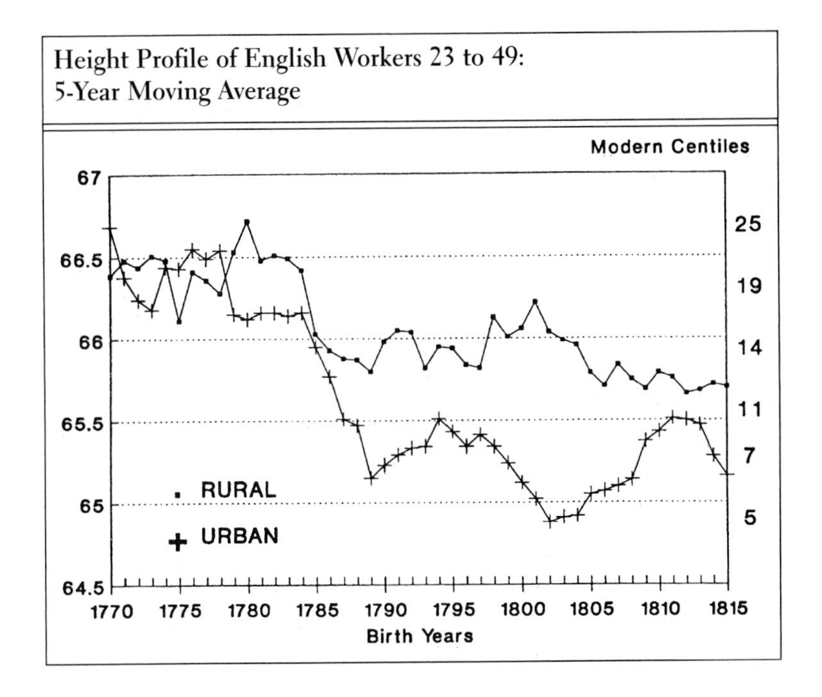

had fallen to centile 6, which approached the level of Creole slaves in Trinidad in 1813. The rural birth cohorts also experienced declining living standards: they began the 1780s sharing the living standards of turn-of-the-century Stuttgart aristocrats but ended up at approximately centile 12, slightly worse off than the Stuttgart middle class. The pessimists' case of deteriorating living standards is thus upheld for the pre-1820 period, particularly among the urban population.

Although there is no single powerful test of selectivity bias, the various tests reported hereafter put at risk the hypothesis that the decline in heights was an artifact of our data. Almost one-third of our convicts were tried in a county other than that in which they were born, but it is not possible to know whether the move occurred during childhood, adolescence, or after maturity. Assuming that all convicts who were tried in the same county as their place of birth were nonmovers, five-year moving averages of height for rural- and urban-born nonmovers showed the same profile as that for the whole sample. The convicts in our sample were convicted and transported after 1816, so those born in the pre-1790 period in [the] figure were older than those born in the 1820s. The lower tail of the distribution for older men—those born before 1790—was not truncated, nor was the upper tail of the distribution overloaded, which would indicate twisting or distortion in the height distributions. We can also reject a possible period effect: that crime became concentrated in poorer and shorter men as the century progressed. Organizing the sample by year of conviction, the distribution of heights for convicts transported before and after 1833 was normal.

The environmental insult causing the sharp fall in final attained heights illustrated in [the] figure was likely to have occurred during childhood, the years of adolescent growth spurt, or some combination of the two. Deficient food inputs, reflected in the higher prices of food relative to manufactured goods during that period, were caused by shortages and dislocations in food supplies resulting from the Napoleonic Wars and poor harvests. J. D. Mingay and E. L. Jones emphasized bad harvests due to the weather as the major cause of rising food prices, while M. Olson, G. Hueckel, J. Mokyr and N. E. Savin, and Jeffrey Williamson focused on the continental blockade and war. The number of harvest failures was significantly higher between 1790 and 1815 than either before or after, and weather was a significant factor in short-run price jumps in 1795, 1800, and 1812. The Napoleonic Wars, which closed or disrupted continental markets, increased the risks and uncertainty of international grain trade. Hueckel estimated that transport and transactions costs accounted for between 25 and 40 percent of the market price of wheat during those years. By the time young men born after 1780 had reached their final height, they had suffered sometime during their growth years from deficient food intake caused by poor harvests, war shortages, or both.

Because urban heights exhibited a different profile than did rural heights, the differences between the two data sets were unlikely to have been simply due to the differential impact of food supplies, though rural workers' access to food supplies meant they fared better than urban workers in times of shortage. Both the smaller average height of urban males and their different time profile relative to rural workers reflect the poorer health standards, substandard housing conditions, and overcrowding in Britain's cities. Although there were no major epidemics during this period, exogenous disease factors in Britain's growing towns and cities constrained urban height. How much of the sharp fall in and different profile of urban relative to rural height was due to disease, environment, congested living conditions, income irregularity, or greater work effort and how much to deficient food supplies is conjectural, but our urban height data identify a significantly greater fall in urban living standards than rural standards after 1780. . . .

Conclusion

Data on per capita income, consumption, and real wages are not robust enough to provide conclusive evidence on changes in living standards during the early years of British industrialization. The anthropometric investigation of human growth offers an alternative approach for assessing pre-1820 living standards. Because the English convicts transported to Australia before 1840 were broadly representative of the working class at home, data on their height can be used to measure changes in English living standards between 1770 and 1815. The height of both rural and urban workers fell significantly after 1780; rural Englishmen born in 1813 were almost 1 inch shorter than cohorts born in 1780, and urban Englishmen were over 1.5 inches shorter in 1802 than cohorts born in the late 1770s. The evidence shows that the growth spurt of English workers was delayed, that their growth continued much longer (at least until the age of 23), and that their final attained height fell from centile 20 in the 1770s to centile 6 for urban-born and centile 12 for rural-born Englishmen near the end of our period.

Using Ireland as a "control economy" relatively untouched by rapid industrialization, we discovered that English workers' growth spurt was delayed by one year and that during their growing years Englishmen were shorter than Irishmen, a gap closed by rural-born but not by urban-born Englishmen at maturation. This evidence suggests that English workers experienced falling living standards during the early years of the British Industrial Revolution.

Food shortages caused by poor harvests and the Napoleonic Wars explain much but not all of the decline in living standards before 1820. Although agricultural workers fared better than town workers during times of food shortage, the different pattern and more pronounced decline in urban heights imply that the poorer work and living environment in English cities also accounted for the shorter stature of urban relative to rural Englishmen. Besides urban-rural differences in height, significant regional variations in living standards were uncovered: workers in London and the south were shorter than workers in the north and the fringe.

E. P. Thompson

Time, Work-Discipline, and Industrial Capitalism

. . . It is true that the transition to mature industrial society demands analysis in sociological as well as economic terms. Concepts such as "time-preference" and the "backward sloping labour supply curve" are, too often, cumbersome attempts to find economic terms to describe sociological problems. But, equally, the attempt to provide simple models for one single, supposedly-neutral, technologically-determined, process known as "industrialization" (so popular today among well-established sociological circles in the United States) is also suspect. It is not only that the highly-developed and technically-alert manufacturing industries (and the way-of-life supported by them) of France or England in the eighteenth century can only by semantic torture be described as "pre-industrial." (And such a description opens the door to endless false analogies between societies at greatly differing economic levels.) It is also that there has never been any single type of "the transition." The stress of the transition falls upon the whole culture: resistance to change and assent to change arise from the whole culture. And this culture includes the systems of power, property-relations, religious institutions, etc., inattention to which merely flattens phenomena and trivializes analysis. Above all, the transition is not to "industrialism" *tout court* but to industrial capitalism or (in the twentieth century) to alternative systems whose features are still indistinct. What we are examining here are not only changes in manufacturing technique which demand greater synchronization of labour and a greater exactitude in time-routines in *any* society; but also these changes as they were lived through in the society of nascent industrial capitalism. We are concerned simultaneously with time-sense in its technological conditioning, and with time-measurement as a means of labour exploitation.

There are reasons why the transition was peculiarly protracted and fraught with conflict in England: among those which are often noted, England's was the first industrial revolution, and there were no Cadillacs,

From E. P. Thompson, "Time, Work-Discipline, and Industrial Capitalism," *Past and Present* 50 (1971).

steel mills, or television sets to serve as demonstrations as to the object of the operation. Moreover, the preliminaries to the industrial revolution were so long that, in the manufacturing districts in the early eighteenth century, a vigorous and licensed popular culture had evolved, which the propagandists of discipline regarded with dismay. Josiah Tucker, the dean of Gloucester, declared in 1745 that "the *lower* class of people" were utterly degenerated. Foreigners (he sermonized) found "the *common people* of our *populous cities* to be the most *abandoned*, and *licentious* wretches on earth":

> *Such brutality and insolence, such debauchery and extravagance, such idleness, irreligion, cursing and swearing, and contempt of all rule and authority . . . Our people are* drunk with the cup of liberty.

. . . [I]rregular labour rhythms . . . help us to understand the severity of mercantilist doctrines as to the necessity for holding down wages as a preventative against idleness, and it would seem to be not until the second half of the eighteenth century that "normal" capitalist wage incentives begin to become widely effective. The confrontations over discipline have already been examined by others. My intention here is to touch upon several points which concern time-discipline more particularly. The first is found in the extraordinary Law Book of the Crowley Iron Works. Here, at the very birth of the large-scale unit in manufacturing industry, the old autocrat, Crowley, found it necessary to design an entire civil and penal code, running to more than 100,000 words, to govern and regulate his refractory labour-force. The preambles to Orders Number 40 (the Warden at the Mill) and 103 (Monitor) strike the prevailing note of morally-righteous invigilation. From Order 40:

> *I having by sundry people working by the day with the connivence of the clerks been horribly cheated and paid for much more time than in good conscience I ought and such hath been the baseness & treachery of sundry clerks that they have concealed the sloath & negligence of those paid by the day.*

And from Order 103:

> *Some have pretended a sort of right to loyter, thinking by their readiness and ability to do sufficient in less time than others. Others have been so foolish to think bare attendance without being imployed in business is sufficient. . . . Others so impudent as to glory in their villany and upbrade others for their diligence. . . .*

> *To the end that sloath and villany should be detected and the just and diligent rewarded, I have thought meet to create an account of time by a Monitor, and do order and it is hereby ordered and declared from 5 to 8 and from 7 to 10 is fifteen hours, out of which take 1½ for breakfast, dinner, etc. There will then be thirteen hours and a half neat service.*

This service must be calculated "after all deductions for being at taverns, alehouses, coffee houses, breakfast, dinner, playing, sleeping, smoaking, singing, reading of news history, quarelling, contention, disputes or anything foreign to my business, any way loytering."

The Monitor and Warden of the Mill were ordered to keep for each day employee a time-sheet, entered to the minute, with "Come" and "Run." In the Monitor's Order, verse 31 (a later addition) declares:

> *And whereas I have been informed that sundry clerks have been so unjust as to reckon by clocks going the fastest and the bell ringing before the hour for their going from business, and clocks going too slow and the bell ringing after the hour for their coming to business, and those two black traitors Fowell and Skellerne have knowingly allowed the same; it is therefore ordered that no person upon the account doth reckon by any other clock, bell, watch or dyall but the Monitor's, which clock is never to be altered but by the clock-keeper.*

The Warden of the Mill was ordered to keep the watch "so locked up that it may not be in the power of any person to alter the same." His duties also were defined in verse 8:

> *Every morning at 5 a clock the Warden is to ring the bell for beginning to work, at eight a clock for breakfast, at half an hour after for work again, at twelve a clock for dinner, at one to work and at eight to ring for leaving work and all to be lock'd up.*

His book of the account of time was to be delivered in every Tuesday with the following affidavit:

> *This account of time is done without favour or affection, ill-will or hatred. I do really believe the persons above mentioned have worked in the service of John Crowley Esq the hours above charged.*

We are entering here, already in 1700, the familiar landscape of disciplined industrial capitalism, with the time-sheet, the time-keeper, the informers and the fines. Some seventy years later the same discipline was to be imposed in the early cotton mills (although the machinery itself was a powerful supplement to the time-keeper). Lacking the aid of machinery to regulate the pace of work on the pot-bank, that supposedly-formidable disciplinarian, Josiah Wedgwood, was reduced to enforcing discipline upon the potters in surprisingly muted terms. The duties of the Clerk of the Manufactory were:

> *To be at the works the first in the morning, & settle the people to their business as they come in,—to encourage those who come regularly to their time, letting them know that their regularity is properly noticed, & distinguishing them by repeated marks of approbation, from the less orderly part of the workpeople, by presents or other marks suitable to their ages, &c.*
>
> *Those who come later than the hour appointed should be noticed, and if after repeated marks of disapprobation they do not come in due time, an account of the time they are deficient in should be taken, and so much of their wages stopt as the time comes to if they work by wages, and if they work by the piece they should after frequent notice be sent back to breakfast-time.*

These regulations were later tightened somewhat:

> *Any of the workmen forceing their way through the Lodge after the time slow'd by the Master forfeits 2/-d.*

and McKendrick has shown how Wedgwood wrestled with the problem at Etruria and introduced the first recorded system of clocking-in. But it would seem that once the strong presence of Josiah himself was withdrawn the incorrigible potters returned to many of their older ways.

It is too easy, however, to see this only as a matter of factory or workshop discipline, and we may glance briefly at the attempt to impose "time-thrift" in the domestic manufacturing districts, and its impingement upon social and domestic life. Almost all that the masters *wished* to see imposed may be found in the bounds of a single pamphlet, the Rev. J. Clayton's *Friendly Advice to the Poor,* "written and publish'd at the Request of the late and present Officers of the Town of Manchester" in 1755. "If the *sluggard hides his hands* in his bosom, rather than applies them to work; if he spends his Time in Sauntring, impairs his Constitution by Laziness, and dulls his Spirit by Indolence[,]" then he can expect only poverty as his reward. The labourer must not loiter idly in the market-place or waste time in marketing. Clayton complains that "the Churches and Streets [are] crowded with Numbers of Spectators" at weddings and funerals, "who in spight of the Miseries of their Starving Condition . . . make no Scruple of wasting the best Hours in the Day, for the sake of gazing." The tea-table is "this shameful devourer of Time and Money." So also are wakes and holidays and the annual feasts of friendly societies. So also is "that slothful spending the Morning in Bed":

> *The necessity of early rising would reduce the poor to a necessity of going to Bed betime; and thereby prevent the Danger of Midnight revels.*

Early rising would also "introduce an exact Regularity into their Families, a wonderful Order into their Oeconomy."

The catalogue is familiar, and might equally well be taken from Baxter in the previous century. If we can trust Bamford's *Early Days*, Clayton failed to make many converts from their old way of life among the weavers. Nevertheless, the long dawn chorus of moralists is prelude to the quite sharp attack upon popular customs, sports, and holidays which was made in the last years of the eighteenth century and the first years of the nineteenth.

One other non-industrial institution lay to hand which might be used to inculcate "time-thrift": the school. Clayton complained that the streets of Manchester were full of "idle ragged children; who are not only losing their Time, but learning habits of gaming," etc. He praised charity schools as teaching Industry, Frugality, Order and Regularity: "the Scholars here are obliged to rise betimes and to observe Hours with great Punctuality." William Temple, when advocating, in 1770, that poor children be sent at the age of four to work-houses where they should be employed in manufactures and given two hours' schooling a day, was explicit about the socializing influence of the process:

> *There is considerable use in their being, somehow or other, constantly employed at least twelve hours a day, whether they earn their living or not, for by these means, we hope that the rising generation will be so habituated to constant employment that it would at length prove agreeable and entertaining to them."*

Powell, in 1772, also saw education as a training in the "habit of industry"; by the time the child reached six or seven it should become "habituated, not to say naturalized to Labour and Fatigue." The Rev. William Turner, writing from Newcastle in 1786, recommended Raikes' schools as "a spectacle of order and regularity," and quoted a manufacturer of hemp and flax in Gloucester as affirming that the schools had effected an extraordinary change: "they are . . . become more tractable and obedient, and less quarrelsome and revengeful." Exhortations to punctuality and regularity are written into the rules of all the early schools:

Every scholar must be in the school-room on Sundays, at nine o'clock in the morning, and at half-past one in the afternoon, or she shall lose her place the next Sunday, and walk last.

Once within the school gates, the child entered the new universe of disciplined time. At the Methodist Sunday Schools in York the teachers were fined for unpunctuality. The first rule to be learned by the scholars was:

I am to be present at the School . . . a few minutes before half-past nine o'clock.

Once in attendance, they were under military rule:

The Superintendent shall again ring,—when, on a motion of his hand, the whole School rise at once from their seats;—on a second motion, the Scholars turn;—on a third, slowly and silently move to the place appointed to repeat their lessons,—he then pronounces the word "Begin."

The onslaught, from so many directions, upon the people's old working habits was not, of course, uncontested. In the first stage, we find simple resistance. But, in the next stage, as the new time-discipline is imposed, so the workers begin to fight, not against time, but about it. The evidence here is not wholly clear. But in the better-organized artisan trades, especially in London, there is no doubt that hours were progressively shortened in the eighteenth century as combination advanced. Lipson cites the case of the London tailors whose hours were shortened in 1721, and again in 1768: on both occasions the mid-day intervals allowed for dinner and drinking were also shortened—the day was compressed. By the end of the eighteenth century there is some evidence that some favoured trades had gained something like a ten-hour day.

Such a situation could only persist in exceptional trades and in a favourable labour market. A reference in a pamphlet of 1827 to "the English system of working from 6 o'clock in the morning to 6 in the evening" may be a more reliable indication as to the general expectation as to hours of the mechanic and artisan outside London in the 1820s. In the dishonourable trades and outwork industries hours (when work was available) were probably moving the other way.

It was exactly in those industries—the textile mills and the engineering workshops—where the new time-discipline was most rigorously imposed that the contest over time became most intense. At first some of the worst masters attempted to expropriate the workers of all knowledge of time. "I worked at Mr. Braid's mill," declared one witness:

> *There we worked as long as we could see in summer time, and I could not say at what hour it was that we stopped. There was nobody but the master and the master's son who had a watch, and we did not know the time. There was one man who had a watch. . . . It was taken from him and given into the master's custody because he had told the men the time of day.*

A Dundee witness offers much the same evidence:

> *[I]n reality there were no regular hours: masters and managers did with us as they liked. The clocks at the factories were often put forward in the morning and back at night, and instead of being instruments for the measurement of time, they were used as cloaks for cheatery and oppression. Though this was known amongst the hands, all were afraid to speak, and a workman then was afraid to carry a watch, as it was no uncommon event to dismiss any one who presumed to know too much about the science of horology.*

Petty devices were used to shorten the dinner hour and to lengthen the day. "Every manufacturer wants to be a gentleman at once," said a witness before Sadler's Committee,

> *and they want to nip every corner that they can, so that the bell will ring to leave off when it is half a minute past time, and they will have them in about two minutes before time. . . . If the clock is as it used to be, the minute hand is at the weight, so that as soon as it passes the point of gravity, it drops three minutes all at once, so that it leaves them only twenty-seven minutes, instead of thirty.*

A strike-placard of about the same period from Todmorden put it more bluntly: "if that piece of dirty suet, 'old Robertshaw's engine-tenter,' do not mind his own business, and let ours alone, we will shortly ask him how long it is since he received a gill of ale for running 10 minutes over time." The first generation of factory workers were taught by their masters the importance of time; the second generation formed their short-time committees in the ten-hour movement; the third generation struck for overtime or time-and-a-half. They had accepted the categories of their employers and learned to fight back within them. They had learned their lesson, that time is money, only too well.

In all these ways—by the division of labour; the supervision of labour; fines; bells and clocks; money incentives; preachings and schoolings; the suppression of fairs and sports—new labour habits were formed, and a new time-discipline was imposed. It sometimes took several generations (as in the Potteries), and we may doubt how far it was ever fully accomplished:

irregular labour rhythms were perpetuated (and even institutionalized) into the present century, notably in London and in the great ports.

Throughout the nineteenth century the propaganda of time-thrift continued to be directed at the working people, the rhetoric becoming more debased, the apostrophes to eternity becoming more shop-soiled, the homilies more mean and banal. In early Victorian tracts and reading-matter aimed at the masses one is choked by the quantity of the stuff. But eternity has become those never-ending accounts of pious death-beds (or sinners struck by lightning), while the homilies have become little Smilesian snipets about humble men who by early rising and diligence made good. The leisured classes began to discover the "problem" (about which we hear a good deal today) of the leisure of the masses. A considerable proportion of manual workers (one moralist was alarmed to discover) after concluding their work were left with

> *several hours in the day to be spent nearly as they please. And in what manner . . . is this precious time expended by those of no mental cultivation? . . . We shall often see them just simply annihilating those portions of time. They will for an hour, or for hours together . . . sit on a bench, or lie down on a bank or hillock . . . yielded up to utter vacancy and torpor . . . or collected in groups by the road side, in readiness to find in whatever passes there occasions for gross jocularity; practising some impertinence, or uttering some jeering scurrility, at the expense of persons going by.*

This, clearly, was worse than Bingo: non-productivity, compounded with impertinence. In mature capitalist society all time must be consumed, marketed, put to *use*; it is offensive for the labour force merely to "pass the time."

But how far did this propaganda really succeed? How far are we entitled to speak of any radical restructuring of man's social nature and working habits? I have given elsewhere some reasons for supposing that this discipline was indeed internalized, and that we may see in the Methodist sects of the early nineteenth century a figuration of the psychic crisis entailed. Just as the new time-sense of the merchants and gentry in the Renaissance appears to find one expression in the heightened awareness of mortality, so, one might argue, the extension of this sense to the working people during the industrial revolution (together with the hazard and high mortality of the time) helps to explain the obsessive emphasis upon death in sermons and tracts whose consumers were among the working-class. Or (from a positive stand-point) one may note that as the industrial revolution proceeds, wage incentives and expanding consumer drives—the palpable rewards for the productive consumption of time and the evidence of new "predictive" attitudes to the future—are evidently effective. By the 1830s and 1840s it was commonly observed that the English industrial worker was marked off from his fellow Irish worker, not by a greater capacity for hard work, but by his regularity, his methodical paying-out energy, and perhaps also by a repression, not of enjoyments, but of the capacity to relax in the old, uninhibited ways.

There is no way in which we can quantify the time-sense of one, or of a million, workers. But it is possible to offer one check of a comparative kind. For what was said by the mercantilist moralists as to the failures of the eighteenth-century English poor to respond to incentives and disciplines is often repeated, by observers and by theorists of economic growth, of the peoples of developing countries today. Thus Mexican paeons in the early years of this century were regarded as an "indolent and child-like people." The Mexican mineworker had the custom of returning to his village for corn planting and harvest:

> *His lack of initiative, inability to save, absences while celebrating too many holidays, willingness to work only three or four days a week if that paid for necessities, insatiable desire for alchohol—all were pointed out as proof of a natural inferiority.*

He failed to respond to direct day-wage incentives, and (like the eighteenth-century English collier or tinner) responded better to contract and sub-contract systems:

> *Given a contract and the assurance that he will get so much money for each ton he mines, and that it doesn't matter how long he takes doing it, or how often he sits down to contemplate life, he will work with a vigour which is remarkable.*

In generalizations supported by another study of Mexican labour conditions, Wilbert Moore remarks: "Work is almost always task-orientated in non-industrial societies . . . and . . . it may be appropriate to tie wages to tasks and not directly to time in newly developing areas."

The problem recurs in a dozen forms in the literature of "industrialization." For the engineer of economic growth, it may appear as the problem of absenteeism—how is the Company to deal with the unrepentant labourer on the Cameroons plantation who declares: "How man fit work so, any day, any day, weh'e no take absen'? No be 'e go die?" ("How could a man work like that, day after day, without being absent? Would he not die?")

> *[T]he whole mores of African life, make a high and sustained level of effort in a given length of working day a greater burden both physically and psychologically than in Europe.*

> *Time commitments in the Middle East or in Latin America are often treated somewhat casually by European standards; new industrial workers only gradually become accustomed to regular hours, regular attendance, and a regular pace of work; transportation schedules or the delivery of materials are not always reliable.*

The problem may appear as one of adapting the seasonal rhythms of the countryside, with its festivals and religious holidays, to the needs of industrial production:

> *The work year of the factory is necessarily in accord with the workers' demands, rather than an ideal one from the point of view of most efficient production. Several attempts by the managers to alter the work pattern have come to nil. The factory comes back to a schedule acceptable to the Cantelano.*

Or it may appear as it did in the early years of the Bombay cotton-mills, as one of maintaining a labour force at the cost of perpetuating inefficient methods of production—elastic time-schedules, irregular breaks and meal-times, etc. Most commonly, in countries where the link between the new factory proletariat and their relatives (and perhaps land-holdings or rights to land) in the villages are much closer—and are maintained for much longer—than in the English experience, it appears as one of disciplining a labour force which is only partially and temporarily "committed" to the industrial way-of-life.

The evidence is plentiful, and, by the method of contrast, it reminds us how far we have become habituated to different disciplines. Mature industrial societies of all varieties are marked by time-thrift and by a clear demarcation between "work" and "life." But, having taken the problem so far, we may be permitted to moralize a little, in the eighteenth-century manner, ourselves. The point at issue is not that of the "standard-of-living." If the theorists of growth wish us to say so, then we may agree that the older popular culture was in many ways otiose, intellectually vacant, devoid of quickening, and plain bloody poor. Without time-discipline we could not have the insistent energies of industrial man; and whether this discipline comes in the forms of Methodism, or of Stalinism, or of nationalism, it will come to the developing world.

What needs to be said is not that one way of life is better than the other, but that this is a place of the most far-reaching conflict; that the historical record is not a simple one of neutral and inevitable technological change, but is also one of exploitation and of resistance to exploitation; and that values stand to be lost as well as gained. The rapidly-growing literature of the sociology of industrialization is like a landscape which has been blasted by ten years of moral drought: one must travel through many tens of thousands of words of parched a-historical abstraction between each oasis of human actuality. Too many of the Western engineers of growth appear altogether too smug as to the gifts of character-reformation which they bring in their hands to their backward brethren. The "structuring of a labour force," Kerr and Siegel tell us,

> *. . . involves the setting of rules on times to work and not work, on method and amount of pay, on movement into and out of work and from one position to another. It involves rules pertaining to the maintenance of continuity in the work process . . . the attempted minimization of individual or organised revolt, the provision of view of the world, of ideological orientations, of beliefs.*

Wilbert Moore has even drawn up a shopping-list of the "pervasive values and normative orientations of high relevance to the goal of social development"—"these changes in attitude and belief are 'necessary' if rapid economic and social development is to be achieved":

> *Impersonality: judgement of merit and performance, not social background or irrelevant qualities.*
> *Specificity of relations in terms of both context and limits of interaction.*
> *Rationality and problem-solving.*
> *Punctuality.*
> *Recognition of individually limited but systematically linked interdependence.*
> *Discipline, deference to legitimate authority.*
> *Respect for property rights.*

These, with "achievement and mobility aspirations," are not, Professor Moore reassures us,

> *suggested as a comprehensive list of the merits of modern man. . . . The "whole man" will also love his family, worship his God, and express his aesthetic capacities. But he will keep each of these other orientations "in their place."*

It need cause no surprise that such "provision of ideological orientations" by the Baxters of the twentieth century should be welcome to the Ford Foundation. That they should so often appear in publications sponsored by UNESCO is less easily explained. . . .

Michael B. Miller

The Bon Marché

. . . [P]aternalism was interjected into the Bon Marché's work environment because of the tensions and difficulties which that environment produced. This is a subject that requires a deeper look at the Boucicauts' work policies and the conditions they created for the Bon Marché employee.

The strains the new work system generated as the Bon Marché expanded into a full-scale department store could be seen in the large number of persons who left on their own. For example, 43 percent of the group who entered in 1873—the year after the first section of the new building was opened—left before five years, and of these a considerable portion did so in the first year. To be sure, the reasons behind this flight could be as varied as the causes for dismissal (and many reentered the store). Women often left to get married and army draftees might frequently not return, although quite a few did as their jobs remained available. There were also clerks who had been sent by their fathers to learn the new merchandising practices, and who then returned to the provinces to assume control of the family business. Others simply felt that they had learned enough to begin their own store, and left "to establish" themselves. But for the most part departures were simply listed as "left voluntarily" and probably reflected, as did the large numbers of persons who were fired for insubordination or failure to respect the rules, a feeling of discontent with the work system itself.

The tensions of working in a department store were illustrated by the salesclerks' pay. Many clerks entered the Bon Marché because overall

From Michael B. Miller, *The Bon Marché: Bourgeois Culture and the Department Store, 1869–1920* (Princeton: Princeton University Press, 1981).

salaries were far higher than what one could earn in the smaller stores or small shops. Nor did the status temptations of a middle-class career entail financial sacrifices. This was a white-collar curse that would come only with the following century. Compared to other working men, most of whom were fortunate to earn five or six francs a day, department store clerks were considerably well off. An income of 3,500 to 4,000 francs a year in nineteenth-century France was sufficient to enable one to live a modest bourgeois existence, especially if one was fed on the job. Annual salaries rather than daily wages were still another attractive feature. But the Bon Marché salary, for all its promise and security, nevertheless entailed a great deal of uncertainty and stress for the salesclerk.

The principal problem was the commission. This, admittedly, did not affect office clerks who worked on straight salary. They often entered at several hundred francs a year, received rather large annual increases so that they might earn over 2,000 francs after five years, and, if they stayed long enough, eventually rose to perhaps somewhere between 3,000 and 4,000 francs. But the fixed salary of sellers was often quite low. While there were a number of sellers who entered at or attained the relatively high pay of from 2,000 to 3,000 francs a year, they were the exception and may not have been on commission at all. Most sellers began at a salary that fluctuated from 300 to 800 francs and some entered *au pair* and received no pay for the first several months. Annual increases were customary, but a maximum of from 1,200 to 1,500 francs appears to have been the norm. Thus salesclerks were dependent upon their commissions to escape a working-class standard of living, and this in turn meant that they were at the mercy of the clientele's whims. The fate was not enviable. How many nightmare stories must have circulated daily through the halls of the great store, recounting the exploits of those shoppers who had to try on every dress or shoe or glove in the house, only to purchase in the end a mere trifle at best, or nothing at all, or perhaps several thousand francs worth of goods, all of which were returned the following morning? How many customers were garroted, guillotined, hung by their thumbs daily—in the wishful minds of frustrated sellers? The fantasies of newcomers who had lowest priority in "the line"—a system of rotation for waiting on clients—must have been especially gruelsome.

Commissions also posed a series of conflicts for salesclerks. There were conflicts between each other and between competing departments over the quest for commissions, conflict with office clerks who received bonuses for detecting faulty commission claims, and conflicts between the desire to sell as much and as often as possible and the need to maintain a posture of honesty at all times.

Even if the insecurity, conflicts, and forced tempo produced by commissions could be offset by the greater salaries one could earn, not all clerks who averaged perhaps 3,600 francs a year lived far beyond the precarious edge. For many it was an unstable life. Bachelors often congregated in special hotels for clerks. Others who had their own lodgings changed their addresses with great frequency (to avoid paying rents?). Occasional requests to the House for aid suggest that salaries offered little leeway for coping with unexpected needs. In some respects these conditions were a consequence of the clerks' adopted life style. Employees were notorious habitués of the music halls and cabarets, and their average annual expense on clothing and cleaning might reach 400–500 francs. Yet clerks were also expected to be well dressed for work, and all had middle-class pretensions, so that even the frugal employee was obliged to spend a fair percentage of his salary on his attire.

Employees who might work fifteen to sixteen hours per day in small shops also entered the Bon Marché for its shorter workload. But the hours were long, nevertheless. In the summer the work day extended from 7:30 in the morning until perhaps 9:00 at night, and in the winter from 8:00 in the morning until 8:00 at night (by 1889 the latter hours were maintained year around). And if the work day was shorter, the pace was harder. During busy seasons there were few slack moments for clerks or garçons, and on days of great sales the intensity of the tempo could be absolutely maddening. At no time were salesclerks permitted to sit down. Overtime work—without reimbursement—was not unusual. Nor did Sunday closings always mean Sunday holidays. At least in the early years, some or all of the work force were required to spend the day preparing new displays or working on other similar chores. By 1882 this practice apparently had changed, for there are references in Zola to Sunday outings by clerks. Still, certain services like delivery continued to work on Sunday, while on the Sundays before big expositions or on inventory Sundays it is likely that most, if not all, employees were expected to work at the House.

Health conditions were another matter of concern. Department stores as a group were criticized for their unsanitary conditions, particularly in regard to poor ventilation and the great quantities of dust that accumulated in back rooms and offices. Tuberculosis rates of commercial employees were reputedly among the highest in Paris. This may have fit the romantic self-image some department store clerks held of themselves, but the consequences were nevertheless dire. Dossiers of Bon Marché personnel entering before 1907 show that perhaps as many as one-fifth left for reasons of fatigue, health, or because of death. It is not surprising, therefore, that the Bon Marché and other stores gradually adopted a policy of not hiring persons over thirty, or that Madame Boucicaut set fifty years as the retirement age when she founded a pension fund. Many employees were well used up by that time.

The tensions of working at the Bon Marché could also be seen in the lure, and disappointments, of the Boucicauts' promotion policy. Undoubtedly most clerks came to the Bon Marché with dreams of one day entering the power structure of the store. Yet only a few persons could ever expect to rise to the level of administrator, and later director, and all the ranking positions together never comprised more than perhaps 10 to 12 percent of the work force. Many employees who entered in the 1860s did rise with expansion. But those who came after 1869 found that opportunities were far less available. By the time Zola visited the Bon Marché, there were over 2,500 employees and only 200 or so managerial positions.

But perhaps the greatest difficulty that employees encountered at the Bon Marché was the severe regimentation of the House and the impersonality of its bureaucratic organization. Most employees found their identity with the firm as a whole limited to the prescribed procedures that they followed as they carried out their specialized tasks. Thus it was far more difficult for the individual employee to develop a sense of a personal relationship with the House than it was in smaller firms or especially in the traditionalist small shops. When the employee did break out of the rigid specialization, he did so as a pawn, shifted about for specific needs, as on the occasion of great sales when clerks were at a premium and administrators arranged the wholesale transfer of personnel. At the same time, however, the employee was extremely vulnerable to the workings of all the organization and hence to the performance of persons whom he did not know and who worked in sections of the store that he might never enter. This was especially so for salesclerks, whose pay was dependent on the smooth functioning of the depot and delivery, and also the office where commissions were computed. But all employees were subject in some way to the interdependency of a system where a change in hours for a particular service, or even a delay on a given day, could affect another's work schedule and perhaps lead to overtime.

Authority could be equally impersonal. Unlike the small shops where authority was no less pervasive but where it emanated directly from the *patron*, the Bon Marché rarely brought the clerk into contact with Boucicaut himself. Orders were passed through a series of hierarchical levels, each of which demanded absolute obedience. It was also, as has been seen, an authority that regarded the employee merely as an instrument and used him accordingly, discarding him with little hesitation when he was ineffective or insufficiently tractable. It did so as well with little grace. Most clerks were fired with a brief "pass to the cashier, monsieur." In its most extreme form, authority at the Bon Marché was impersonal through its reliance on procedures that bound the employee from arrival when he presented a token of presence and submitted to roll call until departure, when a bell rang and he left through a specified door. Hence there was little room for individual initiative, and this regimentation was enforced by a corps of internal police—the inspectors—who were certainly the most detested persons in the store. These men maintained a constant surveillance over the personnel, exercised absolute authority to preserve absolute order, and were notorious for their ruthlessness.

The extent to which the system could be depersonalizing was most apparent in the conditions of that sub-group of employees, the garçons. These grown men who did the bulk of the physical labor and were paid less than the others—they generally began at 600 francs and received annual 100-franc increases up to perhaps 2,000 francs, with a few exceptions in a higher range—were obliged in almost every respect to surrender their individuality. They were attributed a demeaning title and were dressed in livery to appeal to the clientele. They also were given numbers which they wore on their uniforms and by which they could be identified. There was, in effect, an almost military character to their organization, even to the point where foremen chosen among them were known as corporals. Some were lodged in the store and slept on tops of counters or spread their folding beds wherever they could find sufficient space. To be sure, these "accommodations" were likely to be no worse than the miserable hovels most garçons had probably once called home, or the farm. But then garçons had, after all, come to Paris seeking a better life, and one would be hard put to see sleeping in a department store as the mark of a man on the rise. Not a few garçons, along with coachmen who shared many of their conditions, were fired for drinking.

The Boucicauts created, therefore, a very ambivalent world for their employees. On the one hand, they offered their work force the prospect of rising to dizzying heights within their organization and of working conditions that were perhaps better than those any other store in Paris could provide. Zola noted that the ambition of all clerks was to be accepted either at the Bon Marché or at the Louvre, and that a return to the smaller stores was looked on as a "downfall." But work conditions at the Bon Marché were also laden with tensions, and if commissions, promotions, procedures, and dismissals could go far towards adapting employees to the bureaucratic and competitive world of a *grand magasin*, they alone could never build complete organization men who would also feel a sense of personal attachment to such a world, or to the firm and *patron* that represented it to them.

And yet integration of this sort was the essential issue that the Boucicauts faced in their relationships with their personnel. It was the essential issue because absolute respect for authority, energetic pursuit of orders, courteous and professional service of clients, and the efficient processing of flows ultimately hinged on some feeling of identity between the lives of the employees and the goals of the organization. And it was also the essential issue because it touched on a matter that ran still deeper than the specific needs of the Bon Marché, although the fortunes of the firm were tied to this as well.

Department stores were creating not only a new kind of work force but a new kind of middle-class man. The middle-class dream had always envisioned a bourgeoisie open to all those whose birth or hard work or education entitled them to a place in it. But in the past the vision of an expanding bourgeoisie had also assumed a corresponding expansion of independent situations. Many bourgeois who came from the lower echelons of the class or worked their way up from the working-class fringe might begin their middle-class careers in salaried positions. Yet, with the exception of those who entered government service, the position of employee was rarely seen as more than a stepping stone in the stream towards independent proprietorship. Department stores, insurance companies, big banks, and other big operations like railroads, however, forced, a change in this current. Middle-class careers continued to expand, but now more and more they were being channeled into permanently salaried positions with an organization and within an impersonal and hierarchical work environment. The men who entered these careers continued to identify with bourgeois culture and to pursue the conventions of a bourgeois life style. But neither bourgeois respectability nor bourgeois status could cloak the reality of an occupational milieu remarkably similar to that of the working class (Zola was in the habit of referring to department stores as "the great steam engine"). Unmistakably, the emergence of white-collar work in mass proportions and under bureaucratic circumstances signaled a qualitative shift in middle-class life. For many it was a disturbing shift as well. Indeed if the white-collar worker was to become such a volatile factor in European society by the turn of the century, it was largely because of the strains that his working life placed on his pretensions. Thus, integration of the work force was the critical issue at the Bon Marché not only because the success of the firm depended in the end on the employee's adaptation to his new work environment, but also because it touched on the question of whether white-collar workers could be effectively reconciled to the middle-class world that they would now have to inhabit. Of this too ultimately hung the fate of the house, for not until the underpinnings to a new bourgeois culture were set firmly in place would its institutional representations themselves be secured.

To establish these underpinnings, to create integrated relationships between the employees and their work was, then, the most vital purpose that paternalism was to serve in the Boucicauts' efforts to build organization men. Like a number of their industrial contemporaries, the Boucicauts recognized that a new, institutionalized paternalism, reproducing in its own way the family relations of the traditional business household, could be adapted to far larger, far different, kinds of enterprises as a means of retaining a community spirit within an impersonal and rationalized work environment. The idea may have been a simple one, but its implementation was complex, for the Boucicauts never sought merely to counterpoise bureaucracy with a paternalistic veneer. Rather, they endeavored to blend the one with the other, restructuring and reorienting old household values to correspond to the style and the goals of their rationalized work system. In this way they could correlate their paternalism with their firm's structure and purpose, thus projecting an image of an internal work community to tie the personnel to the House, its leadership, and its dynamic aspirations. Basically wedded to the French household tradition, the Boucicauts were to cope with fundamental changes in their culture, not by abandoning its practices and its tenets, but by redefining these to fit their new needs and new ends. . . .

Nor is it difficult to see the spectre of control lurking just beneath the surface of these programs. If employees ate their meals at the store, then they were not likely to extend their breaks beyond the time allotted.

If employees spent their evenings in the store rather than in the cabarets and music halls, then they were also not likely to stay out late at night or to arrive late for work the following morning. And if employees accepted Bon Marché authority over their private lives, then they were equally not likely to question that authority when it was exercised during working hours at the House.

More important, paternalism that encouraged thrift, that sought to broaden the employees' minds, to refine their sensibilities, and to protect their virtue fell directly in line with the great dream of all nineteenth-century employers to check the development of working-class consciousness by turning their workers into bourgeois themselves (what, after all, could be more properly bourgeois than a piano in the living room?). Admittedly the battle in department stores, where most clerks had middle-class origins and middle-class pretensions, was already half won. But it was the other half—the prospect of what might become of this identity as white-collar conditions more and more approximated those of the working-classes—that quite rightly preoccupied the Boucicauts' minds. For bourgeois culture in the late nineteenth century, one of the great dilemmas was how to continue to expand its ranks without simply creating a new enemy in its midst. This is why so many white-collar employers sought to shore up the traditional bourgeois orientations by insisting on dress codes for their employees (at the Bon Marché, men were not only expected to be properly attired, but to wear top hats upon their arrival and departure). It is also one of the reasons why the Boucicauts so ardently sought to cultivate gentlemanly behavior among their personnel. This too, they hoped, would affect the drift of a "vague class, floating between the worker and the bourgeoisie."

Indeed, all of the Boucicauts' paternalistic programs were able to exert their draw on this drift by reinforcing a rigid distinction that existed within the House—and French society—between "employees" and "workers." The former term applied only to those persons who earned a fixed salary, and thus the men and women employed in the workshops, the individual workers like locksmiths and the several hundred women who cut catalogue samples, all of whom were paid an hourly or daily wage or perhaps were paid by piecework, were placed in the separate category of *ouvriers* or workers. The distinction was an important one, for it was strictly maintained linguistically and it suggested a separate class identity that meshed with a difference in function, even though both groups were, in reality, engaged in machine-like or semi-skilled work. But what gave the distinction particular meaning at the Bon Marché was that by limiting their paternalism to their employees alone, the Boucicauts could structurally confirm these status divisions, thereby erecting still further barriers between their employees and their workers. To be sure, the role of employees like garçons was somewhat vague here. But too much confusion between them and the clerks was avoided through such mechanisms as separate titles and separate dining rooms. And, characteristically, when a pension fund for workers was created in the 1890s, it was administered as a totally separate service.

But it was the overall implications of these programs—their catching up of the employees' lives in a larger store world where household conditions were at once reproduced and equated with the business goals of the firm—that again was most striking. By transforming the building in which one worked into the House in which one might learn and play and perhaps even live, and by structuring each of these experiences to correspond to the objectives pursued in one's daily work patterns, the Boucicauts essentially could repeat the same kind of message they had proffered with the provident fund: that the lives of the employees and the life of the House were one and the same. . . .

Sweated Industry, ca. 1900 This moving photograph shows an English family making cheap toys at home for low wages. Women and children were the backbone of sweated industry, and this husband may be filling in while unemployed. (*University of Reading, Institute of Agricultural History and Museum of English Rural Life*)

PART

Gender, Family, and Class

In the 1960s, much of the most dynamic research into the Industrial Revolution emanated from the field of New Social History, which concentrated on how ordinary people experienced large structural developments like industrialization, working-class formation, and urbanization. Today, the cutting edge of historical inquiry mixes these concerns with what some are calling the New Cultural History, a growing interest in how people gave meaning to their world. The most fruitful arena in this merger concerns the centrality of gender and the family to the process of industrialization. The historians who conduct this research focus on two principal issues: the role of sexual difference in shaping how men and women experienced and reacted to industrialization and the importance of gender as a constitutive element of the new systems of meaning derived from those experiences. In the first case, contemporary research builds on the work of early-modern historians who emphasize the operations of the family economy, especially the importance of each member's labor to the family's survival. By removing work from the home setting, the Industrial Revolution forced families to devise new strategies for survival. At the same time, the very different demands placed on men and women in and out of the household, as well as the rise of new cultural standards for appropriate gendered behavior, complicated this quest. The result was a hardening of the divide between men and women as it related to work and the economy. In studies concerned with the second issue, historians argue that gender—the set of meanings attached to sexual difference—also formed an essential component of the justifications proffered for the Industrial Revolution's impact on society. It bolstered the middle class's assertion of position and influence and validated the new power relations established in the workplace. But these historians also reveal the increasing tensions arising from these ideals, for families frequently failed to live up to these exacting standards.

In the first selection, an early and influential work in women's history, Louise A. Tilly and Joan W. Scott examine the impacts that the Industrial Revolution wrought on women's work and family relations. As manufacturing mechanized and moved out of the home, the family economy gave way to the family wage economy, in which survival depended not on each member's labor, but on the wages each member could contribute. This altered the relationship of daughters and mothers to their families. For daughters, opportunities to find employment outside of the household introduced greater freedoms and a new sense of self, but such independence often came at the high price of increased vulnerability. Many a young girl started her work life in domestic service but ended it in prostitution. Married women faced the increased difficulty of combining household and wage labor. The former often prohibited them from seeking the latter, a pattern reinforced by employers' reticence in hiring married women for fear that pregnancy and family demands would hinder their productivity. As a result, paid labor was closely bound to a woman's life-course. Most women worked before marriage, but withdrew if necessary during motherhood, only to return in old age. Nevertheless, society expected working-class women to remain economically valuable to their families, forcing many into unskilled, temporary, low-paid jobs, especially if that employment allowed them to stay home.

In her research, Elinor Accampo addresses similar concerns, but in a vastly different setting. Unlike Scott and Tilly's more general approach, Accampo focuses on one community. Using the technique of family reconstitution among ribbon weavers and metal workers in Saint Chamond, France, she explores alterations in family size and dynamics in the transition from proto-industrial to factory labor. Among her conclusions, Accampo argues that workers reduced their family size (and thus participated in what scholars have labeled the demographic transition to lower birthrates in industrialized nations), but not for the same reasons that prompted the middle class to restrict its fertility. Unlike bourgeois families that invested more emotional value in their individual children and placed more emphasis on raising their standard of living by having fewer of them, workers had fewer children as a response to the strains that industrialization placed on their families. No longer able to combine household and productive labor, but similarly unable to forego the wages that married women could earn, these families chose a conscious strategy of contraception as a means of survival. At the same time, poor living conditions also produced lower birthrates among working-class couples. In other words, smaller family size among Saint Chamond's workers was the result of voluntary and nonvoluntary circumstances.

Industrialization also weakened working-class families by destroying traditions of skill transference from father to son and by reducing their ability to survive independently. Married couples with children could rarely earn enough income to remain off the city's charity rolls, which opened their homes to much more intrusion than they had previously experienced. In the process, the paternalistic practices adopted by their employers influenced working-class organization and politics. In this manner, Accampo is able to skillfully draw connections among industrialization, family life, and politics.

The importance of gender as a tool for constructing meaning is an essential component of the last two selections. According to Leonore Davidoff and Catherine Hall, the domestic ideology that arose in nineteenth-century Britain became a unifying cultural ideal that cemented together the very disparate groups within the middle class. Whether small shopkeepers, professionals, or factory owners, all ascribed to a system of belief that relegated women to the home, effectively removing them from most public forms of economic life. It was unseemly for women to receive any type of formal occupational training and inappropriate to place them in close proximity to a large, male work force. To become middle class, then, meant upholding these domestic ideals. Moreover, these principles achieved legitimization in laws that limited women's use of their own property—giving gender a material as well as a cultural significance.

Nevertheless, like their working-class sisters, middle-class wives and mothers continued to fulfill significant economic roles. They brought both capital and contacts into their marriages and maintained the economic viability of many family businesses by preserving an all-important image of respectability. In addition, many lower-middle-class families remained dependent on female labor in some form or another—usually made more acceptable if the business was still linked in some way to the home. Finally, some women, widows and spinsters, had no choice but to participate actively in the economy, a position made much more difficult due to prevailing legal and cultural restrictions. The contradictions between ideology and these continuing practices highlight the true significance of gender in middle-class formation; it gave new meanings to female economic roles. In the end, domestic ideals limited women's economic possibilities and reduced the value of the contributions many women continued to make.

According to Sonya O. Rose, these gender ideals influenced working-class women and men, too. Employers used gender to define some jobs as skilled and others as unskilled. And gender became an important tool in setting wages. All of this had nothing to do with the nature of the work itself. Women's jobs were by definition unskilled and lower paid. Moreover, employers revealed just how arbitrary such decisions were by redefining some tasks as women's work when the need to decrease wages dictated it. In short, then, while some historians have demonstrated how industrialization altered the symbolic importance of sexual difference, Rose illustrates how gender in turn influenced the process of industrialization.

This influence is perhaps most evident in the development of paternalism, which Elinor Accampo and Michael Miller note in their selections. To Rose, gender and family ideals justified the labor-discipline noted by E. P. Thompson and the harsh living conditions Accampo examines because these ideals attached new workplace roles to something as natural and seemingly unquestionable as sexual difference. By fusing gender and familial rhetoric with the logic of industrial capitalism, paternalism grounded the new economic relationships created by the Industrial Revolution in a supposedly natural order. And like the modified notions of time-discipline, those ideals and the new economic order they validated became accepted facts of life. When working-class men began to demand a ten- and eight-hour workday, they also insisted on the "family wage," adopting the ideal that men worked to support a family while women toiled for "pin money."

Louise A. Tilly and Joan W. Scott

Women, Work, and Family

Early industrialization did not create dramatic changes in the types of jobs women did. Yet the changes associated with economic and urban growth did alter the location of work and increased the numbers of women working for wages. Most significant, in fact, was the spread of wage labor which accompanied industrialization. The decline of the household mode of production meant that women more often worked away from their homes. The concentration of certain jobs in specific regions or cities, moreover, drew young rural women farther from home than their predecessors had gone to find employment. For increasing numbers of women, as well, the essence of work was earning a wage. Since they were members of family wage economies, their work was defined not by household labor needs, but by the household's need for money to pay for food and to meet other expenses, such as rent. In the family wage economy the interdependence of family members and their sense of obligation to the family unit remained strong. The importance of family membership and family ties continued. As in the past, daughters and wives worked in the family interest. The old rules of the family economy continued to operate in new contexts. But changing conditions, and particularly the spread of wage labor, began to change the relationships of daughters to their families as well as the allocation of married women's time among their productive and household activities. . . .

From Louise A. Tilly and Joan W. Scott, *Women, Work, and Family* (New York: Holt, Rinehart and Winston, 1978).

Daughters in the Family Wage Economy

In the family wage economy a daughter's work continued to be defined by the needs of her family. Young children worked as soon as they were able to, and they were socialized to the notion that the family interest required their participation. As daughters grew older, family circumstances and the existence of job opportunities initially determined the type and location of their work. . . .

. . . [D]aughters of propertyless families in rural areas of England and France typically became domestic servants. Two-thirds of all domestic servants in England in 1851 were the daughters of rural laborers. We have no comparable national figures for France, but local studies reveal a similar pattern. Close to three-fifths of servants in Versailles in the period 1825–53 came from the countryside. So did more than half of Bordeaux's female servants. In Marseille, "virtually all of the city's domestic servants were immigrants." Of all domestic servants married in Marseille in 1864–71, 57 percent were migrants from rural areas. Similarly, in Melun in 1872, 54 percent of domestics were either migrants from rural areas of foreigners. The Sauget family is . . . illustrative. After several years as a farm servant, Juliette Sauget moved with her sister to Amiens, where they both found positions as servants. Another sister entered service in Paris. The Sauget family had four daughters, three of whom became servants. On the other hand, four of its five sons remained in the country.

Parents sent their daughters into service because such jobs were plentiful. The expanding middle-class populations of cities created more demand for household servants. No special skills were required of young girls. They performed a variety of household tasks, ranging from cleaning and caring for children to general assistance in family shops or businesses. The fifteen-year-old servant living in the household of a Parisian launderer in 1852, for example, helped in the laundry as well as with household chores. In addition, service offered a relatively secure form of migration for a girl. Having a place to live and food and clothing eased the adjustment of a rural girl to city life. . . .

Parents' interest in their daughters' jobs came not only from concern for their safety, but from economic motives as well. In the context of rural impoverishment, of tiny holdings inadequate for the support even of a couple, or of landlessness, children became increasingly vital resources. A daughter's departure served not only to relieve the family of the burden of supporting her, but it might help support the family as well. A daughter working as a servant, seamstress, or factory operative became an arm of the family economy, and arrangements were made to ensure her contribution even though she did not live at home. Sometimes emotional ties were sufficiently strong for girls to maintain contact with home. They visited their families, they brought other family members to live with them in the city, and they sent money home. The heroine of Samuel Richardson's novel *Pamela* may have amused many a real servant with her impossible devotion to purity and virtue. But they would have recognized the motives that led her to send money to her parents: "so that you may pay some odd debt with part and keep the other part to comfort you both." Marie R., daughter of a blacksmith in the French department of the Meurthe, entered domestic service in 1836, first in a large town near home, then in Paris. Her goal was to save some money in preparation for marriage. LePlay tells us that she managed to acquire savings and a small trousseau during seven years of work, always, however, "sending a part of her earnings to her mother."

Marie R. was undoubtedly exceptional. Most girls like her probably sent home only an occasional sum. The need to save a dowry, the instability of jobs in domestic service and the garment industry, and the low wages and periodic slumps of the latter particularly, made it unlikely that a girl would have money to spare. It may be, too, that distant daughters more conscientiously maintained ties with their parents when they hoped to receive a share of the family property. Landless parents, on the other hand, had little material hold on their daughters. Yet even when they left home, some daughters seem to have continued or tried to continue to contribute to the family. They remained active members of the family wage economy even though they did not directly draw on the family fund.

In some cases parents formalized a working daughter's responsibility to the family wage economy by arranging to receive her wages from her employer. The familiar option of sending a daughter into service thus was transformed into a family-wage-earning activity. The servant girls working at the Flahaut farm in France during the period 1811–77 are an example of this practice. M. Flahaut did not pay them directly. Instead he sent food or clothing or coal to their parents. Sometimes he paid the rent on their farms. Hubscher tells us that for certain farmers who rented their lands, daughters' contributions were "indispensable, without them it would have been impossible to cultivate the fields they rented." He adds that the " financial support" of the daughters for their parents "seemed absolutely normal" to both parties. It represented a "strong family solidarity which required a mature and economically independent child to contribute to the support of its relatives." Similar arrangements for parents to receive a daughter's wages were made with factory owners, especially those with paternalistic living accommodations. Writing of what he considered "an excellent practice," Villermé described such arrangements in Sedan in 1840:

> *Young people under 20 are not admitted to these pensions without the consent of their parents, to whom they always give all their wages until they reach 15 and sometimes even 20; they are allowed to keep their overtime pay, however, and spend it as they wish.*

Parents might even pay a small sum for a daughter's "apprenticeship" and then receive her wages when she began to earn them. Such control was difficult to maintain, of course. Many a rural girl obviously did lose contact with home. Long-distance migration made it inevitable that a departing daughter might eventually be lost to the family wage economy. What is surprising is that ties of family and the sense of obligation to one's parents long persisted among working girls. . . .

Yet once a girl embarked on her work, family ties changed. Daughters could become more independent of family controls than in the past. The location of work away from home, and the fact that they earned individual wages and lived in cities instead of small village communities, increased the autonomy of working-class daughters. Even if a working girl lived at home, her relationship to her family might change. As a wage earner she learned about money and what it could buy. She could contribute her wages and her knowledge to family decisions and she might claim some measure of influence over the allocation of family resources since her wages were part of those resources. The other side of independence, however, was vulnerability. Working girls earned low wages and their employment was often unstable. The loss of protections once provided by family, village community, and church increased a girl's economic and sexual vulnerability.

Gradually, despite the continuity of family values among rural and urban working families, changes in the organization of production and in the structure of occupational opportunity for women altered the relationships between parents and daughters during the nineteenth century. The results were both more choice and more risk for young women.

The availability in cities of jobs for women meant that girls were not restricted to domestic service. Often service was only the first step, a means of entry into the city. When a girl lost one job, she pursued others. Many a young woman moved back and forth between domestic service and the numerous unskilled trades in a city. Many of the garment trades were seasonal, too, forcing girls to seek other kinds of work in slack periods. When Charles Benoist reported on women's work in the Parisian garment industry, he wrote:

> *Yes, indeed, her budget balances. But with winter comes cold, with unemployment hunger and with sickness death. Irresistably, the question arises, How do these women who number in the thousands in Paris, how do they live? Live! Ask rather how they keep from dying.*

One grim alternative in Paris, London, and many other cities was prostitution. In 1836, Parent-Duchâtelet found that the majority of prostitutes in Paris were recent migrants. Almost one-third were household servants and many initially had been seduced by promises of marriage and then abandoned, pregnant or with an infant. He also remarked on the instability of women's employment which drove them to prostitution when they could not find work. Prostitution, in other words, was a form of employment for women when all else failed. Prostitutes in London told Henry Mayhew in the 1850s that unemployment had driven them to their "shame." One, the mother of an illegitimate boy, explained that she could not find work as a seamstress, and so to keep herself and her son from starving she was "forced to resort to prostitution." Another described the "glorious dinner" her solicitations had brought. And a woman explained her prostitution to the anonymous author of *My Secret Life* as her way of enabling the rest of the family to eat: "Well, what do you let men fuck you for? Sausage rolls" "Yes, and meat-pies and pastry, too."

Prostitution, of course, was a desperate measure. In good times, cities offered women a range of opportunities. Many left a first job in domestic service and found other kinds of employment. Indeed, for some women, the possibilities for earning money in the city, if not actually unlimited, must have seemed extensive to young girls from the country. And these jobs presented an alternative to returning to rural towns and villages where work was scarce and did not pay as well.

The existence of alternatives also meant that girls could reject the physically more demanding work of a farm, for example, and remain in the city, an option which earlier had not been available on the scale it was in the nineteenth century. Le Play's account of the experiences of the daughter of a small propertied peasant in the countryside of Champagne captures the process as it affected one family in 1856:

> *For the past two years, the oldest daughter has been sent to Châlons for part of each year, as an apprentice in a maison de lingerie. She is not paid, but receives her food free. After her apprenticeship is finished, she will be a domestic in a house in some nearby city. When she is at home, she helps her mother with her needlework and replaces her in caring for the household. [The mother was a seamstress and her earnings were "one of the principal resources of the family"] . . . but since she began going to the city, she does certain farm chores only with great repugnance. Despite her resistance, however, she is forced to thresh and to collect manure along the road.*

One cannot but conclude that, for this daughter, permanent departure was only a matter of time.

Another aspect of women's occupations, of course, was that, except in textile factories, wages were low and employment was unstable. Accumulating enough money to send home must have been impossible for many girls. Their consequent inability to help their families undoubtedly diminished contacts and ties with their former homes.

Whether or not they maintained contact, rural girls increasingly did not return home. The migration of the domestic servant, which in the past was often temporary, increasingly tended to become permanent. Even when a girl did keep in touch with her parents, the fact that she did not intend to return home loosened family ties. Rural girls no longer used their work as a means of gaining resources which would enable them to become farm wives. Instead they became permanent urban residents. . . .

Permanent migration of this kind was encouraged not only by expanded opportunities for women to work in cities, but also by changes in families themselves. When families became wage-earning instead of producing units, family members no longer shared a common interest in the property which guaranteed their livelihood. Of course, daughters often had left home in the past and so had not always worked on the land or in the shop. But the resources owned by their parents had had an important influence on their futures in the form of dowries or marriage settlements. When parents had no resources but their own and their children's labor power, they had few long-term material holds on the loyalties of their children. Of course, material considerations were not the only basis of parent-child relationships. The values of the family could and did transcend the conditions which gave rise to them. (Jeanne Bouvier accompanied her mother to Paris simply because she was her mother.) Membership in a family also provided many nonmaterial benefits. Again, Bouvier's experiences are illustrative. Family ties helped her find jobs and negotiate difficulties whenever she moved. But the absence of property often meant there was no reason to return home; indeed, it precluded such a return even if a child desired it.

Even when daughters remained at home, as happened more often in urban families, or when whole families migrated to textile towns, the fact that they earned wages had important effects on family relationships. Family members were no longer bound inseparably to a family enterprise. Instead, the goal became earning enough money to support the minimal needs of the group. The family wage was the sum total of individual member's contributions. Inevitably, in this situation, contributions became individualized. One might work with other family members, but this was not necessary. Children earned wages in textile factories, whether or not they worked alongside their parents. Spinners could hire children who were not their own as reelers and piecers. Ultimately, the wage (however low or unfair) represented remuneration for an individual's labor. . . .

A teen-aged child's ability to earn wages and, particularly in textiles, the importance of those wages for the family meant that children were no longer as dependent as they once had been on their parents. In fact, the roles might sometimes reverse, with parents depending increasingly on their children. In textile towns, for example, where work was most plentiful and most remunerative for young people in their late teens and early twenties, according to Michael Anderson "children's high wages allowed them to enter into relational bargains with their parents on terms of more or less precise equality." "The children that frequent the factories make almost the purse of the family," observed a contemporary, "and by making the purse of the family, they share in the ruling of it." In France, an observer at a later period bemoaned the decline of apprenticeship training and the easy availability of wage labor for children. As their wages increased and sometimes surpassed their parents', he wrote, children assumed they had the right to a say in family matters. "When the father earns more than his children, he still has the right to his authority; from the day they earn as much as he does, they no longer recognize his right to command." Furthermore, by earning wages a child established a measure of potential independence. She could move elsewhere and still earn her keep. Hence, while the ability to earn wages increased the importance to a family of a daughter's labor, it also created the potential for a daughter to leave home at an early age. . . .

Married Women in the Family Wage Economy

Under the family wage economy married women performed several roles for their families. They often contributed wages to the family fund, they managed the household, and they bore and cared for children. With industrialization, however, the demands of wage labor increasingly conflicted with women's domestic activities. The terms of labor and the price paid for it were a function of employer's interest, which took little account of household needs under most circumstances. Industrial jobs required specialization and a full-time commitment to work, usually in a specific location away from home. While under the domestic mode of production women combined market-oriented activities and domestic work, the industrial mode of production precluded an easy reconciliation of married women's activities. The resolution of the conflict was for married women not to work unless family finances urgently required it, and then to try to find that work which conflicted least with their domestic responsibilities. . . .

The sectors in both [France and England] which tended to employ similar proportions of married women were those created by the expansion of the nonmechanized garment trades and by urban growth, which increased the demand for unskilled, casual service workers. In the needle trades piecework could be done at home and so attracted married women. Census data give us no precise indication of the overall numbers of married women in the unskilled, temporary jobs increasingly available as urban populations expanded. Some women who worked at these jobs did not consider themselves formally employed, while others feared that reporting a job to the census taker would bring a visit from the tax collector. Yet it is clear from our analysis of the censuses of Amiens, Roubaix, and Anzin, and from studies of York, Preston, and Stockport, as well as from accounts by contemporaries that married women in both countries earned wages as carters, laundresses, charwomen, peddlers of food, and keepers of cafés and inns. The Sheffield knifemaker's wife described by Le Play in the 1850s prepared "a fermented drink called 'pop' which she bottled and sold in the summer to inhabitants of the city." She undoubtedly told the census taker that she had no occupation. . . .

Patterns of married women's employment reflected employer preferences for workers with no other demands on their time. Single women were more likely to work steadily, for longer periods of time, and without interruptions. Married women were likely to become pregnant and miss work, or their family responsibilities could keep them home. Married women were thus clustered in those jobs which were temporary and episodic, which corresponded to their less certain commitment to wage earning. These jobs were also low-paying, exploiting the usually desperate need that drove a married woman to seek employment and the fact that she had neither the skill nor the organizational support which might command higher wages.

Patterns of married women's employment also reflected household preferences. Men, who could command higher and more regular wages, were the family's primary wage earners. If more money were needed, children would be sent to work. Since the household benefited from the mother's management of domestic affairs and children, she only went to work when need was great, when her husband was unemployed or ill, and when there were no children at home who could work. . . . Full-time work was confined to the years before marriage and, perhaps, to the first year or two of marriage, before children were born. After children were born, women's work followed a more episodic course. Many simply withdrew from wage-earning activity. Others moved in and out of it, depending on family need. This was most often a consequence of what Michael Anderson calls "critical life situations"—crises caused by illness, unemployment, or death of the husband. The arrival of several children could also seriously strain family resources. At this point, too, women sought means of earning some money. Some took jobs outside the home, particularly in textile towns where those were the best-paying opportunities available. Others took on piecework to complete at home. Women workers in the London garment trades followed this pattern into the twentieth century: "Before marriage they go to the shops, and after marriage, if obliged to earn money, take the work home." More often, however, married women with young children improvised cash-producing activities to substitute for full-scale labor participation. As in the past, selling food, doing laundry, and taking in borders were the resort of urban working-class women. "Mrs. Jennings had been in service as cook in a gentleman's family. [When she married,] [i]n order to improve their scanty income, she took in a little washing, and she also washed for myself and fellow lodger." The English straw plaiter Lucy Luck "was in the workroom part of the time and had [her] work at home the other part." In the slow season, at one stage of her life she had to find other ways of earning money. "During that time I have been out charring or washing, and I have looked after a gentleman's house a few times, and I have taken in needlework. This was before any of my children were old enough to work."

As children grew older and found employment, the pressure on their mothers eased. This tended to be the period of lowest wage-earning activity by married women. Old age once again pushed them into the job market. Most crises of illness and unemployment for husbands came at this point, when children had left home and no longer contributed to the family fund. The wife then was the only substitute available for an ailing husband. When he died, she had to become self-supporting. Older women returning to work after long absences took whatever jobs they could find. Their low levels of skill and sporadic employment experience restricted them to unskilled, irregular, and low-paying jobs. Typically, even in textile centers, these were not in factories.

> *The unskilled workwoman at the bottom of the social scale . . . is generally elderly, if not aged, infirm, penniless and a widow, she never expected to have to work for a living, and when obliged to do so has recourse to the only work she ever learned to do [sewing]. She is nervous and timid and takes work at whatever price it may be offered her.*

Younger widows, with children to support, were in a similar, desperate situation.

Yet despite the fact that their work was irregular, married women were still expected to be family wage earners. The economist Nassau Senior routinely included in his calculations of family income, the wages "of the married labourer, those of his wife and unemancipated children." The French reformer Jules Simon, while decrying factory labor for women, nonetheless admitted in 1861 that "women's work is needed by the family." Le Play found that women's activities were "a significant supplement to the earnings of the husband." His and other calculations indicated that women's earnings accounted for from 10 to 50 percent of a family's income. It is clear, too, that women saw themselves as economically productive. A parish report described the rural woman in England, wife of a laborer, who could find no work because of an economic crisis:

> *In a kind of general despondency she sits down, unable to contribute anything to the general fund of the family and conscious of rendering no other service to her husband except that of the mere care of his family.*

This sense of an obligation to contribute economically continued among urban women of the working classes. In a factory town, women who did not take jobs were "looked upon as lazy." There was a work ethic held by women in working-class families that may not have been present among their middle-class counterparts. More exploration is needed of the reality or myth of the "idle middle-class woman" of the nineteenth century. But whether they were idle, as the standard accounts contend, or whether they worked hard, as Patricia Branca has argued, most seem to have remained at home. Some evidence indicates, for example, that middle-class husbands took on two jobs before permitting their wives to seek work. The cultural values of the middle classes may have prevented married women especially from leaving home to work. No such prohibition existed among the working classes, and though married women may have preferred to remain at home when family finances permitted it, they were expected to earn wages if necessary.

Yet increasingly, the contributions from married women were expected only if the wages of other working members were insufficient for household subsistence requirements. Their productive activity, in other words, became a kind of reserve, a last resort. That it was often used does not contradict the point. It only tells us how precarious were the lives of working families, how unstable or poorly paid men's jobs were, and how vulnerable to illness or death, and therefore to poverty, were even financially comfortable households. . . .

Elinor Accampo

Industrialization, Family Life, and Class Relations, Saint Chamond, 1815–1914

. . . The demographic profile of Saint Chamond provides two contradictory images of the working-class family. On the one hand, a logical family formation strategy of voluntary fertility control—whether through coitus interruptus, abstinence, or abortion—enabled the working class, and particularly working-class women, to cope with the new organization of work which had decidedly usurped from them a degree of power they had once exercised. Important here was not just the space in which they performed work, but the regulation of its hours. The introduction of inanimate sources of energy clinched the separation of work and family, home and factory, for which proto-industry had set the stage. To regain some control over their lives, workers adjusted their family strategies. Since children could earn wages only after some years of dependency and their care interfered with the mother's ability to contribute to the family income, fewer children posed less of a relative burden. These workers did not simply try to stop having children after their families had reached some sort of "target size." They also had children far more slowly than had workers in the past.

On the other hand, these workers' demographic profile also presents quite an opposite image. Work schedules interfered with conjugal relations and proper feeding practices, poor diets and disease inhibited fertility and caused infant and child deaths, and early adult deaths put an abrupt end to family formation. This profile hardly affords an image of more freedom or control in family life. Among these workers, low fertility was involuntary. Small families in Saint Chamond resulted from

From Elinor Accampo, *Industrialization, Family Life, and Class Relations, Saint Chamond, 1815–1914* (Berkeley and Los Angeles: University of California Press, 1989).

some couples consciously limiting births, as well as from other couples suffering ill health—and some may have fitted into both categories. In any case, having smaller families preceded having healthier children.

Not all couples who married between 1861 and 1866 exhibited control over their lives by having fewer children. Some had very large families. Just as in the first cohort, certain individuals in the second did not show any sign of pursuing a strategy of family limitation. But male occupations had no apparent influence on family size. Nothing about occupation per se motivated these workers to have large families, nor did it motivate them to have small families, as it had for ribbon weavers. Family formation ceased having anything to do with occupation. Workers in Saint Chamond, and no doubt in other industrial cities as well, began to produce fewer children as a response to an environment that threatened the survival of their families. In this respect the way their pattern of family formation differed from that of ribbon weavers has particular significance; rather than limiting births after attaining a certain family size later in marriage, metal workers and their wives hesitated to have children even at the outset of the marriage.

For most workers in Saint Chamond, restrictions on children's labor and the competition between household responsibilities and employment for women outside the household provide sufficient motivation to delay having children or to have them more slowly. The disruption of the family wage economy, rather than the desire to consume more goods or to preserve a way of life centered on the relationship between family and work, drove couples to have fewer children in whatever manner they could. A key element in this behavioral changes was the transformation of female and child labor. The economy in Saint Chamond had depended on the nimble fingers of women and children since the introduction of silk milling in the sixteenth century. Although child labor came to be restricted in the second half of the nineteenth century, the braid industry was built upon female labor and continued to depend upon it. The role of women's labor in the local economy no doubt helped prevent most male wages from becoming "family wages." At the same time, mechanization changed the relationship between women's labor and family life. Women in the second half of the century experienced greater difficulty earning wages inside or outside the home, and they had to cope with the absence of their husbands from the household. Smaller family size, whether it was due to deliberate effort or to ill health and death, reflected an adjustment to the new relationship between family and work.

Testimony from worker congresses in the 1870s and later indicates that industrialization had similar effects in other working-class communities, and it required some form of family adjustment. Beyond male occupations, numerous factors contributed to the logic of a family economy and family formation strategies, or lack thereof, among workers: most important, perhaps, is the nature of a local economy and the specific ways men's and women's work complemented or competed with family life. The effects of mechanization in Saint Chamond were particularly intense because in addition to eliminating most domestic industry, mechanization simultaneously transformed two major sectors, textiles and metal, and thus restructured the work of men, women, and children all at once. Finally, this examination of urban demography, in support of others that have preceded it, suggests that beyond work, less tangible factors associated with urban living—such as miserable living conditions and disease—discouraged large families. Just as with the first cohort, the logic of any strategy could become useless in the face of death, disease, and economic fluctuations—experiences far more familiar to industrial workers after 1860 than to their proto-industrial predecessors. . . .

The pronounced fertility decline in Saint Chamond over the course of the nineteenth century belies the image of workers as having large families that is presented in both current studies and those of nineteenth-century observers. The disparity, however, is more apparent than real. On the average, couples in the lower classes did have larger families than those in the middle and upper classes. For modern scholars and nineteenth-century social scientists, this fact has obscured the more noteworthy one that workers practiced family limitation. Fertility control among workers needs to be understood in its own context, both for what it can contribute to our knowledge about the fertility transition of the nineteenth century and for what it can tell us about the experience of industrialization among workers.

The terms *demographic revolution* and *fertility transition* imply a relatively sudden event resulting from a cause or set of causes which should be identifiable. In addressing this phenomenon, demographic research has thus far provided more description than explanation. Fertility control began in cities among the upper and middle classes. In France, the Revolution of 1789 accelerated a process that had already begun and helped make it a general phenomenon. The reasons for this spread remain unclear. Family historians generally link decline in family size with new attitudes toward children. Though they note that family life varied enormously by social class, they implicitly share the assumption that among all groups it changed in the same direction: emotional functions replaced economic ones. The lower classes have been considered "laggers" in making the transition to fertility control. Scholars assume that once they did begin to limit fertility, they did so for the same reasons the middle class did. Yet general causes for fertility decline among the European population as a whole have yet to be established empirically, and they remain elusive. The timing of decline among various populations defies generalization. No single factor can explain why urban dwellers, upper classes, peasants, workers, and, most puzzling, the French nation as a whole began to limit family size when they did.

Though the concepts of revolution and transition continue to compel researchers to seek general causes, community studies speak instead to varying, particular causes. Ostensibly, the fertility decline in Saint Chamond corresponds to the broader demographic transition throughout France and Western Europe. Workers behaved like the middle and upper classes in having fewer children. But their reasons for doing so were quite different. The way workers in Saint Chamond experienced decline in family size bears no relationship to factors demographers and historians have, up to this point, associated with the general demographic transition: higher standard of living, lower infant mortality, middle-class professions, and changes in the emotional nature of family life. Indeed, these workers continued to suffer a low standard of living, and infant mortality remained high.

The experience of the Saint-Chamonais demonstrates that fertility control did not spread as a result of upper-class values "filtering downward." It was for reasons of their own that workers tried to avoid having numerous children, and through the nineteenth century those reasons changed. Artisans in the early nineteenth century controlled reproduction because women's work conflicted with childbearing and childrearing. Though wives in families of both nail makers and ribbon weavers assisted their husbands, the work that women performed in ribbon-weaving families was at once more demanding and required more precise timing. Women coped with these demands by sending their children to wet nurses. The avoidance of breast-feeding made these mothers more fertile and thus necessitated more deliberate contraceptive measures. While metalwork made different kinds of demands on the wife's time, it too compelled some women to send their children to wet nurses and to avoid numerous births.

In the industrial context of the second half of the nineteenth century, family formation strategies changed. Birth control—whether through contraceptive efforts or through abortion—became more rigorous and more generalized throughout the population. Although the population of Saint Chamond continued to be a mixed one with regard to reproductive behavior, on the average couples delayed having children at the outset of their marriages and had them more slowly than in the earlier part of the century. They also ended their childbearing at an earlier point in their marriages. Fertility strategies in the industrial context still derived from the organization of work. No longer, however, did strategies have anything to do with work activities per se that earlier had created different patterns among metal and silk workers. The role of women in family formation remained pivotal during the period of large-scale industry: mothers had to leave the home to work in factories for the sake of family survival. But even when women could continue to perform labor in the home, the new organization of work conflicted with childbearing and childrearing because most men left the home to perform labor in rigid twelve-hour shifts. The absence of men from the home rendered the labor women performed there more difficult. While labor had always been divided sexually, the lines between men's and women's work in domestic industry had been far less distinct. Men and women shared tasks associated with both reproduction and production. In the industrial period, the tasks in both these categories became more distinctly gender-segregated and the lines between work and family life hardened. Until working-class women no longer had to earn wages, the new organization of work increased their burden. Since family survival depended on their continued contribution to production, the strategy they adopted to resolve the conflicting demands on their time was to reduce the tasks associated with reproduction.

Examination of the physical, economic, and political environment within which the Saint-Chamonais began to have fewer children demonstrates that smaller families resulted, not from new attitudes toward children, but from an environment that proved socially, economically, and physically hostile to traditional goals centered on a tight relationship between work and family. The logic behind decline in fertility among workers thus diverged completely from that of the middle class. It was, moreover, this very difference in the logic of family formation that governed bourgeois perceptions of working-class family life. Though workers' average family size continued to be larger than that of the middle class, it was not size itself that informed bourgeois perceptions. What disturbed the bourgeoisie was that workers formed their families in the context of poverty and an incomprehensibly different way of life: the need to earn wages, rather than emotional gratification, continued to govern working-class families. . . .

As the need for assistance increased, migration and mechanization of labor made it more difficult for families to meet their own needs. "Chain migration" eased the stress of uprootedness but could not eliminate it. Crises that provoked the move from village to city, such as the death of a parent or a spouse, also made settling in an urban context more difficult. Migration also created a gap between generations that mechanization deepened. In the 1860s, more men and women had parents working in agriculture than their artisanal predecessors had had. Even when the older generation did work in industry of some kind, they could no longer transmit useful skills to their offspring. Children ceased adopting the same occupation as their parents; parents stopped teaching children work skills and passing on traditions associated with work. Certainly, in some cases industrial change opened new doors to the children of these workers, and the break in generational bonds meant upward mobility. But for most workers in the second half of the nineteenth century, industrialization meant fewer opportunities to learn skills. Unskilled work in a continually fluctuating industrial economy forced people to change jobs and residences frequently. Occupational and geographical instability made the establishment of new cultures and associations centered on work difficult at best.

Abbé Cetty labeled this process a "decline of paternal authority" in the working-class home. Whether or not the working-class father lost status among his children, the authority and power of the family vis-à-vis employers did decline. Mechanization of work gave employers, the owners of machines, a greater measure of control over the workplace as well as over the worker. The workplace became an arena for discipline and training, as well as for reinforcing morality through such organizations as the Association des Patrons Catholiques and *cercles catholiques*.

Both physically and culturally, the working-class family became more permeable to middle-class attentions. The experience of industrialization in Saint Chamond conforms to the model of industrial discipline Michelle Perrot formulated: the worker family had in fact served as the original source of industrial discipline. Mechanization transferred the paternalistic set of social relationships from the family to the factory. The "fatherly" presence of the employer in the place of production, the treatment of workers as "children," and acceptance by workers of these social relationships constituted three main elements of industrial paternalism.

Though effective, paternalism in Saint Chamond had limits. The republicanism, strike activity, unions, and socialist and anarchist clubs indicate that the elite did not succeed in exerting complete hegemony over workers. Yet class relations did remain relatively harmonious. On a material basis alone, the effort to help workers, combined with the real need for assistance, helps to explain why class relations in Saint Chamond differed from those in neighboring cities. Whether or not paternalism "succeeded" is less important than understanding how and why it operated.

The study of Saint Chamond demonstrates that paternalism in employer-worker relations cannot be understood without an examination of workers' family lives and material conditions. Mechanization, urbanization, migration, and the values of the bourgeois elite placed workers in a vicious cycle. The uprootedness of moving to the city, the removal of work from the home, and the devaluation of labor resulting from mechanization made it possible for many workers to meet their own needs. The lost ability to pass knowledge from one generation to another, frequent job and residence changes, and insufficient wages made it difficult for workers to form associations that would sustain them both materially and politically. At the same time, the industrial elite of Saint Chamond provided the needed material aid and accompanied it with their own moral and political indoctrination. The provision of aid served as a further obstacle to the formation of independent workers' associations.

The religious orders in Saint Chamond meanwhile enjoyed extensive visibility. They had been an intricate and highly praised part of local history ever since Archbishop Ennemond ventured into the Gier valley in the seventh century. Their alliance with the elite had always been powerful, but it became especially crucial with industrialization and the movement toward democracy. Because clerics administered charity, the Catholic industrialists could manipulate local political sentiment. They equated anticlericalism with the disappearance of material assistance. Anticlericalism thus turned many workers away from support of radical republicans and socialists. As a result, the left wing could not sustain electoral support in local government. Without control over the municipality, the left could not control charitable institutions such as the hospice and the *bureau de bienfaisance*. Lacking municipal support, workers faced yet more obstacles in establishing such key institutions as a Bourse du Travail. They had little choice but to accept help from their reactionary employers.

In Saint Chamond, the specific combination of industries, their simultaneous mechanization, and the Catholicism and monarchism of its industrial bourgeoisie distinguished the experience of its working class during the nineteenth century. The microscopic examination possible only in a local study uncovers mechanisms from which generalizations may be made. From both a demographic and a cultural perspective, where industrialization developed intensively and rapidly, it destabilized the working-class family. Change in family structure constituted a response to, as well as a symptom of, the distress workers experienced. Material conditions among workers, as mortality rates indicate, made family survival more difficult. Workers had two alternatives: they could develop independent mutual aid, or they could depend on employers and the local elite for assistance. Numerous factors determined which route workers followed. In communities that continued to have artisans, independent workers' associations developed more readily. Workers in communities with factory work and many recent arrivals to the city faced more difficulty in forming associations. Provision of employer-sponsored mutual aid and the availability of care from hospice institutions and *bureaux de bienfaisance* in such situations filled a need that workers could not, or did not, meet themselves. Whether workers became militant or passive through this process depended on their opportunities or abilities to become self-reliant as a class.

Leonore Davidoff and Catherine Hall

Family Fortunes

Women's identification with the domestic and moral sphere implied that they would only become active economic agents when forced by necessity. As the nineteenth century progressed, it was increasingly assumed that a woman engaged in business was a woman without either an income of her own or a man to support her. She already shared with the men of her class the spiritual stumbling blocks to active pursuit of business. But unlike a man whose family status and self-worth rose through his economic exertions, a woman who did likewise risked opprobrium for herself and possible shame for those around her. Structured inequality made it exceedingly difficult for a woman to support herself on her own, much less take on dependants. But beyond the negative effects on women who openly operated in the market, the construction of domestic ideology and the lure of new patterns of consumption offered attractive alternatives. . . .

A number of developments fostered the contradiction between women's perceived and actual relation to the economy. One of the most important was the growth of scale, creating divisions between larger and smaller operations. The 26 per cent of Suffolk farms where only family labour was employed would be a vastly different setting for the farmer's wife and female relatives than for a woman like Jane Ransome Biddell whose husband farmed over 1000 acres, and where numerous servants including a housekeeper were employed, releasing her to take part in the cultural and intellectual life of nearby Ipswich. In manufacturing, the cannibalizing of modest independent workshops by larger, better financed concerns, spelt the doom for many female entrepreneurs. As such enterprises were drawn more heavily into the regional or even national market, the tendency was to specialize, to produce for agents or middle men who would consolidate products. The shift to arable farming, for example, meant that in Essex and Suffolk subsidiary activities like dairying sharply declined, precisely the area of farm work which had

From Leonore Davidoff and Catherine Hall, *Family Fortunes: Men and Women of the English Middle Class, 1780–1850* (Chicago: University of Chicago Press, 1987).

been traditionally women's work. Cheese making, which had taken place on almost every farm over a certain size, where the farmer's wife used her own labour augmented by her daughters, nieces, sisters or living-in dairy-maids, shifted to centralized production in other parts of the country. By 1843, when the Royal Commission on Women and Children in Agriculture made its investigation, it was announced that the patience, skill and strength needed to produce cheese made this work unsuitable for women. The preferred activities of corn growing and cattle fattening "give but little trouble to the housewives of the present generations" according to an Essex commentator.

The general trend to supersede craft training and experience was particularly disadvantageous for women, compounded by their exclusion from a more scientific culture. In farming, for example, the introduction of both hand and steam powered machinery, and the use of chemistry for fertilizers increased impediments for women farmers. Larger units of production with more rational work flows implied a larger workforce increasingly made up of day labourers, most of whom no longer had a chance of becoming independent producers, thus destined to remain social inferiors. There was a growing feeling that genteel women, particularly the young and unmarried, should be removed from contact with such a workforce both by physical separation and psychological barriers. With a predominantly male workforce, it was even more difficult for women to wield authority. This is sharply illustrated by changes in farming practice. For a variety of reasons, since the mid eighteenth century, there had been a gradual displacement of female labour from the fields, except for casual seasonal tasks. The suitability of field work, indeed any outdoor work for women, was almost always discussed in moral terms, thus turning attention from the practical questions of directing labour. According to a Suffolk social commentator,

> *Our inquiries have convinced us that it (field labour) is a bad school of morals for girls and that the mixing up with men on whom poverty and ignorance have encrusted coarse and vulgar habits, tends to greatly uncivilise and demoralize women of maturer years; single women whose characters for chastity are blemished, work in the fields, the topics of conversation and the language that is used amongst the men and women are described as coarse and filthy.*

Such attitudes multiplied the problems already faced by farmer's wives who no longer acted as house-mistress overseeing the men's domestic life. Supervision of field work on far-flung acreages meant riding horseback, often alone, to deal with the labourers. While this may have given added status and authority to male farmers, thus "elevated above their work force," it ran contrary to notions of feminine propriety.

These factors bore particularly heavily on women operating in their own right. As long as their economic contribution remained within the family they could continue to be active. It was external relations which raised more acute difficulties. In addition to dealing with a wage labour force, there were also clients, bankers, solicitors and agents. These would be men with increasingly fixed expectations of appropriate feminine behaviour. Many of these men, while willing to act as protectors and intermediaries for dependent women, would neither expect nor countenance their independent economic action.

Within this pattern, certain activities became more closely associated with one or the other gender. Some of these connections stemmed from previous male monopolies through the gild system, even where it had faded to a remnant. The exclusion of women from the ranks of the building trades—joinery, wheelwrights and smiths—had serious consequences since it was from these crafts that engineering, surveying and architecture developed. Other gender typing was of more recent origin. The equation of outdoor activity with men, and the indoors as the setting for respectable femininity affected the division of labour in a myriad of ways from farming, as above, to the expectation that within an enterprise women could do preparation of products and services or finance as long as these activities were kept out of sight.

An effort was made to have certain tasks performed by the expected gender. If a family failed to produce the requisite boy or girl, man or woman, the wider kinship or friendship network could be tapped to make up the deficiency. Among the better off, hired labour of the correct age and sex could be substituted. In lesser establishments, tasks usually assigned to one gender might have to be undertaken by the other, at least behind closed doors. This crossing of such a significant boundary, if made visible, could be taken as a sign of social inferiority when social status was crucial to building a picture of creditworthiness. The equation of women with domesticity came to be one of the fixed points of middle-class status. Yet the development of the market did offer some enticements for women to use their skills if not their capital. It may, indeed, be argued that the concerted attack on any display of female *sexual* independence may have much to do with fears about new opportunities for their *economic* activity.

Women and Property

As Ann Whitehead has succinctly argued, property forms indicate relationships between people mediated by the disposition and control of things. The middle class in this period, far from taking the opportunities afforded by the move away from land as the main form of property, continued to build on the principles of patrilineality, and patriarchy. Middle-class women continued to be on "the margins of ownership" in a manner analogous to the restraints often imposed on working-class women (particularly when married) who had to or wished to sell their labour power within artisan culture. Intense fears surrounded the "impertinent" independent mill girl who refused the paternalistic discipline of domestic service or even the oversight of the parental home, and who might also, it was felt, refuse to fit the role of respectable working-man's wife. A similar if less often expressed alarm surrounded the idea of middle-class women using their skills or property to establish independent careers. It could, in fact, be argued that much of the concern about women working in mines and fields expressed in the 1840s was a transplanted discussion of deep seated uneasiness about the middle class itself. Although he was proud of his daughter who ran a successful school, a Quaker farmer solemnly warned her that she would never marry if she was known "only as a School Mistress."

The relationship of women to property had never been made explicit. While John Locke had directly linked the concept of property ownership to independence, both he and Thomas Hobbes did not clarify how women's control of property and their expected subordination within the family could be reconciled. In legal and practical terms, if anything, women's position had deteriorated from the seventeenth century. As landowners in their own rights, women were vastly underrepresented. They made up only 4 per cent of the 404 landowners in Suffolk at mid century and almost all their land was in small parcels. In the gentry, at least freehold land—real property—had been returned to a woman's control after her husband's death. Middle-class property was . . . mainly in other forms: leasehold and copyhold land, buildings, investments and effects, which had foregone even this limited right. With the ending of customary rights of dower, a development recognized by law in 1833, marriage virtually turned legal control of a woman's property permanently over to her husband. . . .

This is not to say that the *aggregate* of small investments held by women was not an important source of capital in early commercial and industrial development. Quite the contrary; economic historians have begun to recognize that women could make up a substantial proportion of those with financial resources. When as Essex village vestry wanted to build a workhouse school they raised a loan by selling annuities, one-third of which were bought by women. The portfolio of Mrs Henstridge Cobbold (*sic*) from the Ipswich brewing family included bonds in the local canal, rail road and insurance companies as well as the Ipswich Gas Light Company; the last investment was also held by her friend Jane Ransome Biddell whose farmer husband acted as Mrs Cobbold's financial agent. Nor should the above discussion give the impression that some women, at least, did not take an active interest in their own financial affairs; women such as the personal clients of Birmingham's earliest stockbroker, Nathaniel Lea.

Nevertheless women's property, so closely tied to their lifecycle status of daughter, wife and widow, only allowed at most a semi-independence. This limitation was compounded by problems of maintaining their own and their family's status precisely by *not* being openly involved in market activities. Once these overlapping forces are understood, it becomes more understandable why it was so difficult for women to form groups based on mutual interest which also relied on mutual control and manipulation of funds or property. The formation of such groups was a commonplace for middle-class men. Men created and ran societies and organizations grounded on corporate property not only to conduct business but for political, cultural, intellectual and even social life. The bonds forged on the basis of communal control of funds contributed to group loyalties even if only a "kitty" built up for an annual convivial evening at a local inn. There seem to be no female equivalents to these informal or semi-formal groups. Women could only operate property through kinship networks which, by definition, included both sexes. There is some evidence from the wills and census sample that sisters, and to a lesser extent, aunts and nieces, shared property as well as ways of making a livelihood in all-female households, but this was a mainly unmarried minority. The limitations on women's control of property, then, had not only serious implications for individuals but more generally for the ties of women to each other and the possibility of creating any but the most ephemeral alliances to support their mutual interests.

Women's Contribution to the Enterprise

In the earlier part of the period when household and enterprise were so intermingled there was only a narrow line between the prohibition on married women acting in a business capacity and their encouragement to pledge their husband's credit as a housekeeper. As the nineteenth century progressed, however, the view hardened that female relatives were and should be dependents. The move to separate family affairs from business was a potent expression of these changes. The same forces which favoured the rise of the private company and ultimately the business corporation, the development of public accountability and more formal financial procedures also shifted the world of women ever further from the power of the active market.

Within this context, it is not surprising that the transformation of honorary positions into salaried posts which has been observed for men is scarcely discernible for women. There was no precedent for female access to a post such as parish clerk, for example, which became secularized in the nineteenth century. The parish clerk had derived from the clerical assistant to the priest, described in an Essex parish as "a man who is able to make a will or write a letter for anyone in the parish . . . the universal father to give away brides, and the standing god-father to all new born bantlings." Women had to wait until the late nineteenth-century establishment of bureaucratic positions based on meritocratic principles for which they could prepare themselves and to which they could appeal.

A second consequence of economic dependency has been the overshadowing of women's contribution to the enterprise. Recent sociological studies have had to rediscover the vital part played by wives in small businesses and the support systems they provided for many male occupations, the recognition of women as a "hidden investment." But in the nineteenth century female involvement in the enterprise was widespread, not just wives but also daughters, sisters, nieces, mothers, aunts, cousins and occasionally unrelated female "friends." First, there is abundant evidence for the direct contribution of women's capital to the family enterprise. The son of an Essex farmer whose brothers had all become farmers was able to combine his self-education with £800 brought by his wife at marriage to start a successful boys' school. When her father died leaving £600 the school was expanded into purpose-built premises. Among the lower middle class, women were constantly used as sources of small sums to start off a business or as credit. In 1831, an Ipswich baker, facing a series of heavy financial demands, borrowed £4 from two of his sisters-in-law to pay off his flour supplier. . . .

The skills and contacts women brought could enrich male careers. In food manufacturing businesses it was the recipe provided by a sister or a wife which became the secret of success. Some women who had been in domestic service had access to employers' good will. A quondam master might stand guarantor or even give a legacy. A Birmingham bookseller's prosperous business was based on the batch of books given to his sister when she left service. Service gave young women wider horizons and specialized skills. An Essex woman, having been an upper servant in a town family, returned to marry a man from a farming family who had descended to being a wage-paid team man. Marriage to this "remarkable woman" who was able to do dressmaking as well as help run the farm, restored the family to independent farming. Women like these sometimes provided one of the leading elements in commercial success, literacy. A contemporary who admired the wealth and position of an illiterate Birmingham auctioneer noted that:

> *Providence had given him a help-meet who conducted his correspondence, superintended his books, graced his hospitable board, and otherwise, by the ease and unaffected politeness of her demeanour, and the use of good, sound common sense, had contrived to make his name respected and his acquaintance deserved by men of all grades and people of all denominations.*

It has been recognized that personal contacts played a central role in the functioning of both household and enterprise. Men took a keen interest in these affairs, their letters and diaries are filled with gossip about family and friends and their attendance at social gatherings. Nevertheless, women held a special place in building and maintaining relationships. Sisters, aunts, grandmothers and female cousins were ardent matchmakers. They arranged visits for their offspring and themselves paid long visits to relatives. They gave and received gifts. It was the farmer's wife who provided the Christmas goose to be dispensed to patrons and kin. A mill owner's wife admitted that she wrote letters more often than her husband for "he considered it more my province to keep up a correspondence with our distant relatives and friends." The fact that women more often designated people by name when leaving their small properties at death—a locket to a niece, a petticoat to a sister—emphasizes the importance of personal contacts in their lives.

Women's contribution to the enterprise was centred above all in the creation of its personnel. The marriage of sisters and daughters was a prime source of partners. But beyond this, women bore and raised the next generation of sons and nephews, the future partners and entrepreneurs. This task must, indeed, have consumed much time and energy for mothers and the other women involved, particularly as the physical and moral care of children had become a serious and self-conscious issue. The average of seven plus children borne to a family absorbed the married woman's life span from her late 20s (average age at birth of first child was 27.3) to her 40s (average age at birth of last child was 40.6), with birth intervals of fourteen to twenty months. Aunts and older sisters also played a prominent part in raising children. They, like mothers, provided the orderly, disciplined framework which was the basis of the serious Christian household. These women saw moral and religious training as the core of their educational function. They also recognized the importance of understanding the natural world, often seen as an adjunct of the Creator's great design. Even the youngest children were started on the path to habits of self-discipline, fitting for both a commercial and religious future. The daughter of a farmer married to a bank manager looked back in late middle age on the problems of child-rearing. She emphasized the need to arrange the day in a regular pattern of activities with time periods allotted to each. Even for a toddler sitting at a table stringing beads, "there should be a degree of perfectness and even something approaching to business habits encouraged and expected even in these little amusements to give a worth and interest to them. Perfect play is the anticipation of perfect work." . . .

These instances may support the contention that, in a broad sense, women contributed cultural as well as monetary capital to the economic life of the middle class. Both these forms, however, were more indirect than the use of women's labour. Where property and educational resources were more limited, there is abundant evidence that women were working at a wide variety of tasks within the family enterprise. Their general usefulness was recognized in the advice given to young Samuel Courtauld by a business associate of his father: "[I]f a good wife fell in your way I would take her as an assistant even though she may not be rich in the World's wealth."

Occasional or even continuous use of wives', daughters' or sisters' labour was easier when living quarters were near or in the working space. As late as 1854, a letter from the wife of an Essex tradesman assumed the combination of household and commercial tasks: "In settling into my new home and duties here in the business-house, I have earnestly desired to fill my situation rightly, to be enabled to walk before our household in the fear of the Lord." In some cases, the wife would run a business next door to and often related to that of her husband, thus in the directories are found husband and wife teams of a clockmaker and tea dealer, a grocer and pork butcher. In villages, the wife or daughter/sister of a farmer might use the front room as a small shop. At a more elevated level, James Bisset, who was a Birmingham manufacturer of some standing, enjoyed a hobby of collecting to the point where he turned his house into a commercial museum run by his wife. . . .

In their capacity as status bearers for their households, adult women faced a number of contradictory pressures. They were expected to be seen at specified public functions and often had to go from home to pay visits, if not buy household supplies or do errands for the family business. But over the period there was increasing social derogation for women who openly walked or rode horseback except for non-utilitarian recreational or health reasons. In the eighteenth century, a prosperous farmer and brewer's wife thought nothing of riding on horseback the 20 odd miles from her village to the market town to transact her business. But with the growing emphasis on the protection of women, light-wheeled vehicles came to be their acceptable mode of transport, although more expensive to maintain than riding horses. Lack of access to means of mobility and the risks of losing status by being seen in many public places, particularly alone, was a serious disadvantage to a woman doing business.

Such obstacles to physical and social mobility were part of the way status considerations encouraged women to play down selling themselves or their products. Three sisters left in a precarious financial position by the bankruptcy and death of their father, manager for a Suffolk shipping company, turned to writing popular history books. Despite the urging of their guardian and trustee, they often refused payment for their work. For farmers, the various corn, cattle and produce markets were their club where "gossip of the countryside could be exchanged," particularly information about prices, turnover of farms and new farming practices. Not only were such markets off limits for women with pretensions to gentility, but their adjunct, the public house market day "ordinary" was hardly a venue for women. By the 1830s, a Suffolk man commented on the notoriety of a female cattle dealer who sat with other dealers at The Swan, drinking and smoking a pipe and locally known as

"The Duchess," by that date considered an eccentric. The change to formal marketing with its male ambience, from the financing by boards of trustees to the convivial dinners held in their spacious halls, was a serious disincentive to women.

The contributions to the enterprise through women's labour were contradicted by her role in displaying rank through the appearance of a non-working lifestyle. This contradiction was related to the more general conflict between achieving a commodious lifestyle and the more religious or cultural emphasis on education and learning, despite protestations that a religious commitment was compatible with a comfortable home life. This latent controversy was often played out by women who were particularly associated with setting the tone of the family lifestyle. Those groups whose claims were solidly based on property—the manufacturers, tradesmen and farmers—were able to build their material "plant" in a way which was often hard to match for the spokesmen of middle-class values, the clergy. In the countryside, where farmers and clergy formed the backbone of the middle class undiluted by other groups, farmers' female relatives came in for particular criticism for their status pretensions. The wives and daughters of clergymen had seen themselves as leaders of refinement, but nevertheless looked uneasily over their shoulders as wartime prosperity raised the position of their uncultivated neighbours. There was less friction where farmers' families found themselves in areas without resident clergy and playing a leading role against superstition, folk belief and what was viewed as rural ignorance and apathy. Against this they pitted both their intense conversionist religion, commitment to scientific modes of thought and conceptions of respectable behaviour. The less educated or well travelled among the farming group might take an intermediate position on issues such as beliefs in ghosts but on the whole they enthusiastically supported more modern ideals. In the early nineteenth century, a Quaker farmer's wife, recently moved to an extremely remote area in Suffolk and acting as the sole "lady" of the village, took on such a role when she deliberately exposed her young children to smallpox after having them vaccinated to demonstrate the efficacy of the new frightening procedure to the villagers. . . .

Nowhere were the contradictions and their consequences for individual women more evident than in the attitudes towards widows and their livelihood. Having proved their feminine commitment through marriage, widows were given legal and customary sanctions to enter the market. Indeed, they were often expected to be able to support themselves and their dependent children in a reversal of their acknowledged depedency within marriage, a position sometimes brutally thrust upon them. However, they were not expected to aspire beyond self-support. At a time when the unrestrained pursuit of business by men was still a questionable virtue, it was abhorrent in a woman. The Suffolk poet, George Crabbe, celebrated the wife and mother who died young, her place in the garden, the fireside chair, the church pew were hallowed by reverent memories. She is contrasted with the surviving widow, her head full of accounts, ruling her household with a rod of iron, whose sons long for her death. Few widows had the option of remaining in active business with high incomes. Realistically a widow's chances of operating near that level were remote and above all such ambition ran against the grain of feminine propriety. The bankers, solicitors and agents as well as fellow (*sic*) traders, merchants, farmers or manufacturers with whom she would have to deal would have been men with firm ideas of proper feminine behaviour. For those widows who could, it was easier to retire on to a fixed income. In the 1790s, Matthew Boulton wrote to his partner about the sale of an iron manufactory, reporting that the "assigned reason for selling is that many of the company are females, who do not find it convenient to carry on such extensive concerns." By mid century inconvenience had changed to social catastrophy. . . .

The majority of women knew that they would have to work within the household if not the enterprise. It was rather the way their contribution was defined which was significant. The evolution of the concept of work in relation to women's activities is suggestive here. Catherine Marsh, Rev. William Marsh's daughter, growing up first in Colchester and then Birmingham as part of an Evangelical household, was held up as a model of feminine behaviour as she helped her father in his ministerial duties. She wrote letters, saw callers and ran the house after her mother's death. Her friend and biographer recalls that Catherine was always busy, always "working." She defined this term: "Fine needlework in young days and when there was a later fashion for crochet bonnets she quickly made 27 for her friends." "Berlin wool work" first made its appearance in Colchester in 1796 and was seen as initiating the vogue for amateur needlework and "useless" crafts, characteristic of nineteenth-century middle-class women's definition of work.

Women, then, did not necessarily conceive of themselves as "working," but they did have a stern conception of duty, the moral imperatives which made them ever ready family aids. They expected and were expected by others to be on call to help family and friends. After his wife's death, the childless shopkeeper, John Perry, made constant calls on the support of his relatives. Among others, his unmarried niece came to stay to help him "in the department of looking over my linen." Yet some of the more prescient seemed to have been aware of their vulnerable position. The daughters of a silk merchant tried to educate themselves, partly for enjoyment but also, as one wrote, they had "early seen how precarious was the tenure of wealth derived from business with its incessant fluctuations." . . .

Sonya O. Rose

Limited Livelihoods

Gender in the Labor Process

Manufacturers organize production by dividing up the jobs to be done and assigning some workers to jobs that require technical facility and other workers to those that are more routine. Numerous scholars have argued that skill is a social construction, not an objective factor that differentiates one job from another. In the nineteenth century nearly all employers hired men for skilled work and for work that involved what they construed to be "complicated" machinery. They rarely questioned the appropriateness of hiring male workers for such jobs. Skill and the ability to run large, complex machinery were widely believed to be "natural" masculine traits. Generally, industrialists hired women for work that had already been defined as "women's work": jobs that were, relative to men's jobs, low-paid and were believed to require little technical competence or training. Employers reevaluated the gender assumptions behind their hiring practices only when they were forced by competitive market pressures to seek ways of reducing their labor costs. . . .

From Sonya O. Rose, *Limited Livelihoods: Gender and Class in Nineteenth-Century England* (Berkeley and Los Angeles: University of California Press, 1991).

Gender and Skill

Employers and their managers rarely doubted the commonly made association between skilled work and male labor. They structured training and advancement opportunities in their factories that reflected and reproduced this association. With the major exception of cotton weaving . . . , industrialists hired boys for jobs that trained them to do the work of skilled adult men. Girls were not given these jobs. Their work did not lead to more advanced or higher paying positions, but were "dead ends" in the factory.

The lace industry provides a good example of how employers structured work so that women were excluded as a potential source of skilled labor. Until the end of the nineteenth century, when manufacturers adopted special lace machines that made embroidered and braided laces, introducing them to the trade as "women's machines," only males worked lace machinery. The early hand-powered machines varied in size; the larger ones probably were too heavy for most women to operate them productively. Hand-run lace machinery became wider, and by 1841 few narrow lace machines were in use. But the size and heaviness of the machinery alone do not explain the exclusively male appropriation of these tools. When hand machines were turned with a wheel instead of hands and feet, boys were employed to turn the wheel under the supervision of men. Factory inspector R. D. Grainger's report to the 1843 Children's Employment Commission noted that turning the wheel was very hard work for young children who worked at all hours of the night.

When lace was made on steam-powered machinery, a number of boys under the age of eighteen were employed as machine-minders. Inspector Grainger commented that the work consisted "simply in minding or watching the progress of the work and in rectifying errors when they arise; the machine is so perfect that no part of the actual work need be done by the mechanic." Henry Scattergood, for example, started working as a threader when he was eleven and began tending a machine when he was thirteen. Together he and the man he assisted worked two machines. If thirteen-year-old boys were physically capable of operating such lace machines, it should have been possible for a grown woman to do at least that same amount and kind of work.

One reason that women were not considered for such jobs is that a number of the early manufacturers of lace, the men who owned machines and employed operatives to work them, had worked as skilled mechanics before becoming entrepreneurs. In the early years of the factory lace industry it was not uncommon for the twist hand to own his machinery. Independent machine-holders moved from their domestic workshops into factories because they were able to rent steam power. In boom times, twist hands became entrepreneurs, and in bad times manufacturers became twist hands again. Even the men who came from families of moderate wealth and headed giant lace-manufacturing firms had earlier acquired mechanical skills.

Given the development of the lace industry and the background of many manufacturers, it is not surprising that the job of twist hand was perceived as one for males. Yet labor costs were a concern. The trade was subject to wild fluctuations caused by changes in fashion, and it was a fiercely competitive industry, with masters attempting to edge out their neighbors and battling challenges from Continental competitors. In lace making, employers looked to boys rather than women as sources of inexpensive labor to assist lace makers and that employment of boys as assistants guaranteed that twist hands would be men.

The Factory Act of 1861 limited the hours that women and children could work in lace factories. Eighteen was the stipulated age at which males ceased to be subject to regulation in other textile industries, but for the lace industry the age was sixteen. Lace manufacturers had insisted that boys from the age of sixteen be allowed to work the same hours as adult men. Mr. Heymann, a major Nottingham lace manufacturer, told parliamentary commissioners who had investigated the industry that it was essential for boys from the age of sixteen to work the same hours as adult men in order to supply skilled labor to the trade. He said, "If legislation prevented our transferring lads at sixteen to the machines, they would go away into other trades, and the best of them would get on those trades, and we should never see them again." Working men opposed the exemption, arguing that boys under eighteen could learn the trade during legally restricted hours by operating the numerous "small, simple machines" that were available. One workman said that the boys should work at the less remunerative work until they were eighteen because it would be better for them from "a moral point of view"; otherwise "they become men too soon." Neither the employers nor the workmen even mentioned the possibility that girls or women could work these machines.

Both employers and working men believed that there was a natural progression in a male's career in the lace industry. A boy worked first as a threader, and then either on the small lace machines or as an assistant to an adult male twist hand on larger machines. Next he moved on to become a twist hand in his own right. Girls had no such career progression. They began their work in lace factories as bobbin winders and they remained bobbin winders, or perhaps they did the job of removing the lace from the machine after it was loomed (called "jacking off"). In any case, they remained in ancillary processes at low wages. To employers and workmen alike, the trade of twist hand was the work of men, which excluded both boys and women. The controversy over whether or not boys sixteen to eighteen should be subject to the factory acts was one concerning a supply of low-waged workers for the lace trade, framed as a debate about when it was appropriate for boys to become men. . . .

Gender and Technology

In addition to structuring career ladders in a way that prevented women from acquiring particular technical skills, employers also adopted "gendered" technology. Machines designed to be worked by skilled workers were built to be operated by people with the hands, height, and weight of an average male, unless a manufacturer had in mind reducing labor costs by replacing men with women and therefore contracted with a machine maker to build a machine that would be suitable for female bodies. Studies of gender and technology in the twentieth century show that men gain a sense of masculinity from their association with machines. In the nineteenth century the technology itself was gendered.

Not all machinery was thought to be solely appropriate for male operatives. Throughout the nineteenth century, in a variety of industries manufacturers introduced machines that were designed to be marketed as "women's machines." These machines were designed to require little training or stamina of the operatives who would run them. In the hosiery industry the invention of circular frames, attributed to the engineer Marc Isambert Brunel, was aimed at use by women, and employers bought them as "ladies' machines" from the earliest years of the factory industry—although male operatives contested women's employment on them from the start. In the lace industry manufacturers introduced the Schiffle, a machine, widely used by women on the Continent, that made embroidered and braided laces. In the carpet industry, the machine that produced Royal Axminster carpets was thought by employers to be one especially suitable for women's work. As one of the employers remarked when the men's union disputed the continued hiring of women to work on the Axminster looms, "[T]here could be no denying that the Axminster was a girl's loom and not fit for a man at all."

When labor costs were an issue, employers were more likely to be successful in battles with the unions over the substitution of women for men if they could find a new machine designed specifically for women. A new machine was appropriate for women's labor if the running of it required little training. If the machines were large and heavy or required technical know-how, industrialists assumed that men should run them.

Manufacturers, however, did not always reserve machines requiring strength for men. For example, in Kidderminster, the center of the carpet trade, when manufacturers tried to employ women on any machine that made carpets or could possibly be used for making carpets, male carpet weavers protested vigorously. . . . However, they made no objection to women making rugs on the Chenille handloom. Weaving on this loom was physically taxing. As a female weaver said, "it needed bone and muscle" to do the work. Lottie Mary Cooper, born in 1890, remembered visiting her mother in the factory where she wove cashmere rugs on a Chenille handloom:

> *I can see our mother now, working at her loom, there wasn't a stool to sit on, only a bar held by ropes. You couldn't sit on it properly, only lean back against it while your feet worked the treadles. It was very hard work operating the treadles which worked the heddles. . . . You could always tell someone who'd been working on the weaving all their lives for they walked in a special way, all that treadling.*

Even though the work required strength, both employers and the members of the all-male union thought of it as women's work. Men in Kidderminster had other sources of employment that were better paid; they were not interested in rug making.

Employers, then, hired men for work defined as skilled; they structured the labor process in such a way that only men could learn the skills; and ordinarily they purchased machinery built with male bodies in mind. Usually women worked at jobs that required little or no formal training. However, when faced with sufficient pressure to lower production costs, industrialists hired women for jobs for which they had previously employed men, sometimes purchasing special "women's machines." . . .

Paternalism as a Managerial Strategy

Paternalism was a set of practices that relied on a familial metaphor in which the employer was the head and father and working men and working women were his dependent children. From the 1850s until after the turn of the twentieth century, paternalistic factory regimes proliferated in family-owned and -operated factories in Lancashire and elsewhere. Industrialists who implemented such workplace regimes hoped to instill in their workpeople feelings of obligation and gratitude that would produce harmonious industrial relations. Worker resentment of harsh working conditions and strict supervision, economic insecurity and persistent poverty, were evident to the employer classes in the cities and the factory communities of the industrial north. The Chartist uprisings and the bitter Preston strike and lockout of 1853–1854 undoubtedly led some industrialists to realize that their economic success depended on the cooperation of workers, and that this could not be exacted by coercion. Paternalism evolved as a management strategy to dampen the conflict between labor and capital in the workplace by putting a positive face on capitalist authority.

Most scholars have viewed paternalism as a mechanism of class control by employers. Judy Lown has enriched the study of paternalism by demonstrating how management strategies at the Courtauld silk mills, which primarily employed women workers, were constituted as a set of patriarchal practices. Paternalist employers of both women and men did structure their workplaces in order to diminish worker resistance and enhance worker loyalty, but they used gender distinctions between women and men as workers and as members of families as a template for structuring their enterprises. Paternalist practices, then, both represented gender distinctions and structured gender divisions and relations. . . .

Paternalism and the Reproduction of Gender Relations

Paternalist industrialists shaped their factories using as a model the inequalities of status and authority that existed in the family. These inequalities were presented as "natural differentiation" in the workplace, just as they were at home. The construction of a paternalistic factory regime with the factory owner and employer as head of the reconstituted "family in work" had specific consequences for the structure of gender relations. Paternalistic employers created a model for appropriate gender relations in the community at large.

The Cadburys of Birmingham are a prime example of employers who structured the factory milieu to symbolize the differences between women and men as workers and as members of families. Cadbury Chocolate at Bourneville was a complete community of semi-detached cottages with gardens. Separate recreational grounds were provided "for men and for girls," and also one for children under the age of twelve. One of the aims of William Cadbury in planning the community was that no child should be further than a five-minute walk from a playground. Every house had at least three bedrooms, a kitchen, a parlor, and a scullery. The Cadburys also provided a boarding house for girls who came from some distance away. At the turn of the century about thirty-four young women lived in the house, sharing six or seven bedrooms, bath and washing rooms, and sitting and dining rooms. Their rent was low, and in addition they were offered a low-priced dinner at the works. . . .

One way [the Cadburys] protected the girls was by strictly segregating them, both at work and in the recreational and educational facilities that they provided. Edward Cadbury wrote that when youth of both sexes were "indiscriminately mixed" in factories under unsatisfactory conditions, grave moral danger would result. He believed moral danger would also be the consequence if married men and women mixed with "single girls and young persons." He advocated careful planning and organization if married women and men were both employed (no married women were employed at the Bourneville works). Cadbury suggested separate entrances for women and men and recommended the construction of separated passageways so both sexes would not use the same hallways in going to and from their separated dining rooms and dressing rooms. At the Bourneville factory, it was forbidden for anyone to be away from their work area without an excuse. Only carefully selected men, wearing badges, were allowed in the girls' work areas. The only times boys and girls and women and men mingled was at the annual gathering of employees, to which the adult men brought their wives; there the assembly heard music written for the occasion, watched plays, and listened to poetry.

The separation and differentiation of the sexes were crucial symbolic and material links in the interlocking chains of paternalistic practices that made up the Bourneville plan. The education scheme was carefully designed to prepare young male and female workers for their different destinies with the firm. Deserving boys earned an apprenticeship to a skilled trade in the factory. Girls were prepared for marriage and motherhood and were rewarded with a gift of money when they left the works to be wed, after which time they ordinarily could not return; the Cadburys only rehired a few married or widowed women in "poor circumstances" to work as cleaners for an hour or two each morning.

Cadbury's scheme for organizing work was, perhaps, the ultimate in paternalistic plans to reinforce gender distinctions and to cast the relationship between employer and employee in a familial mold. Although not all employers could afford such measures, however, many employers adopted some of them. For example, W. Atkinson, formerly a worker himself, was head of a brass foundry in Birmingham that employed both women and men. Atkinson had the women leave the shop five minutes before the men, an arrangement he considered to be orderly and useful. At the Dog and Ship Biscuit Company in London, the employer objected "on principle" to women and men working together, as "there is too much larking." At this factory employing six hundred men and seventy girls and young women, women and men were segregated both by work process and physically. One or two "staid men" were used to lift or carry where the women worked. Women were supervised by forewomen, and their dining, wash rooms, and kitchen were shut off from the rest of the factory and men were forbidden to use the stairs in the women's section. Thomas Adams, a Nottingham lace manufacturer who employed large numbers of women in the preparation of lace for sale, built a warehouse in 1855 which was touted as providing idyllic working conditions. In addition to work rooms, it boasted a library, a classroom, and separated tea rooms, washing facilities, and dining rooms for women and men. Adams, an evangelical, created a chapel within the warehouse premises where a chaplain conducted compulsory services each morning. In Nottingham the story is still told that a Manchester physician visiting his factory "was astonished that his factory girls looked so healthy and fresh—almost as if they had been haymaking rather than lace making." Few employers would have matched the zeal with which Mr. Corbett, a salt manufacturer from Stoke in Worcestershire, reorganized gender relations at his firm. Corbett owned the entire town in which his works were located. There he built for his workpeople cottages and a church and paid the stipend of a clergyman of the Church of England. He restructured his work force, at considerable expense to the business, so that only men would be employed. He wrote to B. L. Hutchins that he did so because he saw

> *[m]en who with their wives earned perhaps 2 pounds a week or 100 pounds a year living in squalor, their children in the streets cursing, lying and stealing and families growing up with the lowest possible tone—not so much immoral or vicious (always free from crime) as depraved and low. It all appeared to me to result from homes without a mother and as soon as a sister was big enough to scrub the house she was drafted off to tap salt which paid better. As this was passing in my mind one evening I saw three women—in hot weather—leaving work later than usual faint and done up. I went to the man at the pan and found him sitting on his shovel, smoking a pipe and fresh as paint. I at once put an end to women's work at those works and . . . I have never employed them again. I believe it to be wrong as a general practice, that is to say, barbarous.*

According to a newspaper description of Corbett, "The people . . . in their appreciation . . . have erected a stained glass window in the adjoining parish church of Stoke Prior to commemorate the circumstance." To refuse employment to all women was a logical extension of paternalism. However, many employers could not afford to reorganize the labor process to eliminate all women in the name of creating working-class gender and family relations on the model of those in the middle-class family. What they could do was to hire only women who were single.

The Marriage Bar

. . . The marriage bar [a rule whereby a woman, once she was married, would have to leave employment] embodied the domestic ideology and the cult of motherhood. It developed as an employer practice in the same milieu as paternalism. It was not the product of an economic calculus. The bar would have been a convenient cost-cutting mechanism in a civil service system or in industries dominated by union seniority rules in the twentieth century. Most of the industries we have been examining, however, paid workers by the piece or paid them an hourly wage for work that was quickly learned, so wages did not increase with the employee's tenure on the job. Numerous accounts of women's work as light and simple suggest that the jobs were such that women could learn them and make their maximum wages after a relatively short time on the job. Only rarely did an employer in the nineteenth century pay his employees a pension; however, even when men were paid a pension, women were not. Thus, there was little or no direct monetary incentive for late-nineteenth-century employers to remove women from their employment when they married. Furthermore, there are indications that in some areas, such as Northampton, the voluntary ban on the employment of married women made women's labor scarce and drove up wages. Some employers complained that the practice of women leaving work when they married meant that firms lost their best workers. The marriage bar is best understood by situating it among . . . other gendered employment practices. . . . It should unquestionably be viewed in the context of the growing public disapprobation for married women's employment. Edward Cadbury, for example, believed that the Factory Acts were not stringent enough regarding married women's employment. He proclaimed, "[W]e are taking the responsibilities of empire upon us without having a race of human beings fit to deal with them." . . .

Suggestions for Further Reading

The literature on the Industrial Revolution is vast and still growing. What follows is meant as an introduction to that literature, including both classics and recent studies.

General Surveys of the Industrial Revolution

Ashton, T. S., *The Industrial Revolution, 1760–1830* (New York: Oxford University Press, 1948).
Berg, Maxine, *The Age of Manufactures: Industry, Innovation, and Work in Britain, 1700–1820* (New York: Barnes and Noble, 1985).
Cannadine, David, "The Past and the Present in the Industrial Revolution," *Past and Present* 103 (1984): 131–172.
Cipolla, Carlo, ed., *Industrial Revolution, 1700–1914*, vol. 3 of *The Fontana Economic History of Europe* (New York: Barnes and Noble, 1976).
Deane, Phyllis, *The First Industrial Revolution* (New York: Cambridge University Press, 1965).
Fisher, Douglas, *The Industrial Revolution: A Macroeconomic Interpretation* (New York: St. Martin's Press, 1993).
Hudson, Pat, *The Industrial Revolution* (London: Edward Arnold, 1992).
King, Steven, and Geoffrey Timmins, *Making Sense of the Industrial Revolution* (New York: Manchester University Press, 2001).
Mathias, Peter, and John A. Davis, eds., *The First Industrial Revolution* (New York: Basil Blackwell, 1989).
Mokyr, Joel, ed., *The British Industrial Revolution: An Economic Perspective* (Boulder, Colo.: Westview Press 1993).
O'Brien, Patrick K., and Roland Quinault, eds., *The Industrial Revolution and British Society* (New York: Cambridge University Press, 1993).
Pollard, Sydney, *Peaceful Conquest: The Industrialization of Europe, 1760–1850* (New York: Oxford University Press, 1981).
Rostow, W. W., *The Stages of Economic Growth* (New York: Cambridge University Press, 1961).
Stearns, Peter N., *Interpreting the Industrial Revolution* (Washington, D.C.: American Historical Association, 1991).
———, *The Industrial Revolution in World History* (Boulder, Colo.: Westview Press, 1993).

The Nature and Origins of Industrialization

Aldcroft, Derek H., and Michael J. Freeman, eds., *Transport in the Industrial Revolution* (Dover, N.H.: Manchester University Press, 1983).

Cameron, Rondo, "*La révolution industrielle manqué*," *Social Science History* 14 (1990): 559–566.

Coleman, D. C. "Proto-industrialization: A Concept Too Many," *Economic History Review*, 2d series, 36 (1983): 435–448.

Crafts, N. F. R., *British Economic Growth During the Industrial Revolution* (New York: Oxford University Press, 1985).

Crouzet, Francois, ed., *Capital Formation in the Industrial Revolution* (London: Methuen, 1972).

Davis, Ralph, *The Industrial Revolution and British Overseas Trade* (Atlantic Highlands, N.J.: Humanities Press, 1979).

Dutton, H. I., *The Patent System and Inventive Activity During the Industrial Revolution, 1750–1852* (Manchester, England: Manchester University Press, 1984).

Flinn, Michael W., *Origins of the Industrial Revolution* (New York: Barnes and Noble, 1966).

Hartwell, R. M., "Was There an Industrial Revolution?" *Social Science History* 14 (1990): 567–576.

———, ed., *The Causes of the Industrial Revolution in England* (London: Methuen, 1967).

Honeyman, Katrina, *Origins of Enterprise: Business Leadership in the Industrial Revolution* (New York: St. Martin's Press, 1983).

Hudson, Pat, ed., *Regions and Industries: A Perspective on the Industrial Revolution in Britain* (New York: Cambridge University Press, 1989).

Kriedte, Peter, Hans Medick, and Jurgen Schlumbom, eds., *Industrialization Before Industrialization: Rural History in the Genesis of Capitalism* (New York: Cambridge University Press, 1981).

Lloyd-Jones, Roger, and M. J. Lewis, *Manchester and the Age of the Factory: The Business Structure of Cottonopolis in the Industrial Revolution* (New York: Croom Helm, 1988).

MacLeod, Christine, *Inventing the Industrial Revolution: The English Patent System, 1660–1800* (New York: Cambridge University Press, 1989).

McKendrick, Neil, "Home Demand and Economic Growth: A New View of the Role of Women and Children in the Industrial Revolution," in Neil McKendrick, ed., *Historical Perspectives: Studies in English Thought and Society in Honor of J. H. Plump* (London: Europa, 1974).

Mokyr, Joel, "Demand vs. Supply in the Industrial Revolution," *Journal of Economic History* vol. 37, no. 4 (December, 1977): 981–1008.

Musson, A. E., and E. Robinson, *Science and Technology in the Industrial Revolution* (Manchester, England: Manchester University Press, 1969).

North, Douglass C., *Structure and Change in Economic History* (New York: Norton, 1981).

Ogilvie, Sheilagh, and Markus Cerman, eds., *European Proto-Industrialization* (New York: Cambridge University Press, 1996).
Schmitz, C. J., *The Growth of Big Business in the United States and Western Europe, 1850–1939* (New York: Cambridge University Press, 1993).

Industrialization in Different Geographic Contexts

Aminzade, Ronald, *Class, Politics, and Early Industrial Capitalism: A Study of Mid-Nineteenth-Century Toulouse, France* (Albany: State University of New York Press, 1981).
Blackwell, William, *The Beginnings of Russian Industrialization, 1800–1860* (Princeton: Princeton University Press, 1968).
Bruland, Kristine, *British Technology and European Industrialization: The Norwegian Textile Industry in the Mid-Nineteenth Century* (New York: Cambridge University Press, 1989).
Dunlavy, Colleen A., *Politics and Industrialization: Early Railroads in the United States and Prussia* (Princeton: Princeton University Press, 1994).
Gordon, David M., *Merchants and Capitalists: Industrialization and Provincial Politics in Mid-Nineteenth-Century France* (Tuscaloosa: University of Alabama Press, 1985).
Herrigel, Gary, *Industrial Constructions: The Sources of German Industrial Power* (New York: Cambridge University Press, 1996).
Lee, W. R., ed., *German Industry and German Industrialization: Essays in German Economic and Business History in the Nineteenth and Twentieth Centuries* (New York: Routledge Press, 1991).
McCaffray, Susan P., *The Politics of Industrialization in Tsarist Russia: The Association of Southern Coal and Steel Producers, 1874–1914* (DeKalb: Northern Illinois University Press, 1996).
McKay, John, *Pioneers for Profit: Foreign Entrepreneurship and Russian Industrialization* (Chicago: University of Chicago Press, 1970).
Merriman, John M., *The Red City: Limoges and the French Nineteenth Century* (New York: Oxford University Press, 1985).
Moch, Leslie Page, *Moving Europeans: Migration in Western Europe since 1650* (Bloomington: Indiana University Press, 1992).
Mokyr, Joel, *Industrialization in the Low Countries* (New Haven: Yale University Press, 1976).
Prude, Jonathan, *The Coming of the Industrial Order: Town and Factory Life in Rural Massachusetts, 1810–1860* (Cambridge: Harvard University Press, 1983).
Sylla, Richard, and Gianni Toniolo, eds., *Patterns of European Industrialization: The Nineteenth Century* (New York: Routledge Press, 1991).
Thomson, J. K. J., *A Distinctive Industrialization: Cotton in Barcelona, 1728–1832* (New York: Cambridge University Press, 1992).
Trebilcock, Clive, *The Industrialization of the Continental Powers, 1780–1914* (New York: Longman, 1981).

Williamson, Jeffrey G., *Coping with City Growth During the British Industrial Revolution* (New York: Cambridge University Press, 1990).

Class Formation and the Work Experience

Berlanstein, Lenard, ed., *The Industrial Revolution and Work in Nineteenth-Century Europe* (New York: Routledge Press, 1992).
Calhoun, Craig, *Before the Working Class: Tradition and Community in English Popular Radicalism, 1790–1830* (Chicago: University of Chicago Press, 1981).
———, *The Question of Class Struggle: Social Foundations of Popular Radicalism During the Industrial Revolution* (Chicago: University of Chicago Press, 1982).
Crew, David, *Town in the Ruhr: A Social History of Bochum, 1860–1914* (New York: Columbia University Press, 1979).
Cunningham, Hugh, *Leisure in the Industrial Revolution, c. 1780–c. 1880* (New York: St. Martin's Press, 1980).
Epstein, James, and Dorothy Thompson, eds., *The Chartist Experience: Studies in Working-Class Radicalism and Culture* (Atlantic Highlands, N.J.: Humanities Press, 1983).
Evans, Richard J., *The German Working Class, 1888–1933: The Politics of Everyday Life* (New York: Barnes and Noble, 1982).
Feinstein, C. H., *Conjectures and Contrivances: Economic Growth and the Standard of Living in Britain During the Industrial Revolution* (New York: Oxford University Press, 1996).
Floud, Roderick, and Kenneth W. Wachter, "Poverty and Physical Stature: Evidence on the Standard of Living of London Boys, 1770–1870," *Social Science History* vol. 6, no. 4 (Fall, 1982): 422–452.
Glen, Robert, *Urban Workers in the Early Industrial Revolution* (New York: St. Martin's Press, 1984).
Haine, W. Scott, *The World of the Paris Café: Sociability Among the French Working Class* (Baltimore: Johns Hopkins University Press, 1996).
Hanagan, Michael P., *The Logic of Solidarity: Artisans and Industrial Workers in Three French Towns, 1871–1914* (Urbana: University of Illinois Press, 1980).
Horrell, Sara, and Jane Humphries, "Old Questions, New Data, and Alternative Perspectives: Families' Living Standards in the Industrial Revolution," *Journal of Economic History* 52, no. 4 (December 1992): 849–880.
Jones, Gareth Stedman, *Languages of Class: Studies in English Working Class History, 1832–1982* (New York: Cambridge University Press, 1983).
Joyce, Patrick, *Work, Society, and Politics: The Culture of the Factory in Later Victorian England* (New Brunswick, N.J.: Rutgers University Press, 1980).
Kelly, Alfred, ed., *The German Worker: Working-Class Autobiographies from the Age of Industrialization* (Berkeley and Los Angeles: University of California Press, 1987).

Kocka, Jurgen, *Industrial Culture and Bourgeois Society: Business, Labor, and Bureaucracy in Modern Germany* (Providence, R.I.: Berghahn, 1999).

Komlos, John, *The Biological Standard of Living in Europe and America, 1700–1900* (Brookfield, Vt.: Variorum, 1995).

Maynes, Mary Jo, *Taking the Hard Road: Life Course in French and German Workers' Autobiographies in the Era of Industrialization* (Chapel Hill: University of North Carolina Press, 1995).

Rule, John, *The Labouring Classes in Early Industrial England, 1750–1850* (New York: Longman, 1986).

Scott, Joan W., *The Glassworkers of Carmaux: French Craftsmen and Political Action in a Nineteenth-Century City* (Cambridge: Harvard University Press, 1974).

Stearns, Peter N., *Paths to Authority: The Middle Class and the Industrial Labor Force in France, 1820–1848* (Urbana: University of Illinois Press, 1979).

Taylor, A. J., ed., *The Standard of Living in Britain in the Industrial Revolution* (London: Methuen, 1975).

Thompson, Dorothy, *The Chartists: Popular Politics in the Industrial Revolution* (New York: Pantheon Books, 1984).

Thompson, E. P., *The Making of the English Working Class* (Harmondsworth, England: Penguin, 1968).

Tilly, Charles, *The Contentious French* (Cambridge, Mass.: Belknap Press, 1986).

Gender and the Family

Anderson, Michael, *Family Structure in Nineteenth-Century Lancashire* (New York: Cambridge University Press, 1971).

Bachrach, Susan, *Dames Employées: The Feminization of Postal Work in Nineteenth-Century France* (New York: Institute for Research in History, 1984).

Canning, Kathleen, *Languages of Labor and Gender: Female Factory Work in Germany, 1850–1914* (Ithaca: Cornell University Press, 1996).

Clark, Anna, *The Struggle for the Breeches: Gender and the Making of the British Working Class* (Berkeley and Los Angeles: University of California Press, 1995).

Coffin, Judith G., *The Politics of Women's Work: The Paris Garment Trades, 1750–1915* (Princeton: Princeton University Press, 1996).

Frader, Laura Levine, "Women in the Industrial Capitalist Economy," in Renate Bridenthal et al., eds., *Becoming Visible: Women in European History*, 2d ed. (Boston: Houghton Mifflin, 1987).

Franzoni, Barbara, *At the Very Least She Pays the Rent: Women and German Industrialization, 1871–1914* (Wesport, Conn.: Greenwood Press, 1985).

Gillis, John R. et al., eds., *The European Experience of Declining Fertility, 1850–1970: The Quiet Revolution* (Cambridge, Mass.: Basil Blackwell, 1992).

Gomersall, Meg, *Working-Class Girls in Nineteenth-Century England: Life, Work, and Schooling* (New York: St. Martin's Press, 1997).
Haines, Michael, *Fertility and Occupations: Population Patterns in Industrialization* (New York: Academic Press, 1979).
Hilden, Patricia Penn, *Women, Work, and Politics: Belgium, 1830–1914* (New York: Oxford University Press, 1993).
Honeyman, Katrina, *Women, Gender, and Industrialization in England, 1700–1870* (New York: St. Martin's Press, 2000).
Hopkins, Eric, *Childhood Transformed: Working-Class Childhood in Nineteenth-Century England* (New York: Manchester University Press, 1994).
Hudson, Pat, and W. R. Lee, eds., *Women's Work and the Family Economy in Historical Perspective* (Manchester, England: Manchester University Press, 1990).
Lynch, Katherine A., *Family, Class, and Ideology in Early Industrial France: Social Policy and the Working-Class Family, 1825–1848* (Madison: University of Wisconsin Press, 1988).
Nardinelli, Clark, *Child Labor and the Industrial Revolution* (Bloomington: Indiana University Press, 1990).
Orthmann, Rosemary, *Out of Necessity: Women Working in Berlin at the Height of Industrialization, 1874–1914* (New York: Garland, 1991).
Seccombe, Wally, *Weathering the Storm: Working-Class Families from the Industrial Revolution to the Fertility Decline* (London: Verso, 1993).
Sharpe, Pamela, ed., *Women's Work: The English Experience, 1650–1914* (London: Edward Arnold, 1998).
Simonton, Deborah, *A History of European Women's Work: 1700 to the Present* (New York: Routledge Press, 1998).
Smith, Bonnie, *Ladies of the Leisure Class: The Bourgeoises of Northern France in the Nineteenth Century* (Princeton: Princeton University Press, 1981).
Stewart, Mary Lynn, *Women, Work, and the French State: Labour Protection and Social Patriarchy, 1879–1919* (Montréal: McGill-Queen's University Press, 1989).
Tuttle, Carolyn, *Hard at Work in Factories and Mines: The Economics of Child Labor During the British Industrial Revolution* (Boulder, Colo.: Westview Press, 1999).
Vicinus, Martha, *Independent Women: Work and Community for Single Women, 1850–1920* (Chicago: University of Chicago Press, 1985).

Credits

Part I

p. 11: From David S. Landes, *The Unbound Prometheus: Technological Change and Industrial Development in Western Europe from 1750 to the Present.* Copyright © 1969. Reprinted with the permission of Cambridge University Press.

p. 17: From William H. Sewell Jr., *Work and Revolution in France: The Language of Labor from the Old Regime to 1848.* Copyright © 1980. Reprinted by permission of Cambridge University Press and the author.

p. 28: From E. A. Wrigley, *Continuity, Chance and Change.* Copyright © 1988. Reprinted with the permisison of Cambridge University Press.

p. 35: From Maxine Berg and Pat Hudson, "Rehabilitating the Industrial Revolution." *Economic History Review*, XLV, 1 (1992): 24–50. Reprinted by permission of Blackwell Publishers and the authors.

Part II

p. 50: From Joel Mokyr, *The Lever of Riches: Technological Creativity and Economic Progress.* Copyright © 1992 by Oxford University Press, Inc. Used by permission of Oxford University Press, Inc.

p. 61: From *How the West Grew Rich* by Nathan Rosenberg and L. E. Birdzell Jr. Copyright © 1986 by Basic Books, Inc. Reprinted by permission of Basic Books, a member of Perseus Books, L.L.C.

p. 71: Robert S. DuPlessis, *Transitions to Capitalism in Early Modern Europe.* Copyright © 1997. Reprinted with the permission of Cambridge University Press.

p. 81: From Jan De Vries, "The Industrial Revolution and the Industrious Revolution," in *The Journal of Economic History*, Vol. 54, Issue 2 (June 1994), pp. 255–263. Reprinted with the permission of Cambridge University Press.

Part III

p. 93: Joel Mokyr, "The Industrial Revolution and the New Economic History," from *The Economics of the Industrial Revolution.* Copyright © 1985. Reprinted with permission.

p. 103: Pomeranz, Kenneth, *The Great Divergence: China, Europe, and the Making of the Modern World Economy.* Copyright © 2000 by Princeton University Press. Reprinted by permission of Princeton University Press.

p. 115: Alexander Gerschenkron, "Economic Backwardness in Historical Perspective," in B. Hoselitz, *The Progress of Underdeveloped Countries.* Copyright © 1952. Published by the University of Chicago Press. Reprinted by permission of the University of Chicago Press.

Part IV

Part V